高校英语选修课系列教材

U0331334

美英报刊选读

主　编　郭　印　毕纪芹
副主编　高公社　马　岩　刘舒展
编　者　张　艳　刘晓茜　吕　慧　李文平

清华大学出版社
北　京

内 容 简 介

本书旨在培养学生阅读美英报刊的能力，促其拓宽视野，了解美英文化，进而提高跨文化交际的能力。教材以美英报刊的基本知识为经线，以美英主流媒体的代表性文章题材为纬线，纵横融合，深入解析。选材包括时政新闻、财经资讯、科技导航、生活百科、体坛风云、文娱在线、艺术名家、教育视窗、旅途人生、全球热点等内容，注重题材广泛性和内容深刻性相结合。每单元均配有思考题，读练融通。倡导以学生为中心的授课方法，注重培养学生思辨能力与创新能力。

图书在版编目（CIP）数据

美英报刊选读 / 郭印，毕纪芹主编. —北京：清华大学出版社，2017（2023.1重印）
（高校英语选修课系列教材）
ISBN 978-7-302-46017-6

Ⅰ.①美… Ⅱ.①郭… Ⅲ.① 英语–报刊–阅读教学–高等学校–教学参考资料
Ⅳ.①H319.4

中国版本图书馆CIP数据核字（2016）第316332号

责任编辑：钱屹芝
封面设计：平　原
责任校对：王凤芝
责任印制：宋　林
出版发行：清华大学出版社
　　　　　网　　　址：http:// www. tup. com. cn，http:// www. wqbook. com
　　　　　地　　　址：北京清华大学学研大厦A座　　邮　　编：100084
　　　　　社 总 机：010-83470000　　　　　　邮　　购：010-62786544
　　　　　投稿与读者服务：010-62776969，c-service@tup.tsinghua.edu.cn
　　　　　质量反馈：010-62772015，zhiliang@tup.tsinghua.edu.cn
印 装 者：北京同文印刷有限责任公司
经　　销：全国新华书店
开　　本：185mm×260mm　　印　　张：15.5　　字　　数：392千字
版　　次：2017 年 8 月第 1 版　　　　印　　次：2023 年 1 月第 8 次印刷
定　　价：65.00元

产品编号：070512-03

前言

　　教育部《高等学校英语专业本科教学质量国家标准》（征求意见稿）中对英语专业的培养目标、知识要求、教学要求等方面做了明确规定：培养目标方面，"教学过程强调实践和应用，人才培养突出人文素质教育，注重开阔学生的国际视野"；知识要求方面，要"了解英语国家的历史和当代社会的政治、经济、文化、科技、军事等基本情况"；教学要求方面，"教学应以能力培养为导向，突出语言综合运用能力和思辨能力的培养"。

　　要达到以上标准，学生应该能较好地理解、诠释、评价原汁原味的英语文本，能以包容的态度、思辨的方法和客观的立场对待英语文本所体现的多元文化现象；提高能和英语文化背景人士进行有效沟通的能力。无疑，《美英报刊选读》对实现以上目标大有助益。

　　《美英报刊选读》是英语专业本科阶段的"美英报刊选读"课程的通用教材。英语专业课程是根据培养目标与规格而设置的，其出发点和宗旨都是提高人才培养质量。此课程设立的直接教学目标在于培养学生阅读美英报纸杂志的能力，长远教学目标在于拓宽学生视野，更多地了解英语国家的文化。本教材服务于英语专业的本科学分制教学改革，与课程建设紧密结合。教材涵盖了美英报刊的基本知识、新闻报道和文化背景介绍，旨在帮助学生：理解美英报刊文章的文体和语言特点，培养阅读美英报刊的能力；拓宽视野，深入了解西方文化，提高跨文化交际能力；加强思辨训练，培养独立思考能力和创新能力。

　　本教材的编写博采众长，选取的文章原汁原味，难度适宜，趣味性强，相配的报刊常识和背景知识由浅入深，循序渐进。主要特色可总结如下：

1）知识性与趣味性相结合。报刊文章的根本目的是为了英语学习效果。良好的学习效果要依托学习者的兴趣与动机。因此，本教材内容的选取，不仅注重选择当前热点，而且注重与学生的现有知识结构和认知水平相结合，从而减少阅读疲劳，激发学习兴趣。

2）广泛性与深刻性相结合。报刊文章阅读既是语言学习，又是文化学习，其中更难的是对文化背景的理解。选材广泛，文章涉及西方国家政治、经济、科技等诸多方面，每个专题配有较为深入的文化背景介绍与相关知识解读。

3）时效性与稳定性的平衡。新闻报道的重要指标之一就是时效性，正因为如此，报刊教材需要常换常新。为了保证教师上课的质量与效度，报刊文章还需要保持相对的稳定性。因此，内容设置上，本教材的报刊文章兼顾了"软新闻"和"硬新闻"，平衡了时效性与稳定性。

4）思辨能力与创新能力并举。美英报刊选读课文直接选材于西方报刊，自然会触及作者的观点。

在选用课文时一方面注重对学生的正面引导，另一方面注重保持文章的完整性，保持原文的风貌。尽可能给学生提供事实性和批判性的文章，以提高其阅读能力和分析能力，同时也兼收一些不同观点的文章以锻炼学生独立思考的能力。教师授课要坚持以学生为中心，鼓励学生结合课后思考题，慎思明辨，勇于发问，想人未想，见人未见，提高学生主动探索和获取知识的能力。

5）线上与线下学习的融合。随着新闻媒体网络化，《纽约时报》、《泰晤士报》、《经济学家》、《时代周刊》等诸多美英主流报刊均免费提供网络版。因此美英报刊选读课程从题材和阅读形式上，已由最初的纸质教材过渡为网络教材，扩大了阅读题材范围，使课内与课外的阅读活动融为一体，互为补充。课外学生根据个人兴趣，通过教材所介绍的网站网址，"无缝"延续报刊阅读，并凭借网络即时答疑沟通，将线上线下阅读活动融为一体。

每单元的内容框架如下：

1）报刊语言特点介绍，本部分旨在帮助学生熟悉了解报刊文章的语言特点，提高该类文体的阅读能力。

2）课文导读与思考，针对本单元的专题和课文进行导入式介绍，启迪学生深入思考。

3）课文，每单元课文集中体现本单元主题，分 A、B 两篇，每篇在 1000 字左右。

4）课文注释，针对课文中的词汇、习语、语法、文化知识的难点给予解释。

5）背景知识延伸阅读，围绕本单元主题筛选材料，帮助学生进一步了解美英文化精髓。

6）课后练习题，练习题的客观题环节主要目的是检验阅读质量，主观讨论环节旨在培养学生的思辨和创新能力。

7）著名报刊介绍，每单元精选并推介一本美 / 英报纸杂志，帮助学生培养阅读原文的习惯。

本教材在内容上从时政新闻（Politics）、财经资讯（Finance）、科技导航（Technology）、生活百科（Lifestyle）、体坛风云（Sports）、文娱在线（Entertainment）、艺术名家（Artists）、教育视窗（Education）、旅途人生（Travel）、全球热点（Global Spotlight）等十个主题展开，全部文章均选材于西方主流媒体。在课文基础上，对美英国家的政党制度、经济情况、科技革命、饮食文化、体育赛事、影视产业、艺术展馆、教育体制、人文景观、宗教影响等专题逐一补充了背景信息，以便于学生深入了解。

在美英报刊知识介绍方面，对当今美英的著名杂志，包括《纽约时报》、《华盛顿邮报》、《今日美国》、《华尔街邮报》、《泰晤士报》、《读者文摘》、《新闻周刊》、《时代周刊》、《卫报》、《镜报》等予以详细介绍。在报刊阅读技巧方面，本书对报刊英语的阅读方法、语言特色、文体风格、修辞手段、话语权力等逐一展开了讲解。内容的安排体现出英语语言知识的层次性，语言技能的系统性，以及语言与文化的关联性。

广大师生在使用本教材时，还需要注意以下几点。

1）在编写过程中，我们兼顾了美英报刊内容，为了保持原汁原味，我们保留了美式英语和英式英语的原貌，而没有做统一处理。

2）本书的编排格式较多地保留了报刊英语的行文格式和特点，比如标题往往仅首词首字母大写，单引号多于双引号等等。

3）本教材每单元教学内容大约需要三课时，加上考试复习，全书共需32学时，供英语专业本科教学一学期使用。

参与本书编写的郭印、毕纪芹、高公社、马岩、刘舒展、张艳均为青岛理工大学人文与外国语学院教师，刘晓茜为齐鲁工业大学（山东省社科院）外国语学院教师，吕慧、李文平为青岛理工大学琴岛学院教师。

所有参编人员都是从事英语专业一线教学工作的高校教师，具有丰富的教学经验和良好的敬业精神，但是由于时间仓促和水平有限，疏漏舛误在所难免，敬请广大师生和专家同仁批评指正。

郭印　毕纪芹

2017 年 6 月

Contents

Unit One
Politics

报刊英语阅读的方法和技巧

　　第二语言习得过程中，阅读是获取知识和信息的重要手段。其中，美英报刊文章因其题材广泛、体裁多样、内容鲜活、语言表达生动自然，为学习者搭建了一个获得各种语言信息的平台。一方面，借助美英报刊阅读，学习者不仅可以扩大报刊词汇，培养和提高阅读外刊的基本能力，而且能增加语言感知的敏锐性，提高英语综合应用能力。另一方面，学习者还能了解西方文化背景知识，增加社会认知能力，进而培养跨文化交流意识，提高综合人文素质，以满足国家和社会对于大学生应具备较高人文素养的要求。

　　社会科技发展日新月异，社会生活各个方面的新事物和新动态迅速涌现，新的词语和表达法也顺应时代潮流，源源不断地出现。报刊英文除了兼具时效性和鲜活性外，其内容丰富多彩、实用性强。可以说，有效阅读美英媒体报刊，是准确把握现代英语脉搏的一条捷径。但是，报刊英语在遣词造句、文章结构、题材体裁等方面，都具有鲜明的特点。这些都决定了报刊文章的阅读策略和技巧与其他种类的阅读会有所不同。

　　下面就英文报刊阅读的方法和技巧方面提出几点建议：

1 学会阅读版面

　　阅读报纸之前，首先要了解报纸的不同版面及各版面的主要内容。版面是每期报刊内容编排布局的整体产物，通过熟悉版面，能够了解每种报纸的主要内容所分布的位置，使进一步阅读具有针对性。美英主流报刊每期都在固定位置刊示报纸内容的索引，对比索引就可以看出报刊之间不同的版面安排。比如，我们对比《卫报》（ *The Guardian* ）、《华盛顿邮报》（ *The Washington Post* ）和《基督教科学箴言报》（ *The Christian Science Monitor* ）的内容索引，即可以看出三者办报风格的异同（其中画线处为三者共有版面）：

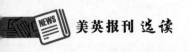

《卫报》 http://www.theguardian.com	《华盛顿邮报》 https://www.washingtonpost.com	《基督教科学箴言报》 http://www.csmonitor.com
UK; World; Sport; Football; Opinion; Culture; Business; Lifestyle; Fashion; Environment; Tech; Travel	Politics; Opinions; Sports; Local; National; World; Business; Tech; Lifestyle; Entertainment; Video; Jobs; WP BrandConnec	World; USA; Commentary; Business; Energy/Environment; Technology; Science; Culture; Books; Take Action

有些报刊的时事新闻部分也视重要性不同提供要闻索引，以方便读者快速了解时事，例如，我们选择不同日期对比了 *The Washington Post* 头版上方的要闻索引（In the News），可以看出时事变化：

Mar. 5, 2016: Louis C.K Trump; Lena Dunham; Eerie noises; Joey Feek dies; O.J. Simpson; Pat Conroy; Bobby Jindal; Han; Erin Andrews; Apple-F.B.I

Oct. 21, 2016: Police hero; Teacher's affair; Duterte; Gorilla bender; Judge's lament; 'To be white'; Infanticide; 'Hipster cop'; WNBA; Josh Brown

Nov. 4, 2016: Church arson; Amelia Earhart; SOS note; Electric cars; Marine's confession; Horror blogger; CMAs; Beyonce; Harvard soccer; Kevin Turner

Dec. 26, 2016: Parents OD'd; Typhoon; Queen Elizabeth II; Jason Miller; 'Generation KKK'; Santa; Pope Francis; Jonathan Allen; Cam Newton; Mike Tomlin

Feb. 6, 2017: Kellyanne Conway; Iranian baby; 'So-called judge'; Trump's calls; N.Y. jogger; Washington state; Schuyler Sisters; Somalia; Super Bowl stats

这样，读者可以根据自己的需要和兴趣来选择不同阅读板块的内容，从而减少盲目性，提高阅读效率。

2 准确把握标题

标题是新闻报道的点睛之笔，用以精要概述全文重点，通常会以不同颜色和字体表示，凝练醒目。快速而高效地理解标题，会对整篇新闻的理解起到提纲挈领的作用。新闻标题在词汇、语法等方面均有显著的特点。比如，在语法方面有两个显著特点：一是某些语法功能虚词的省略倾向，二是标题时态的特定习惯用法。由于新闻报道的是新近或刚刚发生的事情，因此倾向于使用能让读者感受时效性的表达方法。常见标题的时态用法可以概括为以下四种：一般现在时表述新近发生的事实；一般过去时表述往事或历史事实；现在分词表述正在进行的动作；不定式表述未来的行为。

例如

Rupert Murdoch and Jerry Hall marry. (*The Times*, Mar. 6, 2016)

Brazil in crisis as Dilma Rousseff fights to stave off impeachment threat (*The Guardian*, Mar. 20, 2016)

Awaiting a political awakening (*The Washington Post*, Mar. 20, 2016)

Trump to huddle with influential Republicans in D.C. ahead of AIPAC speech (*The Washington Post*, Mar. 20, 2016)

关于传媒大亨默多克和超模杰莉·霍尔（Jerry Hall）结婚的新闻标题用了"历史现在时"（Historical Present）来表达他们已经完婚的事实；同样地，关于巴西总统胡塞夫努力避免弹劾威胁的新闻标题也运用了该时态，让读者感觉这件事情的发生近在眼前。Awaiting a political awakening 使用进行时态表达"正在等待政治觉醒"之义。关于新一届美国总统候选人特朗普将与共和党权力人士在华盛顿特区碰头的新闻则用了动词不定式 to huddle with 表示将来的行为。

3 了解新闻体裁

英文报刊的体裁包括：消息报道、特写及专栏、社论和广告。消息报道就是我们通常意义上的"硬新闻"，结构上一般是典型的"倒金字塔"，即最重要的信息出现在导语中，信息的重要性依次降低。特写着重在某一方面，既要提供事实，也要引起读者的兴趣，因此在文笔上比较讲究。特写包括新闻特写（news features）和一般特写（general features）（廖维娜、杨静，2008），可专门写一人、一事、一情、一景，也可就专门问题写个人的看法，并由此发展成定期发表文章的"专栏"。特写往往以有独到的思想、趣味、观点、风格来吸引读者。报刊上的社论代表报纸或杂志的立场、观点，常是对某一件事做出表态、提出问题或发出号召，对某行为或人物进行臧否褒贬，社论的篇章结构与一般议论文相同，即"论点—论证—论据—结论"。广告是商业宣传的手段，大量使用照片及图画，图文并茂，形式活泼，广告部分的文字语言凝练，善用修辞，表现力强，与广告意图紧密相合。

4 正确处理生词

英文报刊阅读中，不可避免地会遇到一些新词和生词。正确的处理方法包括利用构词法知识、利用上下文语境、利用时事和百科知识等进行合理猜测。

首先，可以合理利用构词法知识。英语中"词缀＋词根"构词法非常普遍，理解基本

的词缀、词根涵义，熟练掌握构词规律，对于由这些词根、词缀组成的单词意思也就容易理解多了。例如 un-employ-ment、con-tribu-tion 等。缩略词的频繁使用是美英报刊文章另一个显著特点。例如：

缩略词	全称	汉语对应词
SALT	Strategic Arms Limitation Talks	限制战略武器会谈
ASEAN	The Association of the Southeast Asian Nations	东南亚国家联盟
APEC	Asia-Pacific Economic Cooperation	亚太经济合作组织
IMF	International Monetary Fund	国际货币基金组织
ADB	Asian Development Bank	亚洲开发银行
WTO	World Trade Organization	世界贸易组织
OPEC	Organization of Petroleum Exporting Countries	石油输出国组织（欧佩克）
UNESCO	United Nations Educational, Scientific and Cultural Organization	联合国教科文组织
IAEA	International Atomic Energy Agency	国际原子能机构
IEA	International Energy Agency	国际能源机构
NATO	Northern Atlantic Treaty Organization	北大西洋公约组织
IOC	International Olympic Committee	国际奥林匹克委员会

其次，可以通过上下文猜测单词意义。任何新闻都是一个语篇，有一定的语域（register）。在特定的语域内，语言的使用是紧密相关的。生词的意义通常和语域是相契合的，具有可推测性。根据上下文，正确推测贴合具体语境的单词意义，是阅读的重要方法之一。例如，Campaign manager for Trump denies manhandling protester，虽然读者有可能对 manhandle 一词有些陌生，但是通过上下文中"竞选总干事否认____抗议者"不难猜出"粗暴对待"（physically hold or push）之义。

再次，合理利用时事和百科知识进行推测。熟知西方国家政治经济和人文地理等方面的专有名词，以及一些知名企业和组织的中英文对应名称，对报刊阅读能力的提高会很有帮助。如：White House 白宫（指代美国政府）、No. 10 Downing Street 唐宁街 10 号（英国首相官邸和办公处，指代英国政府）、Elysee 爱丽舍宫（法国总统官邸和办公处，指代法国政府）、Capitol Hill 美国国会大厦（指代美国国会）、Buckingham 白金汉宫（是英国君主在伦敦的主要寝宫及办公处，指代英国皇室）、Pentagon 五角大楼（指代美国国防部）、Wal-Mart Stores（沃尔玛商店）、J.P. Morgan Chase（摩根大通银行）、AIG（American International Group，美国国际集团）等。

5 养成良好的阅读习惯

英文报刊阅读中，除非特殊需要，一般应努力避免"指读""笔读""唇读""默读"，以及过于依赖词典等阅读习惯。所谓"指读"或"笔读"，是指习惯用手指或笔指着逐词阅读。

眼球的运动远比手指灵活，速度也更快，所以"指读"和"笔读"一定程度上是在迫使眼睛跟着手指移动，势必会降低阅读速度。同时，眼睛所涉及的阅读范围不应是单个词语，而应该是一些意群（meaning cluster），由于一个句子通常由若干结构不同的意群构成，这样也会提高阅读效率。如果英语学习过于依赖有声朗读练习，忽略速读泛读练习，逐渐养成了出声朗读、动唇拼读或在心里默默拼读的习惯，这些都会降低大脑处理语言信息的速度。另外，阅读过程中碰到生词是正常的，频繁查单词不仅会影响阅读兴趣，而且自己根据语境猜词义的阅读技能也得不到锻炼和提高。

　　总之，语言的学习是一个漫长的实践过程。通过阅读美英报纸杂志，可以有效培养语感，提高阅读理解能力，增强精读、略读等阅读技能。同时，阅读使学生能在信息激增的时代，积极有效地获取并积累有价值的信息，体味西方文化，培养正确的跨文化交流意识。

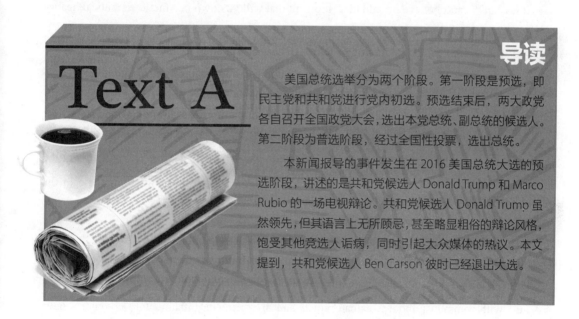

导读

美国总统选举分为两个阶段。第一阶段是预选，即民主党和共和党进行党内初选。预选结束后，两大政党各自召开全国政党大会，选出本党总统、副总统的候选人。第二阶段为普选阶段，经过全国性投票，选出总统。

本新闻报导的事件发生在 2016 美国总统大选的预选阶段，讲述的是共和党候选人 Donald Trump 和 Marco Rubio 的一场电视辩论。共和党候选人 Donald Trump 虽然领先，但其语言上无所顾忌，甚至略显粗俗的辩论风格，饱受其他竞选人诟病，同时引起大众媒体的热议。本文提到，共和党候选人 Ben Carson 彼时已经退出大选。

Debating Trump: Whatever happened to civility in politics?

The Republican debate Thursday night sank to a new low in modern campaign discourse. But for Donald Trump, at least, it's working[1].

By Linda Feldmann

Washington—Ben Carson[2] could see it coming a mile away.

Two days before Thursday's Republican presidential debate[3] on Fox News[4], Dr. Carson called on the candidates to come together and agree to conduct themselves with civility.

"I am confident that the five remaining candidates can rise above the sophomoric attacks of

past encounters and have a serious discussion about substantive issues," Carson said.

The next day, the famed neurosurgeon opted out of the debate, and, effectively, the campaign. And on Thursday night, the four remaining Republicans staged a debate that arguably sank to a new low for off-color public discourse in a televised American presidential campaign event.

The schoolyard taunts that had come to mark campaign events in recent days, mostly between Donald Trump[5] and Marco Rubio, seeped onto the debate stage—and into rhetoric not suitable for family viewing.

Mr. Trump called Senator Rubio "little Marco." He called Ted Cruz "lyin' Ted[6]." And then he fired back on Senator Rubio's charge earlier in the week that he has "little hands" with a crude retort defending his masculinity[7].

It was an "I can't believe he said that" moment that will go down in American political history for its sheer shock value.

"You're inviting the question, should we now have language warnings on presidential debates?" says Kathleen Hall Jamieson, director of the Annenberg Public Policy Center[8] at the University of Pennsylvania.

Insulting political language is nothing new. In the 19th century, Ms. Jamieson notes, such attacks came in printed form, with the posting of "broadsides" that cast aspersions[9]. But "in the mass media age, with a large viewing audience, we have not had anything comparable to the Republican debates," Jamieson says.

This is politics in the age of Trump—a campaign style that tracks the larger decline of public discourse and decorum. And for Trump, at least, it's a way of campaigning that works. He's the front-runner for the Republican nomination. From the moment Trump announced his campaign last June with comments about Mexican rapists and drug dealers, inflammatory comments have been central to his brand—and his appeal.

For the rapt American viewing audience—both fans and detractors—it makes for compelling TV. Longtime Republican political practitioners have watched with fascination and horror, as their party undergoes a hostile takeover by a man who is neither especially conservative nor a loyal Republican.

"The spectacle is irresistible," says Matt Robbins, president of the group American Majority, which trains aspiring political candidates. "He is breaking all the rules... but it could not be done by anyone else. It is not replicable."

Ultimately, Mr. Robbins adds, Trump is "riding a wrecking ball through the heart of this movement, which is itself the heart of this party. It's very sad."

For Rubio[10], getting sucked into Trump-style campaigning, the effect may just be to harm his image. As the youngest candidate in the GOP field[11], and youthful in appearance, Rubio has worked hard to show that he's ready for the job of president. In his debate appearances, he has consistently shown mastery of policy, arguing that foreign policy is his strength.

Now, spending most of his debate time on the attack, he seems to be undercutting his argument. It may be that Rubio feels he has nothing to lose: Polls show he is well behind in the winner-take-all Florida primary on March 15, his home-state contest, and if he loses, his campaign is likely over.

Still, it's one thing to attack Trump as a "con artist" over his past, including the legal battles he's fighting over the defunct Trump University. It's another to fling insults at the billionaire reality TV star over the size of his hands. The origins of the "small hands" comment go back to 1988, when *Spy* magazine called Trump a "short-fingered vulgarian."

The Donald, it should be noted, does not seem to have especially short fingers, though few can dispute the second part of the epithet.

Trump's thin skin has raised questions about his suitability for the presidency—a job like no other that, history has shown, requires a temperament that can withstand constant testing. But in his quest for the presidency, his style has served him well. It may be, in the age of reality TV and radio shock jocks, Trump's at-times coarse language is just chalked up as part of the show.

Maybe, some Republicans say, his over-the-top campaign style is an act[12], and if successful, a President Trump would behave in a more dignified fashion.

To secure the GOP nomination, Trump still has to win over many more voters. He has won 10 of the first 15 nominating contests, but in a still-large, divided field, he hasn't won a majority of votes in any of them.

Now, with Carson's decision to drop out, there's a new bloc of voters up for grabs. At the annual Conservative Political Action Conference, being held this week outside Washington, D.C., voters wearing Carson buttons stood near his booth in the exhibition hall and contemplated their choices.

One woman, who declined to be named, said she now wasn't planning to vote, because there's no one left for her to support. She doesn't like how Cruz treated Carson, and she feels Rubio is too much like Obama, issuing scripted remarks with a TelePrompTer[13].

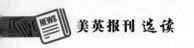

What about Trump? "He isn't a conservative," she said. "He's for eminent domain, and he doesn't want to defund Planned Parenthood[14]."

Tim Donney, a retiree from Newtown, Penn., said he doesn't like the way Trump "demonizes" and attacks anyone who disagrees with him. "It's his way or the highway," he said Thursday afternoon.

But Mr. Donney said he's still open to voting for Trump. "It depends on how he acts," he said.

That was before Thursday night's debate.

（From *The Christian Science Monitor*, Mar. 4, 2016）

NOTES

1. 共和党周四晚上的党内辩论让美国当代竞选用语的文明程度"跌入新低"（sank to a new low），但是对于 Donald Trump 来说，这样的竞选风格至少是很奏效的。这是本篇新闻的副标题，补充说明了标题中提到的美国大选辩论中的语言修养问题。

2. Ben Carson 本·卡森，共和党人，美国传奇神经外科医生，《恩赐妙手》(*Gifted Hands: The Ben Carson Story*) 原型。2014 年 11 月，宣布参选美国总统。2016 年 3 月 4 日，本·卡森正式宣布，自己将退出竞选。

3. Republican presidential debate 是指共和党内部总统候选人之间的辩论，在大选的预选（primary election）阶段进行。同一党内的竞选人要通过辩论来表达自己观点，同时反驳对方，展现自己的优势，提高选票支持率。最终胜出者将代表本党角逐总统宝座。

   美国总统大选的两党候选人通过电视进行辩论，通常在两党全国代表大会结束之后和大选投票正式开始之前这段时间进行。最早追溯于 1960 年共和党候选人尼克松与民主党候选人肯尼迪的精彩电视辩论。从 1976 年开始，美国两党的总统候选人的全国电视辩论，这种"近距离体验民主政治"，成为大选的一个惯例。大选辩论是总统候选人公开宣传政见、展示自身魅力并赢得选票的最佳时机。

4. Fox News 福克斯新闻频道。该频道从早上五点开始，每小时开始和结束的时候都会提供最新的新闻报道。节目内容包括新闻人物、追踪报道事件的最新消息。

5. Donald Trump 唐纳德·特朗普于 1946 年 6 月 14 日出生于美国纽约，是一名商人、作家和主持人。曾经是美国最具知名度的房地产商之一，人称"地产之王"。2015 年 12 月 7 日，唐纳德·特朗普入围美国知名新闻周刊《时代》2015 年度人物的候选名单。2016 年 3 月 2 日，在美国大选共和党初选"超级星期二"共获得 7 个州胜利，遥遥领先。此后，支持率逐渐上升，一路赶超，于 2016 年 11 月 8 日，击败民主党候选人希拉里·克林顿（Hillary Clinton），当选为美国第 45 任总统，2017 年 1 月 20 日宣誓就职。

6. Donald Trump 给参议员 Rubio 起绰号为"小马克"，称另外一名共和党的候选人 Ted Cruz 为"撒谎的泰德"。Trump 在总统竞选过程中，以其语言上的不羁为特有风格。知名脱口秀主持人 Jon

Stewart 把 Trump 称为"有钱、疯狂而又自大的莽兽"（a rich, crazy, egotistical monster）。

7. 1988 年，《名利场》（*Vanity Fair*）杂志主编和《密探》（*Spy*）杂志的联合创刊人 Graydon Carter 发文将 Trump 讥讽为"短指土豪"（short-fingered vulgarian），笑其指短手小，在此次共和党党内总统候选人竞选中，作为候选人之一的参议员 Marco Rubio 利用这一典故开涮，嘲笑 Trump "人大手小不可靠"，回应其对自己的戏谑。

8. Annenberg Public Policy Center 美国宾夕法尼亚大学的安伦博格公共政策中心。

9. 侮辱性的竞选语言不是新把戏。贾米森女士指出，在 19 世纪时，这种攻击就以印刷品的形式，张贴"抨击（broadsides）"，以诋毁中伤对手。

10. Marco Rubio 国会议员，共和党人，于 2015 年 4 月份宣布参加 2016 年的美国总统竞选。2016 年 3 月 15 日宣布退选。

11. GOP (Grand Old Party) 大老党，美国共和党的别称。

12. 一些共和党人认为 Donald Trump 过火的竞选风格只是一种作秀。over-the-top 的意思是"过火的，荒唐的，荒谬的"（far more than usual or expected）。

13. TelePrompTer 讲词提示机，讲词提示器。因记不住或担心忘记演讲内容，一些演讲者习惯于依赖这种机器。本文指 Marco Rubio 同奥巴马总统演讲时一样，借助于讲词提示器帮助，一些选民对此持有看法。

14. Planned Parenthood，是一家提供生殖健康医疗服务的非营利组织，每年大约为 270 万女性提供各种医疗检查，帮助预防和治疗性传播疾病、提供避孕与堕胎服务等。

USEFUL WORDS

aspersion	[əsˈpɜːʃən]	*n.*	the act of aspersing. *cast ~s on sb/sb's honor* 对某人 / 某人的名誉加以诽谤
asperse		*v.*	(formal) to slander; say false or unkind things about（正式用语）诽谤；中伤
bloc	[blɒk]	*n.*	[C] a group of countries that work closely together because they have similar political interests（政治利益一致的）国家集团
broadside	[ˈbrɔːdsaɪd]	*n.*	[C] the whole of a ship's side above the water; (fig) strong attack of any kind made at one time against one person or group 船舷（吃水线以上之全部船侧）；（喻）对某人或某团体所做的一次猛烈攻击
civility	[səˈvɪləti]	*n.*	[U] politeness 礼貌；客气 ~ *to*（对人）有礼貌
coarse	[kɔːrs]	*adj.*	vulgar; not delicate or refined 粗鲁的；粗俗的
contemplate	[ˈkɒntəmpleɪt]	*v.*	to look at (with the eyes, or in the mind) 注视；沉思
decorum	[dɪˈkɔːrəm]	*n.*	[U] right and proper behavior, as required by social custom 社会习俗所要求的正当而合乎礼仪的行为；礼貌

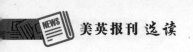
defunct	[dɪ'fʌŋkt] *adj.*	(formal) no longer existing, operating or being used 不再存在的；不再起作用的；不再使用的
detractor	[dɪ'træktər] *n.*	a person who tries to make sb's reputation, etc, smaller 损毁某人之名誉者；贬低者
eminent	['emɪnənt] *adj.*	(of a person) distinguished; (of qualities) remarkable in degree （指人）著名的，卓越的；（指品质）优良的
epithet	['epɪθet] *n.*	[C] 1) an adjective or phrase that is used to describe sb/sth's character or most important quality, especially in order to give praise or criticism（尤用于褒贬人或事物特征或性质的）表述形容词，修饰语 2) (especially North American English) an offensive word or phrase that is used about a person or group of people 别称；绰号；诨名
inflammatory	[ɪn'flæmətɔːri] *adj.*	If you accuse someone of saying or doing inflammatory things, you mean that what they say or do is likely to make people react very angrily. 使人激愤的；煽动性的
neurosurgeon	[ˌnjʊroʊ'sɜːdʒən] *n.*	someone who does surgery on the nervous system (especially the brain) 神经外科医生
opt	[ɑːpt] *v.*	to select as an alternative 选择；做出抉择 ~ out 决定不参加；退出
rapt	[ræpt] *adj.*	so interested in one particular thing that you are not aware of anything else 全神贯注的；专心致志的
retort	[rɪ'tɔːrt] *v.*	to answer back quickly, wittily or angrily (esp. to an accusation or challenge)（对控诉或挑战）立即机智地或愤怒地反击
rhetoric	['retərɪk] *adj.*	(art of) using words impressively in speech and writing 修辞；修辞学
seep	[siːp] *v.*	(of liquids) to ooze out or through; trickle（指液体）渗出；漏出
sophomoric	[ˌsɒfə'mɒrɪk] *adj.*	childish and not very sensible 稚的；不明智的；不切实际的
substantive	[səb'stæntɪv] *adj.*	having an independent existence; real; actual. 独立存在的；真正的；实际的
taunt	[tɔːnt] *n.*	[C] remark intended to hurt sb's feelings; contemptuous reproach 辱骂；讥笑
temperament	['temprəmənt] *n.*	[C] a person's or an animal's nature as shown in the way they behave or react to situations or people（人或动物的）气质；性情；性格；禀性
ultimately	['ʌltɪmətli] *adv.*	1) in the end; finally 最终；最后；终归 2) at the most basic and important level 最基本地；根本上
vulgarian	[vʌl'geriən] *n.*	a person, esp a rich person whose manners and tastes are bad 粗俗的人，（尤其是）粗俗的有钱人

EXERCISES

I. Vocabulary

Choose among the four alternatives one word or phrase that is closest in meaning to the underlined part in each statement.

1. I am confident that the five remaining candidates can rise above the <u>sophomoric</u> attacks of past encounters and have a serious discussion about substantive issues

   A. hazard   B. insulting   C. inspiring   D. childish

2. The next day, the famed neurosurgeon <u>opted out</u> of the debate, and, effectively, the campaign.

   A. dropped out   B. kicked out   C. expelled out   D. popped out

3. The schoolyard <u>taunts</u> that had come to mark campaign events in recent days, mostly between Donald Trump and Marco Rubio, seeped onto the debate stage—and into rhetoric not suitable for family viewing.

   A. assails   B. ridicules   C. strikes   D. squeezes

4. This is politics in the age of Trump—a campaign style that tracks the larger decline of public discourse and <u>decorum</u>.

   A. decency   B. calmness   C. kindness   D. perseverance

5. The Donald, it should be noted, does not seem to have especially short fingers, though few can dispute the second part of the <u>epithet</u>.

   A. assault   B. nickname   C. mockery   D. attack

6. Trump's thin skin has raised questions about his suitability for the presidency—a job like no other that, history has shown, requires a temperament that can <u>withstand</u> constant testing.

   A. withdraw   B. repress   C. ravage   D. endure

7. Maybe, some Republicans say, his <u>over-the-top</u> campaign style is an act.

   A. peril   B. exaggerating   C. elementary   D. coarse

8. Now, with Carson's decision to drop out, there's a new <u>bloc</u> of voters up for grabs.

   A. group   B. strip   C. fake   D. chip

9. Trump's at-times coarse language is just <u>chalked</u> up as part of the show.

   A. resulted in   B. due to   C. far-fetched   D. bound to

10. At the annual Conservative Political Action Conference, being held this week outside Washington, D.C., voters wearing Carson buttons stood near his booth in the exhibition hall and <u>contemplated</u> their choices.

    A. verified   B. certified   C. reflected   D. censored

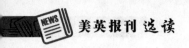

II. Comprehension

Decide whether the following statements are true or false according to the information given in the press clipping. Mark T or F to each statement.

1. The Republican debate Thursday night sank to a new low in modern campaign discourse, which means US election has become more decayed.

2. Mr. Trump called Senator Rubio "little Marco." From that we can see Trump's behavior is rather crude.

3. From the news, we might guess Cruz might be another candidate who is the rival of Trump.

4. Matt Robbins, president of the group American Majority, thinks Trump's campaign style is not so decent.

5. *Spy* magazine called Trump a "short-fingered vulgarian," because Trump does have very short fingers.

6. Trump's coarse language in the campaign is a great advantage in the election, but makes public discourse decline.

7. The candidates mentioned in the news are Trump, Carson and Matt Robbins.

8. Dr. Carson has been very confident, and will continue the campaign until the last moment.

9. One woman, who declined to be named, was for Rubio, for she thought Rubio was like Obama.

10. From the news, we cannot predict which party will win the election.

III. Questions for discussion

1. When Barack Obama, an African American, was elected the President of the United States, some people said that the United States was the most desirable country in the world. Do you agree to this view? Please illustrate your ideas.

2. How much have you learned about the procedures of US presidential election?

3. Please describe what kind of person Donald Trump is, according to the article. Could you explain why he could be finally elected to be the president of a country?

4. The two political parties take turns to be in power in the United States. Some people say both of them represent only the few people who sponsor them in the election. Is it true or false? Please justify your ideas.

美英政党简介

美国

美国是世界上最早出现政党的国家之一，也是实行两党制的代表性国家之一。民主党和共和党是两大主要政党，主导着美国各个层面的政治生态。美国的两党制，与其政治选举制度、国会制度、行政管理制度和司法制度等，联系都非常密切。美国大选期间，报刊上经常出现两党的党徽：驴和象。前者象征民主党，后者则象征共和党。人们往往将两党的这一政治交锋称为"驴象之争"。两党制在一定程度上对于维护美国的政治稳定，保证公民参与政权等方面发挥了较为积极的作用。

民主党（the Democratic Party）起源于 1792 年由托马斯·杰斐逊（Thomas Jefferson）创立的民主共和党（the Democratic-Republican Party）。初期主要由种植园主、农民和一些与南方奴隶主有联系的资本家组成。1828 年该党正式改为现名。民主党在经济上的立场偏左派。1932 年富兰克林·罗斯福"新政"以来，民主党的自由派色彩比较浓，强调国家干预社会经济生活，夸大社会福利保障（金灿荣，1995）。美国总统奥巴马（Barack Obama）是民主党的现任执政领袖，自 2009 年上台后，走的是左翼自由派和进步主义路线。

共和党（the Republican Party）于 1854 年成立，初期主要由反对扩大奴隶制的北方工商业资本家组成。前身亦为民主 - 共和党。该党于 1825 年发生分裂，其中一派组成国家共和党（National Republican Party），1834 年改称辉格党（Whig Party）。共和党的保守派形象更突出，被视为社会保守主义、经济古典主义，比较多地主张发挥市场的作用，强调个人自由，反对国家干预，反对国家承担过多的福利保障职能（金灿荣，1995），在外交、国防问题上则采取强硬的右派态度。

近年来，全国性政党在代表选举和总统竞选中所起的作用逐渐增大。全国代表大会是政党的最高权力机关，每四年举行一次。大会提名下届总统和副总统的候选人，并通过该政党纲领。民主党和共和党的全国委员会是两次全国代表大会期间的主要管理实体，其主要任务是为该党的总统候选人进行选举筹款、开展选情调研、从事政策研究等。该委员会还设有外围组织，如妇女联合会和青年联合会等（周淑真、冯永光，2010）。

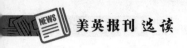

美国历任总统所属党派

任数	姓名（英文）	姓名（中文）	任期	党派
1	George Washington	乔治·华盛顿	1789-1797	无
2	John Adams	约翰·亚当斯	1797-1801	联邦党
3	Thomas Jefferson	托马斯·杰斐逊	1801-1809	民主共和党
4	James Madison	詹姆斯·麦迪逊	1809-1817	民主共和党
5	James Monroe	詹姆斯·门罗	1817-1825	民主共和党
6	John Quincy Adams	约翰·昆西·亚当斯	1825-1829	国家共和党
7	Andrew Jackson	安德鲁·杰克逊	1829-1837	民主党
8	Martin Van Buren	马丁·范布伦	1837-1841	民主党
9	William Henry Harrison	威廉·亨利·哈里森	1841-1841	辉格党
10	John Tyler	约翰·泰勒	1841-1845	辉格党
11	James Knox Polk	詹姆斯·诺克斯·波尔克	1845-1849	民主党
12	Zachary Taylor	扎卡里·泰勒	1849-1850	辉格党
13	Millard Fillmore	米勒德·菲尔莫尔	1850-1853	辉格党
14	Franklin Pierce	富兰克林·皮尔斯	1853-1857	民主党
15	James Buchanan	詹姆斯·布坎南	1857-1861	民主党
16	Abraham Lincoln	亚伯拉罕·林肯	1861-1865	共和党
17	Andrew Johnson	安德鲁·约翰逊	1865-1869	民主党
18	Ulysses Simpson Grant	尤利西斯·辛普森·格兰特	1869-1877	共和党
19	Rutherford Birchard Hayes	拉瑟福德·伯查德·海斯	1877-1881	共和党
20	James Garfield	詹姆斯·加菲尔德	1881-1881	共和党
21	Chester Alan Arthur	切斯特·艾伦·阿瑟	1881-1885	共和党
22	Grover Cleveland	格罗弗·克利夫兰	1885-1889	民主党
23	Benjamin Harrison	本杰明·哈利森	1889-1893	共和党
24	Grover Cleveland	格罗弗·克利夫兰	1893-1897	民主党
25	William McKinley	威廉·麦金莱（利）	1897-1901	共和党
26	Theodore Roosevelt	西奥多·罗斯福	1901-1909	共和党
27	William Howard Taft	威廉·霍华德·塔夫脱	1909-1913	共和党
28	Woodrow Wilson	伍德罗·威尔逊	1913-1921	民主党
29	Warren Gamaliel Harding	沃伦·盖玛利尔·哈定	1921-1923	共和党
30	Calvin Coolidge	卡尔文·柯立芝	1923-1929	共和党
31	Herbert Clark Hoover	赫伯特·克拉克·胡佛	1929-1933	共和党
32	Franklin Delano Roosevelt	富兰克林·德拉诺·罗斯福	1933-1945	民主党

续表

任数	姓名（英文）	姓名（中文）	任期	党派
33	Harry S. Truman	哈里·S·杜鲁门	1945-1953	民主党
34	Dwight David Eisenhower	德怀特·戴维·艾森豪威尔	1953-1961	共和党
35	John Fitzgerald Kennedy	约翰·菲茨杰拉德·肯尼迪	1961-1963	民主党
36	Lyndon Baines Johnson	林登·贝恩斯·约翰逊	1963-1969	民主党
37	Richard Milhous Nixon	理查德·米尔豪斯·尼克松	1969-1974	共和党
38	Gerald Rudolph Ford Jr.	杰拉尔德·鲁道夫·福特	1974-1977	共和党
39	James(Jimmy) Earl Carter	詹姆斯（吉米）·厄尔·卡特	1977-1981	民主党
40	Ronald Reagan	罗纳德·里根	1981-1989	共和党
41	George Herbert Walker Bush	乔治·赫伯特·沃克·布什	1989-1993	共和党
42	Bill Clinton	比尔·克林顿	1993-2001	民主党
43	George Walker Bush	乔治·沃克·布什	2001-2009	共和党
44	Barack Hussein Obama II	巴拉克·侯赛因·奥巴马	2009-2017	民主党
45	Donald John Trump	唐纳德·约翰·特朗普	2017-	共和党

英国

英国是世界上最早确立政党政治的国家，是现代政党政治的发源地，也是实行两党制的典型国家。

17世纪复辟王朝时期，英国诞生了辉格党（Whig Party）和托利党（Tory Party）这两大政党，当时辉格党代表新兴资产阶级和新贵族的利益，主张限制王权，提高议会权力；托利党代表地主贵族利益，维护君主特权。随着资产阶级的发展，辉格党以自由贸易的工厂主为核心，在原来的基础上组成自由党（Liberal Party）。以土地贵族为核心，在原托利党的基础上组成保守党（Conservative Party）。19世纪末、20世纪初，自由党逐步衰落。1924年后，工党（Labor Party）取代自由党，与保守党轮流执政。到20世纪80年代末，英国除保守党和工党两大政党外，还有自由民主党（The Liberal Democrat Party）、苏格兰民族党（Scottish National Party）等。其中，自由民主党是比较重要的第三政党，通常能够获得20%左右的选票。虽然这样的支持率不足以组建政府，但往往能够对保守党和工党的执政前景产生决定性影响。

1979年，保守党在撒切尔夫人（Margaret Thatcher）带领下赢得大选后，致力于反对国有化（nationalization），削弱工会权力，倡导经济自由主义（economic liberalism）。现任首相特蕾莎·梅（Theresa Mary May）是保守党的党魁。而与之相对，工党推动政治体制改革

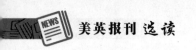

比较积极；经济上推行国有化，强调一定程度的国家干涉，主张建立福利型国家。

英国历任首相及所属党派

任数	姓名（英文）	姓名（中文）	任期	党派
1	Robert Walpole	罗伯特·沃波尔	1721-1742	辉格党
2	Spencer Compton, Earl of Wilmington	威尔明顿伯爵	1742-1743	辉格党
3	Henry Pelham	亨利·佩尔汉姆	1743-1754	辉格党
4	Thomas Pelham-Holles, Duke of Newcastle	纽卡斯尔公爵	1754-1756	辉格党
5	William Cavendish, Duke of Devonshire	德文郡公爵	1756-1757	辉格党
6	Thomas Pelham-Holles, Duke of Newcastle	纽卡斯尔公爵	1757-1762	辉格党
7	John Stuart, Earl of Bute	比特伯爵	1762-1763	托利党
8	George Grenville	乔治·格兰维尔	1763-1765	辉格党
9	Charles Wentworth, Marquess of Rockingham	白金汉侯爵	1765-1766	辉格党
10	William Pitt, Earl of Chatham	查塔姆伯爵	1766-1768	辉格党
11	Augustus Henry Fitzroy, Duke of Grafton	格拉夫顿公爵	1768-1770	辉格党
12	Lord North	诺斯勋爵	1770-1782	托利党
13	Charles Wentworth, Marquess of Rockingham	白金汉侯爵	1782	辉格党
14	William Petty, Earl of Shelburne	谢尔本伯爵	1782-1783	辉格党
15	William Bentinck, Duke of Portland	波特兰公爵	1783	托利党/联合内阁
16	William Pitt	威廉·皮特	1783-1801	托利党
17	Henry Addington	亨利·埃丁顿	1801-1804	托利党
18	William Pitt	威廉·皮特	1804-1806	托利党
19	William Wyndam Grenville, Lord Grenville	格伦维尔勋爵	1806-1807	辉格党联合内阁
20	William Bentinck, Duke of Portland	波特兰公爵	1807-1809	托利党
21	Spencer Perceval	斯潘塞·帕西瓦尔	1809-1812	托利党
22	Robert Banks Jenkinson, Earl of Liverpool	利物浦伯爵	1812-1827	托利党
23	George Canning	乔治·坎宁	1827	托利党
24	Frederick Robinson, Viscount Goderich	戈德里奇子爵	1827-1828	托利党
25	Arthur Wellesley, Duke of Wellington	威灵顿公爵	1828-1830	托利党
26	Earl Grey	格雷伯爵	1830-1834	辉格党
27	William Lamb, Viscount Melbourne	墨尔本子爵	1834	辉格党
28	Arthur Wellesley, Duke of Wellington	威灵顿公爵	1834	保守党
29	Robert Peel	罗伯特·皮尔爵士	1834-1835	保守党
30	William Lamb, Viscount Melbourne	墨尔本子爵	1835-1841	辉格党
31	Robert Peel	罗伯特·皮尔爵士	1841-1846	保守党

续表

任数	姓名（英文）	姓名（中文）	任期	党派
32	Earl Russell	约翰·罗素勋爵	1846-1851	辉格党
33	Earl of Derby	德比伯爵	1852	保守党
34	Earl of Aberdeen	阿伯丁伯爵	1852-1855	保守党 / 联合内阁
35	Viscount Palmerston	帕尔姆斯顿子爵	1855-1858	辉格党
36	Earl of Derby	德比伯爵	1858-1859	保守党
37	Viscount Palmerston	帕尔姆斯顿子爵	1859-1865	自由党
38	Earl Russell	约翰·罗素勋爵	1865-1866	自由党
39	Earl of Derby	德比伯爵	1866-1868	保守党
40	Benjamin Disraeli	本杰明·迪斯雷利	1868	保守党
41	William Ewart Gladstone	威廉·格莱斯顿	1868-1874	自由党
42	Benjamin Disraeli	本杰明·迪斯雷利	1874-1880	保守党
43	William Ewart Gladstone	威廉·格莱斯顿	1880-1885	自由党
44	Robert Gascoyne-Cecil, Marquess of Salisbury	索尔兹伯里侯爵	1885-1886	保守党
45	William Ewart Gladstone	威廉·格莱斯顿	1886	自由党
46	Robert Gascoyne-Cecil, Marquess of Salisbury	索尔兹伯里侯爵	1886-1892	保守党
47	William Ewart Gladstone	威廉·格莱斯顿	1892-1894	自由党
48	Earl of Rosebery	罗斯贝利伯爵	1894-1895	自由党
49	Robert Gascoyne-Cecil, Marquess of Salisbury	索尔兹伯里侯爵	1895-1902	保守党
50	Arthur James Balfour	亚瑟·贝尔福	1902-1905	保守党
51	Henry Campbell-Bannerman	亨利·坎贝尔－班内南爵士	1905-1908	自由党
52	Herbert Henry Asquith	赫伯特·亨利·阿斯奎斯	1908-1916	自由党
53	David Lloyd George	大卫·劳合乔治	1916-1922	联合内阁
54	Andrew Bonar Law	安德鲁·伯纳尔·劳	1922-1923	保守党
55	Stanley Baldwin	斯坦利·鲍德温	1923-1924	保守党
56	James Ramsay MacDonald	拉姆赛·麦克唐纳	1924	工党
57	Stanley Baldwin	斯坦利·鲍德温	1924-1929	保守党
58	James Ramsay MacDonald	拉姆赛·麦克唐纳	1929-1935	工党 / 国民内阁
59	Stanley Baldwin	斯坦利·鲍德温	1935-1937	保守党 / 国民内阁
60	Arthur Neville Chamberlain	尼维尔·张伯伦	1937-1940	保守党 / 国民内阁
61	Winston Leonard Spencer Churchill	温斯顿·丘吉尔	1940-1945 1945	保守党 / 联合内阁 过渡政府

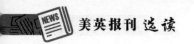
续表

任数	姓名（英文）	姓名（中文）	任期	党派
62	Clement Richard Attlee	克莱门特·艾德礼	1945-1951	工党
63	Winston Leonard Spencer Churchill	温斯顿·丘吉尔	1951-1955	保守党
64	Anthony Eden	安东尼·艾登爵士	1955-1957	保守党
65	Harold Macmillan	哈罗德·麦克米伦	1957-1963	保守党
66	Alec Douglas-Home	道格拉斯－霍姆	1963-1964	保守党
67	Harold Wilson	哈罗德·威尔逊	1964-1970	工党
68	Edward Heath	爱德华·希思	1970-1974	保守党
69	Harold Wilson	哈罗德·威尔逊	1974-1976	工党
70	James Callaghan	詹姆斯·卡拉汉	1976-1979	工党
71	Margaret Thatcher	玛格利特·撒切尔	1979-1990	保守党
72	John Major	约翰·梅杰	1990-1997	保守党
73	Tony Blair	托尼·布莱尔	1997-2007	工党
74	James Gordon Brown	戈登·布朗	2007-2010	工党
75	David William Donald Cameron	戴维·威廉·唐纳德·卡梅伦	2010-2016	保守党 / 联合政府
76	Theresa Mary May	特蕾莎·梅	2016-	保守党

Text B

导读

英国自 20 世纪 70 年代加入欧盟以来，国内一直存在支持派和怀疑派之间的争议。卡梅伦在参加竞选时曾表示，英国将于 2017 年关于是否退出欧盟的问题举行公投。但基于各种考虑，他在 2016 年 2 月 20 日突然宣布，英国将于 2016 年 6 月 23 日举行全民公投。

本篇新闻讲述的就是在此背景下，英国国内不同的态度和争议。尤其是"脱欧派"的立场和言论。文章以英国的 NHS 组织警告"脱欧派"一些不合适的行为开始，禁止他们用 NHS 的标志进行相关宣传活动。进而介绍了当时英国内部"脱欧派"与"留欧派"之间的争议。

Brexit[1] group warned: stop using NHS[2] logo or we' ll sue

By Daniel Boffey

Vote Leave campaign accuses Downing Street of 'bully boy tactics' as it argues that getting out of Europe will help the health service.

Government lawyers acting on behalf of NHS England have threatened to sue the lead Brexit campaign group, Vote Leave[3], over its use of the NHS logo on its leaflets.

The Observer[4] understands that a legal letter was sent on Saturday claiming the use of the trademark breaches guidelines. A spokesman for Vote Leave insisted it would not pull the leaflets and accused Downing Street[5] of "bully boy tactics", adding that Brexit would free up cash for a health service in "financial crisis".

The anti-EU group[6] has been selling and distributing leaflets and letters bearing the white capital letters on a blue background with the message to "Save our NHS" in the top right corner. Below a message to "Help protect your local hospital", it also features Vote Leave's slogan to "Vote Leave, take control" next to a red ballot box.

A central argument of the Vote Leave group—recently given backing by justice secretary Michael Gove, Commons leader Chris Grayling and culture secretary John Whittingdale[7]—is that it wants to "stop sending £350m every week to Brussels and instead spend it on our priorities, like the NHS and science research".

However, the Department of Health wrote to the campaign group last month after receiving complaints about the use of the NHS logo. Under brand guidelines, the NHS logo should be used only in its official communications in support of "core principles and values".

It is understood that the correspondence from Department of Health officials was ignored by Vote Leave, whose campaign director is Gove's former special adviser, Dominic Cummings.

Whitehall sources said the row had subsequently escalated, with lawyers being instructed to threaten legal proceedings, including a possible injunction on the use of the leaflets pending a trial[8]. Other consequences threatened included the destruction of all infringing goods and the payment of damages to the Department of Health.

A spokesman for Vote Leave said the move was further evidence of bullying by Downing Street, which on Saturday was forced to deny suggestions the government might have also played a role in the British Chamber of Commerce's (BCC)[9] decision to suspend its director general, John Longworth, for making pro-Brexit remarks. At the BCC's conference on Thursday, Longworth said

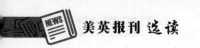

Britain would be left "sitting on the margins" of an "unreformed EU" if voters chose to stay in the EU in the 23 June referendum[10].

Matthew Elliott, Vote Leave's chief executive, said: "Business leaders like John Longworth should be able to speak freely about the dangers of staying in an unreformed EU. He made it clear he was speaking in a personal capacity—as many others will do throughout this debate. It is wrong for No 10 to attempt to gag business leaders. This is the most important debate for 40 years and everyone should be able to speak their mind without fear of retribution."

A No 10 source said any claims about government officials having a role in the affair were not true. He added: "It is a matter for the BCC."

A statement released on Friday by the BCC said it would not "be campaigning for either side ahead of the EU referendum. The BCC will survey chamber member companies across the UK, report their diverse views, and inform the debate".[11]

Government's lawyers have insisted Vote Leave takes the leaflets out of public use by 8 March or it will face a legal battle. The DoH said: "We have informed Vote Leave this is an inappropriate use of the NHS brand."

（From *The Guardian*, Mar. 5, 2016）

NOTES

1. Brexit（一说 Brixit），即 British exit from the EU（英国退出欧盟），是一种略带调侃性的说法。2016 年 1 月 23 日，时任首相卡梅伦就英国是否退出欧盟发表演讲后，该词迅速传播开来。

2. NHS (National Health Service) 英国国家医疗服务体系，始建于 1948 年，是英国社会福利制度中最重要的部分之一。该体系一直承担着保障英国全民公费医疗保健的重任，秉持不论个人收入如何，只根据个人的不同需要，无偿提供全面医疗服务的服务原则。

3. Vote Leave "脱欧派"，指英国主张脱离欧盟的人，主要代表有司法大臣 Michael Gove，在本篇新闻中提到的人物之一，他既是卡梅伦首相的朋友，也是长期以来的"疑欧主义者"。

4. *The Observer*《观察家报》，是一份英国周报，每周日发行，创刊于 1791 年。目前隶属于卫报传媒集团（Guardian Media Group）。

5. 英国首相卡梅伦是"留欧派"最重要的代表，一定程度上代表了英国政府对待是否脱离欧盟的官方态度，因此"脱欧派"指责英国政府威吓那些持脱欧观点的人。No. 10 Downing Street（唐宁街 10 号）位于英国首都伦敦威斯敏斯特（City of Westminster，又译为西敏市），是英国首相官邸和办公室。黑色木门，门上缀有白色的阿拉伯数字"10"。就像白宫代表美国政府一样，唐宁街 10 号通常代表英国政府，有时简为唐宁街（Downing Street）。

6. The anti-EU group "反欧盟集团"，即"脱欧派"（pro-Brexit）。EU(European Union) 指欧洲联盟，是 1992 年成立的政治经济性组织。在英国退出前，一度有 28 个会员国，是世界最有政治影响力的组织之一。在成员国之间贸易、农业、渔业、和区域发展等方面实行统一的政策，实现人员、商品、服务和资本在成员国之间自由流动。欧盟成员国执行统一的外交和安全政策，因此成为当今世界政治经济格局的重要力量，总部设在比利时首都布鲁塞尔。 2016 年 6 月 23 日，英国就欧盟问题举行公投，决定是否仍留在欧盟，结果 "脱欧派" 取得胜利。

7. Chris Grayling 英国内阁大臣。John Whittingdale 是英国文化部长。跟司法大臣 Michael Gove 一样，这两位都是 "脱欧派" 的重要代表，都公开主张英国脱离欧盟。

8. Whitehall 白厅，是英国首都伦敦威斯敏斯特内的一条道路，位于英国议会大厦和特拉法加广场（Trafalgar Square）之间，它连接议会大厦和唐宁街。路两旁集中了一些英国重要的政府部门，如国防部、外交部等。白厅不仅是政府中枢的所在地，也是热门的旅游景点。

9. BCC (The British Chambers of Commerce) 英国商会。已经有 150 年的历史，是一个有着重要影响力的独立商务网络。其宗旨是将英国各地区有影响的商会连为一体。

10. John Longworth 英国商会（BCC）总干事，因发表 "英国退欧" 的言论被停职。在本新闻中提到，这件事引起 "脱欧派" 的不满，他们认为针对 John Longworth 的脱欧言论，英国政府利用权力进行干涉，让商会辞退 John Longworth 的做法不妥。但英国政府对此予以否认，坚持说 John Longworth 被停职，只是商会行为，跟政府无关。

11. 英国商会也透漏消息称，关于英国是否脱离欧盟的公投问题，他们不会倾向任何一方，只会调查英国的商会成员公司的不同意见并上报。

USEFUL WORDS

ballot	['bælət] *n.*	[C] piece of paper, ticket or ball, used in secret voting （秘密投票所用之）选举票（用纸制者或用球者）take a ~ 投票决定
breach	[briːtʃ] *v.*	to break, violate or neglect (of a rule, duty, agreement, etc) 破坏；违反；怠忽
bully	['bʊli] *v.*	to frighten or hurt the weaker by using one's strength or power 威胁；恐吓
Commons	['kɑːmənz] *n.*	the Commons [复数] = the House of Commons （与 the 连用）英国议会下议院
correspondence	[ˌkɔːrəˈspɑːndəns]	*n.* letter-writing; letters 通信；信件；书信
diverse	[daɪˈvɜːs] *adj.*	very different from each other and of various kinds 不同的；多种多样的
escalate	['eskəleɪt] *v.*	to increase, develop, intensify by successive stages 逐渐增加；增强；强大
gag	[gæg] *v.*	to put sth into sb's mouth to prevent from speaking or crying out; silence; (fig) deprive sb of free speech 塞物于某人之口；（喻）禁止发言；剥夺某人之言论自由
infringe	[ɪnˈfrɪndʒ] *v.*	(of an action, a plan, etc.) to break a law or rule （行动、计划等）违背，触犯（法规）
injunction	[ɪnˈdʒʌŋkʃn] *n.*	authoritative order, esp a written order from a law court, demanding that sth shall or shall not be done 必须服从的命令；（尤其指）强制令，禁止令

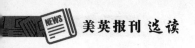
leaflet	['liflɪt]	*n.*	[C] a printed sheet of paper or a few printed pages that are given free to advertise or give information about sth 散页印刷品；传单；（宣传或广告）小册子
referendum	[ˌrefə'rendəm]	*n.*	the referring of a political question to a direct vote of the electorate 公民投票
retribution	[ˌretrɪ'bjuːʃn]	*n.*	deserved punishment 应得的惩罚；报应
row	[raʊ]	1) *n.*	[C] a noisy argument between two or more people 吵架；争吵
		2) *v.*	~ *with sb* (British English, informal) to have a noisy argument 吵架；大声争辩
sue	[suː]	*v.*	to make a legal claim against 起诉；控告

✍ EXERCISES

I. Vocabulary

Choose among the four alternatives one word or phrase that is closest in meaning to the underlined part in each statement.

1. The *Observer* understands that a legal letter was sent on Saturday claiming the use of the trademark <u>breaches</u> guidelines.

   A. blackguards   B. onslaughts   C. violates   D. pursues

2. A spokesman for Vote Leave insisted it would not pull the <u>leaflets</u>.

   A. scripts   B. flyers   C. posters   D. sketches

3. Whitehall sources said the row had subsequently <u>escalated</u>, with lawyers being instructed to threaten legal proceedings, including a possible injunction on the use of the leaflets pending a trial.

   A. ascended   B. accentuated   C. worsened   D. accelerated

4. Brexit would <u>free up</u> cash for a health service in "financial crisis".

   A. separate   B. release   C. loosen   D. entangle

5. Other consequences threatened included the destruction of all <u>infringing</u> goods and the payment of damages to the Department of Health.

   A. intruding   B. violating   C. oppressing   D. surpassing

6. A spokesman for Vote Leave said the move was further evidence of <u>bullying</u> by Downing Street.

   A. deriding   B. whipping   C. reproaching   D. threatening

7. Longworth said Britain would be left "sitting on the margins" of an "unreformed EU" if voters chose to stay in the EU in the 23 June <u>referendum</u>.

   A. demise   B. election   C. public voting   D. striving

8. It is wrong for No 10 to attempt to <u>gag</u> business leaders.

   A. incite   B. advocate   C. restrict   D. perish

9. The BCC will survey chamber member companies across the UK, report their <u>diverse</u> views, and inform the debate.

   A. reverse   B. converse   C. classified   D. various

10. This is the most important debate for 40 years and everyone should be able to speak their mind without fear of <u>retribution</u>.

   A. distribution   B. contribution   C. revenge   D. attribution

II. Comprehension

Decide whether the following statements are true or false according to the information given in the press clipping. Mark T or F to each statement.

1. According to the news, currently most of the people in Britain agree to leave the EU.

2. Michael Gove, justice secretary and culture secretary John Whittingdale are representatives of Vote Leave.

3. John Longworth was suspended from his position as director general, for making pro-Brexit remarks.

4. No. 10 in the news refers to the government of the United Kingdom.

5. Vote Leave should be sued if it did not take the leaflets out of public use by 8 March.

6. Business leaders like John Longworth shouldn't speak freely about the dangers of staying in an unreformed EU.

7. Vote Leave's slogan was "Vote Leave, take control".

8. The BCC will survey chamber member companies across the UK, report their diverse views, and inform the debate and set some restrictions upon Vote Leave.

9. According to Vote Leave, the NHS logo should be used only in its official communications in support of "core principles and values".

10. Downing Street had been bullying Vote Leave for a long time, which led to Vote Leave to protest against British government.

III. Questions for discussion

1. Britain used to be the most powerful country in the world, but for many complicated reasons it has now lagged behind. How would you describe the international image of this country?

2. How much do you know about the relationship between the EU and the UK?

3. In Britain, there are two opposing attitudes towards whether Britain should stay at the EU or not. Please justify the different ideas respectively.

4. If you were David Cameron, the Prime Minister, how would you persuade the Vote Leave to change their idea, and continue to stay at EU?

5. Freedom of speech is one of the rights all citizens are supposed to enjoy. According to the news, do you think there is absolute freedom of speech in the UK? Why or why not?

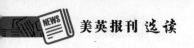

《纽约时报》简介

　　《纽约时报》(*The New York Times*，有时简为 NYT)，创刊于 1851 年 9 月 18 日，是美国的三大主流报纸之一，是美国公认的历史记录性报纸。该报历史悠久，流程完备，在全世界发行，历来以信息灵通、言论权威著称，截至 2016 年 9 月，该报已荣获 117 项普利策奖(Pulitzer Prize)。初期名为《纽约每日时报》(*The New-York Daily Times*)，其创始人是亨利·贾维斯·雷蒙德(Henry Jarvis Raymond)和乔治·琼斯(George Jones)。阿道夫·奥兹 (Adolph Ochs) 家族于 1896 年开始接管经营。

　　该报的宗旨是"天下新闻，宜而印之"(All the News That's Fit to Print)。《纽约时报》在突发新闻、国际局势与政治报道方面享有盛誉。如对于 1912 年豪华客轮"泰坦尼克号"撞上冰山沉没的及时报道；对于第一次世界大战后签订的《凡尔赛和约》(Treaty of Versailles)独家刊载；对于飞行家林白 (Charles Augustus Lindbergh，又译林德伯格) 于 1927年单人驾驶单翼飞机飞越大西洋的报道；对于 1945 年美国向日本广岛投掷原子弹的报道等。在美国的精英报纸中，被称为是"政治精英的内部刊物"，政府部门、社会团体都视其为重要的信息参考材料。《纽约时报》的头版新闻深受美国新闻界的重视，已成为每日重大新闻的标准版本。

　　多年来，浏览《纽约时报》似乎成了美国民众生活中不可缺少的部分。保持地方性，扩展到全国，坚守权威性，是近年来《纽约时报》的主要特点。由于该报风格古典严肃，拘谨保守，版面一片灰色，有时被戏称为"灰衣女士"(The Gray Lady)。

　　该报隶属于纽约时报公司(The New York Times Company)。该报的国际版，原名为 *International Herald Tribune*，现称为 *International New York Times*。2012 年 6 月，开始发行中文版。

　　登录《纽约时报》的官方网站，可以阅读该报刊的电子版。

Unit Two Finance

报刊英语的语言特色

美英报刊是我们了解西方世界的政治、经济、科技和社会文化诸多方面的重要窗口，也是英语学习者，特别是英语专业学生熟悉并掌握纯正英语的良好材料。美英报刊的题材广泛，内容丰富，语言地道鲜活。体裁丰富多样，通常包括新闻报道、解释性报道、调查报道、精确性报道、特写、社论、读者来信和广告等等（王克俊，2007）。以新闻报道为例，受到报刊大众性、经济性、趣味性、时新性和客观性等诸多因素的制约，该类文章在语言运用上形成了独特的风格。

1 报刊文章标题特点

报刊文章标题需要简洁明快，引人注目，要达到这一目的，常用的语言手段有省略、缩略语、简短表达法、多重修饰语、借喻、提喻等。

（一）省略

省略这一手段在新闻标题的撰写方面表现尤为突出。

1. 虚词省略

新闻标题往往只使用实义词（content words）而弱化或省略起语法功能作用的虚词。省略常见于冠词和系动词 be，此外还表现在连词、介词、助动词、人称代词等。如：

Third Spanish Election Expected after Attempt to Form Government Fails（A Third Spanish Election Is Expected after the Attempt to Form a Government Fails）

（*The Guardian*, Sept. 2, 2016）

Number of people displaced by conflict 'equivalent to UK population of 65m'（the number of people displaced by conflicts is equivalent to the UK's population of 65 million）但需要指出的是，

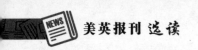

冠词省略不能一概而论，有时也有例外。如：

U.S. role at a crossroads in Mexico's intelligence war on the cartels（at a crossroads 是固定表达，意思是"在十字路口 / 处在紧要关头"）

An American president's approach to a world in turmoil（两个不定冠词同时使用，增加对比效果）

Obama in Athens: 'The current path of globalization needs a course correction'（标题中有直接引语，不能省略）

2. 使用标点符号代替

在新闻英语标题中，冒号使用较多，主要目的有二：一是取代说意动词，连系动词等；二是将主题词提炼出来，用冒号引出解释性语言，大致相当于"on/about + 主题词 + 逗号"。就引号而言，常用单引号代替双引号。

France's burkini debate: About a bathing suit and a country's peculiar secularism（用冒号取代系动词 is）

U.S. general on naval confrontations with Iran: 'The big concern here is miscalculation'（用冒号取代 says；单引号代替双引号）

Bratislava summit: Donald Tusk urges EU leaders not to waste Brexit crisis（用冒号引出 Bratislava 峰会所发生之事）

MH370: debris found in Madagascar in June still not collected by Malaysia（用冒号引出关于马航 MH370 的具体内容）

Donald Trump to Dr Oz: I feel 'as good today as I did at 30'（用冒号引出美国总统候选人 Donald Trump 对保健医生 Dr Oz 所讲的具体内容；单引号代替双引号）

3. 名词用作修饰语

以若干名词作定语的标题常常可以达到双重节省的效果，既节省了动词，也节省了连词或介词。如：

FBI releases Hillary Clinton email investigation documents（FBI releases documents from an FBI investigation into Hillary Clinton's emails）

UK aid money spent trying to boost British role in Malawi oil sector（UK aid money: money of aid from the UK; Malawi oil sector: sector of oil in Malawi）

（二）缩略词

缩略词的大量涌现是现代英语的发展特点，在词汇层面表现尤其突出。无论是在报刊文章的标题还是正文中，政治、军事、经济、文化教育等重要机构的首字母缩略词出现频率都很高（王克俊，2007）。如：

NHS cuts 'planned across England'（*BBC News*, Aug. 26, 2016）

NHS (National Health Service)：（英国）国民保健制度

BBC presenters' pay to be made public（*The Guardian*, Sept. 15, 2016）

BBC (British Broadcasting Station)：英国广播公司

此类缩略词不胜枚举，再如：

CPI (Consumer Price Index)：全国居民消费价格指数

IOC (International Olympic Committee)：国际奥林匹克委员会

ISO (International Organization for Standardization)：国际标准化组织

OPEC (Organization of Petroleum Exporting Countries)：欧佩克，石油输出国组织

GDP (Gross Domestic Product)：国内生产总值

GNP (Gross National Product)：国民生产总值

英文报刊也常用其他形式的缩略词—截短词（clipping），如：

advertisement：ad（截后段）

caravan：van（截前段）

influenza：flu（前后均截）

（三）常用简单词和短词

简单词和短词短小精悍，通俗易懂，能够降低读者的阅读门槛，以争取更大的读者群，同时亦能节省篇幅，因此简单词和短词常常受报刊文章标题的青睐，如：

Diane James wins Ukip leadership election and <u>vows</u> new direction declaring: 'I am not Nigel Lite' (vow: promise) (*The Mirror*, Sept. 17, 2016)

Syrian cease-fire <u>backed</u> by U.S. and Russia gets off to rocky start (back: support) (*The Washington Post*, Sept. 17, 2016)

类似的情况还有很多，比如：

aid: help/assist（帮助，援助）

axe: dismiss/reduce（解雇，减少）

drive: campaign（运动）

due: schedule（安排，预定）

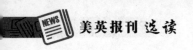

top: exceed（超过）

slump: drop drastically（暴跌）

vie: compete（竞争）

woo: seek to win（争取，追求）

（四）韵音词

韵音词能够赋予语言灵动的乐感和韵律，在标题中使用能够达到让人赏心悦目，甚至过目难忘的效果。以下两例就通过押头韵（alliteration）的修辞手法，达到了这一效果。

Where the river runs red: can Norilsk, Russia's most polluted city, come clean?（*The Guardian*, Sept. 16, 2016）

Colombia's clandestine cannabis growers keen to come out of the shadows（*The Guardian*, Sept. 16, 2016）

（五）使用一般现在时

为强调新闻的真实性和即时性，新闻英语常用一般现在时来表示刚发生或正在发生的事情。

Argentina and UK agree to 'remove obstacles' to Falklands development（*The Guardian*, Sept. 16, 2016）

Hillary Clinton and Donald Trump Give More Details on Their Health（*The New York Times*, Sept. 15, 2016）

📋2 英语报刊正文的词句特点

（一）使用转喻（metonymy）和提喻（synecdoche）

转喻是指用一个与被比喻的事物有联系的词来替换被比喻事物的名称。提喻是用物体的部分名称来指代整体，或以整体名称来指代部分。在美英报刊文章中，常用这两种修辞手段来凝练篇幅，并增加行文的生动性（廖维娜、杨静，2008）。比如：

"The Kremlin saw a tactical opportunity to demonstrate American weakness."（The Kremlin: Russian Government) (*The Washington Post*, Sept. 17, 2016)

"Meanwhile, Paris gets ready to welcome migrants in a new urban center." (Paris: France) (*The Washington Post*, Sept. 17, 2016)

类似的还有很多，比如：

White House：美国或美国政府

Moscow：俄罗斯或俄罗斯政府

Waterloo：滑铁卢战役

Donkey：美国民主党

（二）语言准确具体、生动有趣

具体词表达语义更准确、更生动，因此新闻报道中往往用具体词汇代替抽象词汇。如：

"For hard-hit Italian towns, earthquake rattles deeper fears"中，rattle 意思是 make nervous，但 rattle 是拟声词，较为形象具体，容易给人留下深刻的印象。

Rodrigo Duterte attracts lurid headlines, but to Filipinos he's a breath of fresh air（*The Guardian*, Sept. 16, 2016）"a breath of fresh air"使用了隐喻的修辞手法，比喻杜特尔特给菲律宾带来了清新之气。

使用隐喻的新闻往往借助词汇的联想意义和情感意义，增加语言的趣味性。如：

sexy（性感的）：attractive（吸引人的）或 interesting（有趣的）

divorce（离婚）：break up of relationship（关系破裂）

marriage 或 wedding（结婚、联姻）：close association 或 union（亲密的关系或联盟）

war（战争）：conflict（冲突）、argument（辩论）、quarrel（争吵）、competition（竞争）、contest（比赛）

（三）使用新词

报刊英语常常通过借用行业词汇、旧词新用、创造新词等手段，让语言保持新鲜有趣。

行业词汇，特别是商业词汇、科技词汇等，极大地丰富了新闻语汇，新闻英语有时借用此类词汇表达某种新的含义。如：

Secretary of State Hillary Rodham Clinton's shuttle diplomacy yielded a short-term victory that experts say may translate to greater diplomatic leverage for the administration down the road. 此 处 shuttle diplomacy 指的是"穿梭外交"，即为解决某一问题，一国代表频繁来往于有关国家和地区之间的外交活动。

The fusion dining experience has become trendy in recent decades, but it's an ancient tradition. 该句中 fusion 原指"核聚变；熔化"，此处指"融合（joining together）"。

有时旧词词义经过变化，也会产生新鲜活泼的用法，如：plastic 在"塑料"的基础上

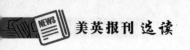

发生转义，可以表示"信用卡"。此外，报刊英语也偶有使用俚语、行话的情况，使文章更加生动亲切。如：

Malawi's new president has wasted no time in sacking the country's police chief in a move described by observers as the start of a "cleanup" of the old guard. 该句中 sack 是英语俚语，表示"解雇"之义。

不少新闻写作人员为了增加文章的吸引力，在语言上刻意求新，不断创造新鲜词汇和表达法。如：dawk（中间派）是 dove（温和派，鸽派）和 hawk（好战派，鹰派）的混成词，类似的还有 Abenomics（Abe + economics，安倍经济学），Brexit（British + exit，英国脱欧）等。

（四）使用套嵌结构（embedded structure）

套嵌结构由于能够使语句传递多层信息，是报刊英语的常见句式。插入语是最常见的套嵌结构形式，插入语两端往往用逗号或破折号标识。如：

However, a group of Republican state attorneys general has challenged the Clean Power Plan, <u>a key part of Obama's climate plan</u>, and the case is awaiting a hearing in an appellate court. （*The Washington Post*, Sept. 3, 2016）

该句中，"a key part of Obama's climate plan"用作"the Clean Power Plan"的插入语，前后均用逗号隔开。

Except for the United States and China, many of the countries that have already joined the accord tend to be smaller ones who are particularly worried about rising seas—the Bahamas, the Maldives, the Marshall Islands—but don't emit a lot of greenhouse gases. （*The Washington Post*, Sept. 3, 2016）

该句中，"the Bahamas, the Maldives, the Marshall Islands"用作"smaller ones"的插入语，前后均用破折号隔开。

综上，美英报刊文章题材广泛、体裁多样、内容丰富、信息即时、语言鲜活，英语学习者若能养成经常浏览阅读的习惯，"博观而约取，厚积而薄发"，必有助于掌握纯正地道的英语。

Text A

导读

波多黎各自治邦（英语：The Commonwealth of Puerto Rico，西班牙语：Estado Libre Asociado de Puerto Rico）是美国属地，位于加勒比海的大安的列斯群岛东部，首府为圣胡安。

波多黎各持续多年的经济衰退导致失业率达 12%，贫困率高达 45%，当地政府常年依靠大举发行市政债券来弥补财政缺口和维持经济运转，最后造成债务负担大幅攀升。2016 年 6 月 30 日，时任美国总统奥巴马签署一项波多黎各债务重组法案，以帮助波多黎各解决约 720 亿美元的债务负担。上述法案并不会为波多黎各提供任何直接金融救助，而是授权成立一个联邦监督委员会来监督波多黎各的财务规划和债务重组情况，同时禁止债权人在 2017 年 2 月前向波多黎各提起债务诉讼，从而为波多黎各重组债务和平衡预算提供时间（高攀、郑启航，2016）。

然而，为了维持必要的服务项目和设施，波多黎各政府宣布无法支付 7 月 1 日到期的债务，这是该政府目前最大的市政债务违约之一。根据美国联邦法律，作为美国属地的波多黎各不能宣布申请破产保护，只能设法通过谈判与债权人达成协议。无疑，解决错综复杂的波多黎各债务问题，将是个艰巨的任务。

Despite emergency measures, Puerto Rico[1] defaults on debt payments

By Steven Mufson

President Obama signed into law on Thursday a bill designed to rescue Puerto Rico's economy and restructure its staggering debt burden.

Nonetheless, in order to maintain essential services, Puerto Rico's government defaulted on roughly $1 billion of debt payments that came due Friday in one of the largest ever municipal bond defaults[2].

"The fiscal situation of the Commonwealth on the last day of fiscal year 2016 is dire," the government said in a release Friday morning.

Meanwhile, the island's state-owned electric utility said it had reached a deal with its biggest creditors to avert a default for the time being—although it would mean as much as 24 percent hikes in electricity rates by early next year.

Although the Senate on Wednesday approved legislation to set up a federally appointed oversight board designed to bring balance to Puerto Rico's budget and manage its debts, the island

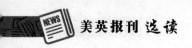

still faced about $2 billion of debt payments due Friday and more in the months ahead while the oversight board gets up and running.

"It's not going to be an easy period," Treasury Secretary Jack Lew said[3]. He added that although the legislation includes a temporary stay on bondholder lawsuits, Puerto Rico would have to negotiate lasting restructuring terms with its creditors on a voluntary basis.

"The bill doesn't solve any problems. It gives you a framework," said another person involved in negotiations who spoke on the condition of anonymity to protect his business relationships.

The Puerto Rico Electric Power Authority (PREPA) said Thursday that it would make Friday's payments by tapping cash on hand and floating $264 million worth of new bonds at high interest rates. The bonds will pay an average of 8.46 percent and help the power authority make a total of $417 million in payments while leaving some money for capital improvements and operations.

The agreement was joined by the holders of 70 percent of PREPA's debts and included Syncora Guarantee[4], one of the firms insuring a portion of the utility's bonds. That put PREPA over the two-thirds mark needed to appeal to the oversight board to enforce a deal even if some creditors remain opposed to it.

PREPA has also obtained permission from the island's energy commission to make two series of electricity rate increases that would total 4.4 cents a kilowatt hour, roughly a 24 percent jump in rates that are already among the highest in the nation. A person involved in the talks said that because the utility generates electricity by burning oil, the rates had fallen over the past two years because of lower oil prices. Rates had peaked earlier at 28 cents a kilowatt hour.

Puerto Rico's government said it simply did not have the $780 million needed to meet interest costs and the repayment of general obligation bonds[5] due Friday, even though the general obligation bonds are supposed to be backed by the full taxing authority of the commonwealth.

The Commonwealth said it expected to end the month of June with approximately $200 million of cash in its operating account and about $150 million more in funds that were clawed back from state-owned corporations.

Puerto Rico's governor, Alejandro García Padilla[6], issued two executive orders Thursday evening blocking the transfer of tax revenues to half a dozen other agencies with payments due Friday, thus forcing defaults by the Metropolitan Bus Authority, the Public Buildings Authority, Convention Center District Authority, the Puerto Rico Industrial Development Company, the

Commonwealth's Employee Retirement System, and the University of Puerto Rico.

García Padilla has said that the territory must first pay for essential services—education, police, sanitation, among them.

In a lawsuit filed June 21, a group of hedge funds[7] led by Jacana Holdings argued that the general obligation bonds must be paid first. "The Puerto Rico Constitution explicitly guarantees that the Constitutional Debt will be paid first, on time, and in full from all of the Commonwealth's available resources—ahead of any and all other expenditures," the filing said.

But the congressional legislation, known as PROMESA, retroactively issues a stay on such lawsuits, rendering the hedge fund filing moot for now. The stay expires in February 2017.

In the meantime, it makes little sense for the Puerto Rican government to make partial payments.

"In a restructuring, the first rule is 'Cash is king,'" said Susheel Kirpalani, a partner at Quinn Emanuel Urquhart & Sullivan[8], representing bondholders in COFINA, a financing arm of the Puerto Rican government. "To pay interest would be 180 degrees opposite of restructuring 101."

Kirpalani said that COFINA bonds are backed by the island's sales tax and that $400 million of those revenues have been placed into an account at the Bank of New York Mellon[9].

The Puerto Rican highway authority also has enough money in a reserve account to meet Friday's payments.

The Puerto Rican government said that even after taking extraordinary measures, the balance in the Treasury's account is projected to fall below approximately $95 million later this year, "a dangerously low cash position for a government that funds services to millions of Puerto Ricans."

"It kind of reminds me of an International Monetary Fund[10] program for Puerto Rico—without the funding," said Sarah Glendon, senior vice president and head of sovereign research at Gramercy, a hedge fund that does not currently hold any Puerto Rico securities. "Usually, the IMF gives funding and then says you have to do all these structural reforms. PROMESA is not giving any funding but simply a framework for getting the economy back on track."

Lew said that one of the long-term issues that concerned him was the fate of Puerto Rico's pension plans, which currently have a $43 billion shortfall in funding. Under current law in Puerto Rico, pensioners there had virtually no protections. Ideally, he said, they would be on equal footing with bondholders and other creditors. The PROMESA bill instructs the oversight board to make sure pensions are adequately funded, though what that means is not clear.

(From *The Washington Post*, June 30, 2016)

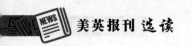

📖 NOTES

1. Puerto Rico 波多黎各自治邦（The Commonwealth of Puerto Rico），位于加勒比海的大安的列斯群岛（Greater Antilles）东部。包括波多黎各岛及别克斯（Vieques Island）、库莱夫拉（Culebra Island）等小岛。北临大西洋，南濒加勒比海、东与美属、英属维尔京群岛隔水相望，西隔莫纳海峡同多米尼加共和国为邻。首府为圣胡安（San Juan）。波多黎各面积 13，790 平方千米，目前人口约 367.4 万。其中西班牙人和葡萄牙人的后裔占 76.2%。作为美国自治区，波多黎各没有国家主权，其人民具有美国公民身份，但是不能参与美国总统选举。

2. municipal bond 市政债券（又称市政证券），是指州、市、县、镇、政治实体的分支机构、美国的领地、以及它们的授权机构或代理机构所发行的证券。市政债券起源于 19 世纪 20 年代的美国，当时由于城市建设需要，地方政府部门开始通过发行市政债券筹集资金，到了 20 世纪 70 年代以后，市政债券在世界部分国家逐步兴起（安义宽，2003）。市政债券一般可分为两类，一般责任债券（general obligation bonds，或 GOs）和收益债券（或收入债券）（revenue bond）。一般责任债券是由州、市、县或镇（政府）发行的，均以发行者的税收能力为后盾（以一种或几种方式的税收），其信用来自发行者的税收能力。收益债券是由为了建造某一基础设施依法成立的代理机构、委员会和授权机构所发行的债券，其偿债资金来源于这些设施有偿使用带来的收益（安义宽 2003；王劲松 2009）。

3. Jack Lew 杰克·卢（Jacob Joseph "Jack" Lew），1955 年 8 月 29 日生于纽约，美国第 76 任财政部长，2013 年 2 月 28 日起上任。杰克·卢毕业于乔治敦大学法学院（Georgetown University Law Center），获法学博士学位（J.D.），历任克林顿总统特别助理（Special Assistant to the President）、立法事务副主任（Associate Director for Legislative Affairs）、管理及预算办公室（the Office of Management and Budget）副主任、主任、纽约大学业务执行副校长（Executive Vice President for Operations at New York University）、花旗集团首席运营官（COO at Citigroup）、负责管理和资源的副国务卿（Deputy Secretary of State for Management and Resources）、白宫幕僚长（White House Chief of Staff）等职。

4. Syncora Guarantee 西克拉担保公司（Syncora Guarantee Inc.），是一家为全球债券发行机构提供金融担保的公司，是西克拉控股有限公司（Syncora Holdings Ltd.）的全资拥有子公司。其业务范围包括为美国市政债券（US municipal bonds）、资产担保证券（asset-backed securities）等；此外，也涉足一些其他的风险投资，比如未来现金流证券化（future flow securitizations）、银行存款保险（bank deposit insurance）、债务抵押债券（collateralized debt obligations，CDOs) 等。

5. general obligation bonds 一般责任债券。详见注 2。

6. Alejandro García Padilla 亚历山大·加尔西亚·帕迪利亚，第 11 任波多黎各自治邦总督，生于 1971 年 8 月 3 日。此前曾历任波多黎各消费者事务部部长（Secretary of Consumer Affairs），参议员，人民民主党（Popular Democratic Party）主席。由于支持率不高，他在任期内宣布不谋求连任。

7. hedge fund 对冲基金，又称"避险基金""备择基金"或"另类基金"。其操作宗旨在于利用期货、期权等金融衍生产品以及对相关联的不同股票等资产或标的物进行实买空卖、风险对冲、在一定程度上规避和化解投资风险（唐军、李政，2011）。比如，基金管理者购入某股票时，同时购入这种股票的一定价位和实效的看跌期权（put option）。这样当股票价位跌破期权限定的价格时，卖方期权的持有者可将所持有的股票以期权限定的价格卖出，从而使股票跌价的风险得到对冲。

8. Quinn Emanuel Urquhart & Sullivan 昆毅律师事务所，是美国著名的商业诉讼律师事务所，专业致力于商事诉讼与仲裁。公司成立于 1986 年，由 John B. Quinn，Eric Emanuel，David Quinto 和 Phyllis Kupferstein 联合创始，总部位于美国洛杉矶。截至 2016 年，共有超过 650 位律师、在全球 10 个国家拥有 19 家事务所。

9. Bank of New York Mellon 指纽约银行梅隆公司（The Bank of New York Mellon Corporation），由纽约银行有限公司 (The Bank of New York Company, Inc.，NYSE: BK) 和梅隆金融公司（Mellon Financial Corporation，NYSE: MEL）于 2007 年 7 月合并而成，是一家资产管理和证券服务领域的全球领先企业。

10. International Monetary Fund 国际货币基金组织（简称：IMF），根据 1944 年 7 月在布雷顿森林会议（Bretton Woods Conference）签订的《国际货币基金协定》，于 1945 年 12 月 27 日在华盛顿成立。与世界银行同时成立，并列为世界两大金融机构，其职责是监察货币汇率和各国贸易情况，提供技术和资金协助，确保全球金融制度运作正常（熊易，2016）。其总部设在华盛顿。现任 IMF 总裁是前法国财政部长克里斯蒂娜·拉加德（Christine Lagarde），任期自 2011 年 7 月 5 日开始。

USEFUL WORDS

anonymity	[ˌænəˈnɪməti] *n.*	the state of not being known or identified by name, e.g. as the author or donor of something 匿名；作者不详；匿名者
appeal	[əˈpiːl] *v.*	~ *(to sb) (for sth)* (here) to make a serious and urgent request（此处）呼吁；吁请；恳求
back	[bæk] *v.*	If you back a person or a course of action, you support them, for example by voting for them or giving them money. 支持；资助
claw (back)	[klɔː] *v.*	to recover through taxation money paid out, especially in state benefits（政府）用增税等办法收回（已支付的国家福利）
commonwealth	[ˈkɑːmənwelθ]	*n.* 1) the Commonwealth, an organization consisting of the United Kingdom and most of the countries that used to be part of the British Empire 英联邦（由英国和大多数曾经隶属于大英帝国的国家组成）2) (North Amercian English) an independent country that is strongly connected to the US （与美国联系紧密的）自治政区
default	[dɪˈfɔːlt] *v.*	If a person, company, or country defaults on something that they have legally agreed to do, such as paying some money or doing a piece of work before a particular time, they fail to do it. 不履行；未支付
dire	[ˈdaɪə(r)] *adj.*	1) Dire is used to emphasize how serious or terrible a situation or event is. 严峻的；严重的；可怕的 2) If you describe something as dire, you are emphasizing that it is of very low quality. 极其糟糕的；质量低劣的

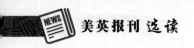

fiscal	['fɪskl] *adj.*	Fiscal is used to describe something that relates to government money or public money, especially taxes（政府）财政的；国库的；（尤指）税收的
float	[fləʊt] *v.*	~ *sth.* to sell shares or bonds to the public 公开发行（股票或债券）
footing	['fʊtɪŋ] *n.*	If something is put on a particular footing, it is defined, established, or changed in a particular way, often so that it is able to develop or exist successfully. 立足点；基础
moot	[muːt]	1) *v.* If a plan, idea, or subject is mooted, it is suggested or introduced for discussion. 提出（计划、主意或主题）供讨论 2) *adj.* If something is a moot point or question, people cannot agree about it. 有争议的；尚未达成一致的；未决的
oversight	['oʊvərsaɪt]	1) *n.* If there has been an oversight, someone has forgotten to do something which they should have done. 疏忽 2) *adj.* An oversight committee or board is responsible for making sure that a process or system works efficiently and correctly. 监督的
project	['prɑːdʒekt] *v.*	to estimate what the size, cost or amount of sth. will be in the future based on what is happening now 预测；预计；推想
render	['rendər] *v.*	You can use render with an adjective that describes a particular state to say that someone or something is changed into that state. For example, if someone or something makes a thing harmless, you can say that they render it harmless. 致使；造成
shortfall	['ʃɔːrtfɔːl] *n.*	an amount by which something falls short of what is required 缺口；差额；亏空
staggering	['stægərɪŋ] *adj.*	Something that is staggering is very surprising. 令人大吃一惊的；令人震惊的
tap	[tæp] *v.*	~ *(into) sth,* to make use of a source of energy, knowledge, etc. that already exists 利用，开发，发掘（已有的资源、知识等）

EXERCISES

I. Vocabulary

Choose among the four alternatives one word or phrase that is closest in meaning to the underlined part in each statement.

1. Nonetheless, in order to maintain essential services, Puerto Rico's government defaulted on roughly $1 billion of debt payments that <u>came due</u> Friday in one of the largest ever municipal bond defaults.

   A. owed and payable immediately or on demand

   B. capable of being assigned or credited to

C. was the proper or deserved amount of sth.

D. was regular fee for an organization

2. "The fiscal situation of the <u>Commonwealth</u> on the last day of fiscal year 2016 is dire," the government said in a release Friday morning.

A. a nation or its people considered as a political entity

B. an official title used by the US states of Kentucky, Massachusetts, Pennsylvania, and Virginia

C. a self-governing territory associated with the United States, such as Puerto Rico.

D. an organization consisting of the United Kingdom and most of the countries that were previously under its rule.

3. He added that although the legislation includes a temporary <u>stay</u> on bondholder lawsuits, Puerto Rico would have to negotiate lasting restructuring terms with its creditors on a voluntary basis.

A. a judicial order forbidding some action until an event occurs or the order is lifted

B. brace consisting of a heavy rope or wire cable used as a support for a mast or spar

C. a thin strip of metal or bone that is used to stiffen a garment

D. continuing to be in a place or a position for a short time

4. The Puerto Rico Electric Power Authority (PREPA) said Thursday that it would make Friday's payments by <u>tapping</u> cash on hand and floating $264 million worth of new bonds at high interest rates.

A. hitting   B. producing   C. attaching   D. using

5. The Puerto Rico Electric Power Authority (PREPA) said Thursday that it would make Friday's payments by tapping cash on hand and <u>floating</u> $264 million worth of new bonds at high interest rates.

A. drifting   B. fluctuating   C. financing   D. selling

6. That put PREPA over the two-thirds mark needed to <u>appeal to</u> the oversight board to enforce a deal even if some creditors remain opposed to it.

A. formally request   B. be desirable   C. challenge   D. apply to

7. The Commonwealth said it expected to end the month of June with approximately $200 million of cash in its operating account and about $150 million more in funds that were <u>clawed back</u> from state-owned corporations.

A. regained   B. held   C. scratched   D. attacked

8. "In a restructuring, the first rule is 'Cash is king,'" said Susheel Kirpalani, a partner at Quinn Emanuel Urquhart & Sullivan, representing bondholders in COFINA, a financing <u>arm</u> of the Puerto Rican government.

A. section   B. weapon   C. limb   D. equipment

9. The Puerto Rican government said that even after taking extraordinary measures, the balance in the Treasury's account is <u>projected</u> to fall below approximately $95 million later this year.

A. imagined   B. planned   C. transformed   D. estimated

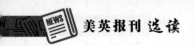

10. The PROMESA bill instructs the <u>oversight</u> board to make sure pensions are adequately funded, though what that means is not clear.

    A. mistake   B. supervising   C. responsibility   D. job

II. Comprehension

Decide whether the following statements are true or false according to the information given in the press clipping. Mark T or F to each statement.

1. President Obama signed into law on Thursday a bill to urge Puerto Rico to pay its debts.

2. For the sake of military purposes, Puerto Rico's government defaulted on roughly $1 billion of debt payments that came due Friday.

3. Puerto Rico's state-owned electric utility has implied that electricity rates would rise sharply early next year.

4. The Senate has done nothing to bring balance to Puerto Rico's budget.

5. The text implies that instead of a dramatic increase in electricity rates, there should have been a decrease in the past two years.

6. Puerto Rico's governor, Alejandro García Padilla, insisted that the Commonwealth should pay off all the debts in due time.

7. According to García Padilla, the salaries of civil servants should be paid first; otherwise, the Commonwealth could not function properly.

8. According to the text, the congressional legislation has made it clear that general obligation bonds should be paid first .

9. For the time being, there is little reason for the Puerto Rican government to pay the debts in part.

10. A subsequent issue along with the default is whether pensions could be adequately funded.

III. Questions for discussion

1. Puerto Rico's government said it simply did not have the $780 million needed to meet interest costs and the repayment of general obligation bonds due Friday, even though the general obligation bonds are supposed to be backed by the full taxing authority of the commonwealth. Can you explain why?

2. When governments and banks can't meet their obligations to creditors, one easy fix to the problem could be to issue more bonds with central banks. Why can't Puerto Rico just issue new bonds that get added to Central Bank balance sheets?

3. Why can't Puerto Rico seek emergency liquidity from the World Bank or the International Monetary Fund (IMF)?

4. Part of the territory of the U.S. as Puerto Rico is, it is different from other states of this country in many ways. Can you elaborate on the differences?

5. Why is it so important for the pensions to be adequately funded?

二战以来的美英经济概览

美国和英国分属美洲和欧洲，美国是当今世界唯一的超级大国，英国也属于世界经济强国。根据世界银行（World Bank）公布的数据，2015 年世界 GDP 总量为 73.434 万亿美元，美国 GDP 为 17.947 万亿美元，约占世界 GDP 总量的 24%，这一比例与 1960 年（40%）相比有明显下降。英国 GDP 为 2.849 万亿美元，约占世界 GDP 总量的 4%，比 1960 年（5%）略有下降。对比中国的经济发展情况，2015 年 GDP 为 10.866 万亿美元，约占世界 GDP 总量的 15%，比 1960 年（4%）有极大改善。

美、中、英国家经济实力对比

项目 国家	2015 年（单位：美元）				1960 年（单位：美元）		
	GDP 排名	GDP 总量 （亿美元）	占世界总量百分比	人均 GDP	GDP 总量 （亿美元）	占世界总量百分比	人均 GDP
美国	1	179470	24	55,836.8	5433	40	3,007.1
中国	2	108660	15	7,924.7	591.84	4	88.7
英国	5	2849	4	43,734	723.28	5	1,380.3
世界		734340	100	9995.6	13650	100	449.6

一、美国经济概览

二战结束以来，美国作为唯一的超级大国，是经济贸易自由化的积极倡议者与推动者，同时利用自身经济优势向其他国家频繁实施单边经济制裁（economic sanctions），阻止这些国家获取经济全球化的"和平红利"（peace dividend），以实现美国利益或安全目标（储昭根，2015）。目前，虽然美国在世界经济中的相对地位不断下滑，但仍然是世界头号经济强国。其经济发展可以大致分成"经济繁荣—危机调整—持续发展—震荡前行"四个阶段：

（1）持续发展时期（二战结束至 20 世纪 60 年代）。二战后初期美国通过 1944 年确立的"布雷顿森林体系"（Bretton Woods System）、1947 年成立的"关税及贸易总协定"（General Agreement on Tariffs and Trade，GATT）、1948 年开始实施的"马歇尔计划"（The Marshall Plan）等确立了其世界经济霸主地位。从 1955 至 1968 年，美国的国民生产总值（GNP）

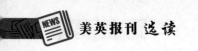

以每年4%的速度增长，特别是美国西部、南部经济呈现繁荣景象。这一时期的经济发展得益于一系列因素，包括：美国政府对经济加强了干预；为应付冷战而加强的国民经济军事化极大地刺激了经济的增长；战后技术革命推动了经济的迅速发展；利用经济优势地位，扩大商品输出和资本输出，充分利用国外的廉价资源（特别是石油资源），以获取高额利润（张宏菊，2010）。

（2）危机和经济调整阶段（20世纪七八十年代），1973年10月，第四次中东战争（The Arab–Israeli Conflict）爆发，阿拉伯石油生产国削减石油输出量，造成油价飞涨，对包括美国在内的西方国家经济带来了负面影响。此外，美国在外部也承担着不少压力：欧共体和日本经济的迅速发展；与苏联展开的争霸斗争中处于劣势；第三世界国家经济迅速发展；身陷侵越战争的泥潭。以上原因导致美国经济相对实力下降。自20世纪80年代以来，美国的财政赤字（budget deficit）占值GNP的比例不断攀升，到1992年，美国、德国和日本的商品出口在世界出口总额中所占比重已相当接近，分别为12.1%，11.6%和9.2%。此时的美国成为了世界头号负债国和贸易赤字国，在国际市场上的竞争能力受到愈来愈严重的挑战（储昭根，2015）。

（3）新经济发展时期（20世纪90年代至2001年"911恐怖袭击事件"）。在本阶段，美国经济持续稳定发展，发展速度名列西方发达国家前列，进入新经济时代。这一阶段发展的特点是由过去依赖传统产业，转化为以教育、科技为支撑的信息化，以及跨国经济合作的有力推动。

在克林顿执政时期，美国经济有了较大发展，由高达2900亿美元的财政赤字发展为国库盈余5590亿美元，实现了20世纪60年代以来的最低通胀，失业率也降至美国30年来的最低。1992年8月，美、加、墨签署"北美自由贸易协定"（North American Free Trade Agreement，NAFTA），该协议于1994年正式生效。1994年12月，由美国发起，建立"美洲自由贸易区"（Free Trade Area of Americas，FTAA）。1993年起，努力开启促进亚太经济合作一体化。美国通过努力推行经济一体化，以抗衡来自欧盟、日本和德国经济发展所带来的挑战。美国在重视经济自由和经济外交的同时，常常使用经济制裁的手段来应对各种竞争和挑战。据统计，仅克林顿政府时期，美国就针对35个国家实施了61次制裁。

（4）震荡前行阶段（"911"恐怖袭击以来）

"911事件"（2001年9月11日）是发生在美国本土的最为严重的恐怖袭击行动。对于此次事件的财产损失各方统计不一，但可以肯定的是，该事件对美国普通民众带来极大的心理冲击，美国经济和政治上长期一国独大让普通民众所产生的安全感受到严重削弱。

小布什（George Walker Bush）时期的经济安全和经济援助政策，是与反恐行动紧密联系起来的。小布什敦促国会批准了"2002年贸易法"，重新确立起间断了8年的重要贸易授权（即"快速审批权"）。

奥巴马时期，美国除了加大小布什政府的经济刺激力度之外，大力实施金融改革，通过改变华尔街的游戏规则以解决金融和经济安全问题。在奥巴马的艰苦努力下，美国国会通过了"大萧条"以来最全面、最严厉、最彻底的金融改革法案——多德—弗兰克法案（The Dodd-Frank Wall Street Reform and Consumer Protection Act）（储昭根，2015）。奥巴马称，这是历史上最强的消费者金融保护制度，将为美国的家庭和企业带来更大的经济安全，美国人民将不再为华尔街的错误埋单。

奥巴马政府致力于推进全球经济再平衡，实现金融监管国际化，通过国际经济合作来解决危机。在奥巴马建议下，2009 年的匹兹堡峰会声明宣布 G20 取代 G8，成为永久性国际经济协作组织与"国际经济合作的主要平台"。奥巴马政府还努力推动"跨太平洋伙伴关系协议"（TPP）和"跨大西洋贸易与投资伙伴协定"（Transatlantic Trade and Investment Partnership，TTIP）两大贸易协定与机制建设，试图主导并重塑世界经济格局。

2008 年 9 月 15 日，美国雷曼兄弟公司（Lehman Brothers Holdings）申请破产保护，金融危机开始席卷全球，全球经济自此步伐艰难，分化加剧。自 2009 年起，美国经济发展一直低于经济危机前3%—4%的增长速度，远逊于 1950-1960 年和 1995-2001 年的两次经济复苏。

金融危机后的美国经济增长表现出与以往诸多不同的新特征，多对矛盾并存。这一趋势的实质是美国经济处于"结构转型期"与"技术创新积聚期"两期叠加的新阶段。经济结构的调整和技术创新需要时间，其在夯实美国实体经济基础、增强发展潜力的同时，会加剧结构性失业和社会分化。页岩油气的大规模开采、大量失业及隐性失业人口压低工人工资、技术进步和数字化生产压低生产成本，令美国国内通胀缺乏上涨动力。预计上述新特征短期内不会消失，将成为美国经济的"新常态"，其持续时间将主要取决于美国经济何时成功转型及重大技术革命何时出现（余翔，2015）。

二、英国经济概览

英国是最早开始工业化进程的资本主义国家。1850 年，英国在世界工业总产值中占39%，在世界贸易中占 21%。经过两次世界大战，其经济力量遭到严重削弱。二战后，主要依赖美国的援助来恢复发展经济。尽管如此，由于英国工业发展历史较长，国民经济体系和工业体系较为完整，目前仍属于经济实力较强的国家。

（一）低速稳定发展（1946-1967）

1945 年至 1951 年，尽管有美国的贷款和资本支持，但是工业技术改造和工业部门建设需要时间，生产效率的提高也不能立竿见影，在出口贸易额没有迅速增长的情况下，必须进口急需的生产设备、原料和生活资料，这样就增大了国际贸易逆差。1949 年 9 月，英国

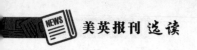

政府被迫宣布英镑贬值 30.5%。从二战结束到 20 世纪 50 年代，英国从战时经济走向和平时期经济。在 20 世纪 50 年代，英国经济领域发生了重大变化，主要表现为五个方面：1）结束了配给制度；2）居民实际收入得以增加；3）消费品的国内需求扩大；4）分期付款消费制度盛行；5）消费者权益得到重视。

第二次世界大战以后的 20 年，英国 GDP 低速稳定增加，私人投资的 GDP 占比有较大提高。这一阶段虽然增长是经济趋势，但期间也出现了几次小幅衰退（如：1952、1955、1958、1961）。

（二）"英国病"的激化与缓解（1967-1997）

所谓"英国病"（British Disease），是指在二战结束后，英国经济出现的滞涨状态。继 1949 年英镑贬值之后，1967 年发生了严重的英镑危机。1973 年石油危机，1973-1974 年股市出现崩盘，在 20 世纪 70 年代的十年里，失业率、通货膨胀率和贸易赤字居高不下，英国经济增长率在西方发达资本主义国家中相对滞后，也使英国在国际贸易和金融中的地位进一步削弱。

1979 年，撒切尔夫人当选为英国首相，率领保守党奉行新自由主义（neo-liberalism）经济主张，在 20 世纪 80 年代，多数国有工业和公用事业都完成了私有化。随着多项宏观与微观经济政策的成功实施，经济开始复苏，"英国病"得到有效缓解。1988 年，GDP 一度实现 5% 的增长，一跃而成为欧洲经济增长最快的国家之一。在 20 世纪 90 年代，经济平均增速为 2.2%。

（三）震荡增长期（1997 年以来）

1997 年，布莱尔（Tony Blair）率领工党，赢得大选。在布莱尔执政的 10 年里，英国经济连续 40 个季度实现经济增长，在 2000 年至 2009 年，英国 GDP 每年平均增速为 1.7%，制造业每年平均收缩 1.2%，但是，服务业出现了较快增长，每年平均增速为 2.6%。

但是，近年来的两大事件对英国经济带来了连续的影响，一是 2008 年的金融危机，使英国 GDP 于 2008 和 2009 年连续两年出现负增长（2008 年为 -0.47%；2009 年为 -4.19%），虽然到 2014 年（2.99 万亿美元）恢复到了 2007 年（2.97 万亿美元）的水平，但是 2015 年又降到了 2.849 万亿美元。二是 2016 年 6 月，英国举行全民公投，决定退出欧盟。该事件对英国经济的长期影响还有待观察，但是其直接导致了英镑贬值，2016 年一季度英国 GDP 为 4742 亿英镑，约合 5527 亿欧元，同期法国 GDP 为 5554 亿欧元。从这一角度来说，英国第五大经济体的地位并不稳固。

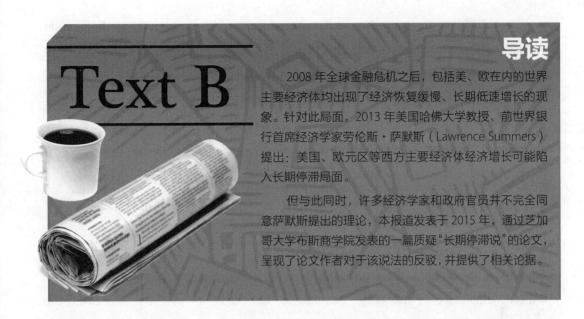

导读

2008 年全球金融危机之后，包括美、欧在内的世界主要经济体均出现了经济恢复缓慢、长期低速增长的现象。针对此局面，2013 年美国哈佛大学教授、前世界银行首席经济学家劳伦斯·萨默斯（Lawrence Summers）提出：美国、欧元区等西方主要经济体经济增长可能陷入长期停滞局面。

但与此同时，许多经济学家和政府官员并不完全同意萨默斯提出的理论，本报道发表于 2015 年，通过芝加哥大学布斯商学院发表的一篇质疑"长期停滞说"的论文，呈现了论文作者对于该说法的反驳，并提供了相关论据。

Lots of economists believe in "secular stagnation[1]" —but it may be overblown

Author Unknown

Is America stuck in a rut of low growth, feeble inflation and rock-bottom interest rates? Lots of economists believe in the idea of "secular stagnation", and they have plenty of evidence to point to. The population is ageing and long-run growth prospects look dim. Interest rates, which have been near zero for years, are still not low enough to get the American economy zipping along.

A new paper published by the University of Chicago's Booth School of Business[2], however, reckons that secular stagnation is not quite the right diagnosis for America's ills.

A country in the grip of secular stagnation cannot find enough good investments to soak up available savings. The drain on demand from these underused savings leads to weak growth. It also leaves central banks[3] in a bind.

If the real (i.e. inflation adjusted) "equilibrium" interest rate[4] (the one that gets an economy growing at a healthy clip) falls well below zero, then central bankers will struggle to push their policy rate low enough to drag the economy out of trouble, since it is hard to push nominal (i.e. not adjusted for inflation) rates[5] deep into negative territory.

Worse, in the process of trying, they may end up inflating financial bubbles, which lead to unsustainable growth and grisly busts.

Stagnationists argue that this is not a bad description of America since the 1980s. Real interest

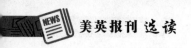

rates have been falling for years, they note, a sign of a glut of savings. Recoveries from recent recessions have been weak and jobless.

The authors of the Chicago paper dispute this interpretation of events. Stagnationists are right, they note, that real interest rates have been falling, and have in fact been negative for much of the past 15 years. But low real rates do not necessarily imply that future growth will be weak, as many economic models assume.

The authors examine central-bank interest rates, inflation and growth in 20 countries over 40 years. They find at best a weak relationship between economic growth and the equilibrium rate. If there is a long-run link, they argue, it tends to be overshadowed by other factors.

After the Second World War, for example, government controls on rates ("financial repression") prevented the market from having its say. In recent years short-run woes have dragged down the equilibrium rate, such as the "50-miles-per-hour headwinds" that Alan Greenspan[6], the chairman of the Federal Reserve[7], described in 1991, when bad loans pushed big American banks to the brink of insolvency. The authors note that such stormy periods are usually short-lived, and that when the headwinds abate the equilibrium rate tends to pop back up.

They also reckon the stagnationists are misinterpreting some of the evidence. Growth in the 1990s was not illusory, they argue. The stockmarket boom only really got going in 1998, after America's unemployment rate had already fallen below 5%.

The expansion of the 2000s[8] looks like a better example of secular stagnation. Rising house prices made Americans feel flush, propelling consumer spending. Expanding credit added about one percentage point to growth each year, says the paper.

Yet the behavior of the economy in this period looks more like a product of distortion than stagnation. At the time China and oil-producing states were running enormous current-account[9] surpluses with America and building up large foreign-exchange reserves[10]. Expensive oil and rising Chinese imports placed a drag on growth that more or less offset the boost from housing. The American economy would not necessarily have grown any faster or slower, just more healthily.

What about the situation now? Some of the distorting forces of recent years are slowly fading. Household finances are certainly in better shape after a long period of deleveraging. That is helping to power a consumer-driven recovery in America that will eventually lead to higher interest rates.

On the other hand, stagnationists argue that the effects of demographic change are intensifying. Baby-boomers[11] approaching retirement may be stashing more money away. Longer lifespans continue to spur saving. Experts of Cambridge University have found that the increase in life expectancy over the past 40 years in rich and middle-income countries has raised the desired stock of savings by two times GDP.

Global conditions must also be taken into consideration. The authors of the Chicago paper calculate that over the long term, America's real interest rate tracks the one prevailing across the world as a whole. Yet since about 2000 the real rate in America has generally been well below that of the world as a whole. The authors argue that thanks to the mobility of international capital that gap should soon close.

On their best estimates America's equilibrium rate has probably fallen a little, relative to the average from the 1960s until 2007 of about 2%. But, they argue, the decline is smaller than many stagnationists believe, and the rate is almost certainly positive. Nor is a lower rate now a sign that growth will permanently fall below past averages.

That is still no reason to breathe easy. A low equilibrium rate raises the risk that central-bank interest rates will sometimes become stuck at zero, leaving an economy in a prolonged slump. Even if the risk of secular stagnation is overdone, the authors reckon that the Fed has good reason not to raise rates too soon.

（Excerpt from *The Economist*, Mar. 7, 2015）

NOTES

1. secular stagnation 长期增长停滞，以凯恩斯理论为基础，"长期增长停滞"的说法最早来自美国经济学学会主席阿尔文·汉森（Alvin Hansen）。在 1939 年的演讲中，他认为大萧条并不是暂时的经济下滑，而是人口增长减速、储蓄过剩、投资不足引发的永久性失业和经济停滞。

2. University of Chicago's Booth School of Business 芝加哥大学布斯商学院（原芝加哥大学商学院），创建于 1898 年，是美国最好的商学院之一，以其多位学者荣获诺贝尔经济学奖而著称于世。2008 年 11 月正式更名芝加哥大学布斯商学院，以纪念"有效市场假说"创立者尤金·法玛的弟子、芝大商学院校友大卫·布斯（David Booth）向学院捐赠 3 亿美元。

3. central bank 中央银行，是国家最高货币金融管理组织机构，在各国金融体系中居于主导地位。国家赋予其制定和执行货币政策、对国民经济进行宏观调控、对其他金融机构乃至金融业进行监督管理的权限，地位非常特殊。

4. equilibrium interest rate 均衡利率，是指保持货币流通中货币供给与货币需求一致时的利率。real interest rate 实际利率，是指剔除通货膨胀率之后储户或投资者得到利息回报的真实利率。

5. nominal rate 此处指 nominal interest rate, 名义利率，由中央银行或其他提供资金借贷的机构公布的、未调整通货膨胀因素的利率，即利息的货币额与本金的货币额之间的比率，是指包括补偿通货膨胀风险的利率。

6. Alan Greenspan 艾伦·格林斯潘（1926.3.6-），美国犹太人，出生于纽约市。1948 年获纽约大学经济学学士学位，1950 年获经济学硕士学位，1977 年获经济学博士学位。1987 年 8 月被里根总统任命为联邦储备委员会主席。1991 年 7 月，布什总统任命格林斯潘继续担任联邦储备委员会主席。1996 年 2 月，克林顿总统提名他连任联邦储备委员会主席。2000 年 1 月，克林顿总统再次任命他为美联储主席。2004 年 6 月，受小布什总统提名，开始第五个任期。任期跨越六届美国总统，被公认为美国国家经济政策的权威和决定性人物。1998 年 7 月，格林斯潘被授予美国"和平缔造者"奖。2002 年 8 月，英国女王授予格林斯潘"爵士"荣誉称号，以表彰他对"全球经济稳定所做出的杰出贡献"。

7. Federal Reserve 美国联邦储备委员会，是美国联邦储备系统（Federal Reserve System，简称 Fed）的核心机构，其办公地点位于美国华盛顿特区（Washington D.C.）。该委员会由七名成员组成（主席和副主席各一名，委员五名），须由美国总统提名，经美国国会参议院批准方可上任，任期为 14 年（主席和副主席任期为四年，可连任）。美国联邦储备系统负责履行美国的中央银行的职责，主要由联邦储备委员会、联邦储备银行及联邦公开市场委员会等组成，同时有约 3000 家会员银行与三个咨询委员会（Advisory Councils）。

8. the 2000s 该表达方法有"21 世纪前 10 年"、"21 世纪"和"2000—2999 年"三种可能的理解，其中"21 世纪前 10 年"属于通常的理解，也是本文中的意思。该阶段世界经济处于前所未有的变化中，呈现"新、变、乱"特征，"新"于全球治理机构，"变"于国际力量格局，"乱"于金融危机后遗症治理。后危机时期，新兴大国群体性崛起，多极化进程加速推进，全球发展不平衡加剧；可谓大危机潜藏大风险，推动大变革，孕育大机遇。

9. current-account 经常账户（现金账户），反映一国与他国之间的实际资产流动，与该国的国民收入账户有密切联系，是国际收支平衡表中最基本、最重要的部分（那明，2014）。包括货物（goods）、服务（services）、收入（income）和经常转移（current transfer）四个项目。国际收支中的经常账户（现金账户）是指贸易收支的总和（商品、服务的出口减去进口），减去生产要素收入（如利息、股息），然后减去转移支付（如外国援助）。经常项目的顺差（盈余）增加了一个国家相应金额的外国资本净额，逆差（赤字）则恰好相反。

10. foreign-exchange reserve 外汇储备，为了应付国际支付的需要，各国的中央银行及其他政府机构集中掌握的外汇资产。外汇储备的具体形式包括政府在国外的短期存款或其他可以在国外兑现的支付手段，如外国有价证券，外国银行的支票、期票、外币汇票等。外汇储备用于清偿国际收支逆差，以及干预外汇市场以维持该国货币的汇率（王明明，2009）。

11. baby-boomer "婴儿潮"一代，指出生于生育高峰期的一代人，此处特指美国第二次世界大战后的"4664"现象，即在 1946—1964 年 18 年间，美国出现"婴儿潮"，共有约 7600 万人出生，约占当前美国总人口的三分之一，是美国社会的中坚力量。成长在经济大繁荣时期的"婴儿潮"一代所积累的财富极其可观。资料显示，截至 2008 年末，"婴儿潮"一代掌握了 13 万亿美元的投资性资产与 50% 的可支配收入，财富总额约为 40 万亿美元，占美国家庭总财富的 70% 左右。

USEFUL WORDS

abate	[ə'beɪt] *v.*	to become much less strong or severe 减弱
deleverage	['diːvərɪdʒ] *v.*	(of an organization) to reduce the ratio of debt capital to equity capital（机构）减债
demographic	[ˌdeməˈgræfɪk] *adj.*	of or relating to demography, the study of the changes in numbers of births, deaths, marriages, and cases of disease in a community over a period of time 人口统计学的
dispute	[dɪ'spjuːt] *v.*	to say that a fact, statement, or theory is incorrect or untrue 反驳
distortion	[dɪ'stɔːrʃn] *n.*	1) the changing of the shape, appearance or sound of sth so that it is strange or not clear 变形；失真 2) the twisting or changing of facts, ideas, etc. so that they are no longer correct or true 歪曲；曲解
drain	[dreɪn] *n.*	a gradual depletion 流失
equilibrium	[ˌiːkwɪˈlɪbriəm] *n.*	a balance between several different influences or aspects of a situation 平衡
feeble	['fiːbl] *adj.*	1) very weak 虚弱的；衰弱的 2) not effective; not showing determination or energy 无效的；缺乏决心的；无力的
grisly	['grɪzli] *adj.*	shockingly repellent; inspiring horror 可怕的；厉害的
illusory	[ɪ'luːsəri] *adj.*	(formal) not real, although seeming to be 虚假的；幻觉的；迷惑人的
inflation	[ɪn'fleɪʃn] *n.*	a general increase in the prices of goods and services in a country 通货膨胀
offset	['ɔːfset] *v.*	to use one cost, payment or situation in order to cancel or reduce the effect of another 抵消；弥补；补偿
prevail	[prɪ'veɪl] *v.*	to be larger in number, quantity, power, status or importance 胜过；获胜；占优势
repression	[rɪ'preʃn] *n.*	the use of force to restrict and control a society or other group of people 镇压；压制
rut	[rʌt] *n.*	being fixed in a way of thinking and doing things, and difficult to change 惯例
soak	[soʊk] *v.*	~ *up,* to use a great deal of money or other resources 耗费（金钱或资源）
stagnation	[stæg'neɪʃn] *v.*	to stop developing or making progress 停滞；不发展；不进步
stash	[stæʃ] *v.*	to save up as for future use 存放，储藏

EXERCISES

I.   Vocabulary

Choose among the four alternatives one word or phrase that is closest in meaning to the underlined part in each statement.

1. Is America stuck in a rut of low growth, <u>feeble</u> inflation and rock-bottom interest rates?

   A. weak   B. long-run   C. temporary   D. strong

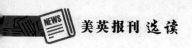

2. A country in the grip of secular stagnation cannot find enough good investments to <u>soak up</u> available savings.

    A. absorb   B. submerge   C. consume   D. swallow

3. The <u>drain</u> on demand from these underused savings leads to weak growth.

    A. drip   B. exhaustion   C. loss   D. drought

4. Worse, in the process of trying, they may end up inflating financial bubbles, which lead to unsustainable growth and grisly <u>busts</u>.

    A. vigor   B. attacks   C. wishes   D. depressions

5. The authors of the Chicago paper <u>dispute</u> this interpretation of events.

    A. refute   B. discuss   C. prove   D. disagree

6. They find <u>at best</u> a weak relationship between economic growth and the equilibrium rate.

    A. all the best   B. at most   C. at present   D. most of all

7. After the Second World War, for example, government controls on rates ("financial <u>repression</u>") prevented the market from having its say.

    A. impression   B. distress   C. suppression   D. mistress

8. Such stormy periods are usually short-lived, when the headwinds <u>abate</u> the equilibrium rate tends to pop back up.

    A. allay   B. reverse   C. accumulate   D. stop

9. Growth in the 1990s was not <u>illusory</u>, they argue.

    A. credible   B. illusive   C. real   D. faraway

10. Yet the behavior of the economy in this period looks more like a product of <u>distortion</u> than stagnation.

    A. divergence   B. derivation   C. disturbance   D. deformation

11. Baby-boomers approaching retirement may be <u>stashing</u> more money away.

    A. slashing   B. withdrawing   C. depositing   D. dashing

12. The authors of the Chicago paper calculate that over the long term, America's real interest rate tracks the one <u>prevailing</u> across the world as a whole.

    A. dominating   B. controlling   C. predicting   D. revealing

II. Comprehension

Decide whether the following statements are true or false according to the information given in the press clipping. Mark T or F to each statement.

1. Ageing population, bright long-run growth prospects and rock-bottom interest rates are the evidence for the idea of "secular stagnation" in America economy.

2. Judging from the news, not all of American economists believe that secular stagnation is quite the right diagnosis for America's ills.

3. If the real "equilibrium" interest rate has been negative for a long time, central banks will fall into a bind.

4. As many economic models assume, low real rates imply that future growth will be weak.

5. The authors from the University of Chicago's Booth School of Business note that stormy periods like "50-miles-per-hour headwinds" are usually short-lived.

6. "The 2000s" in the news refers to the bad economic situation in the year of 2000.

7. Expensive oil and rising Chinese exports worked together to place a drag on the growth of American domestic economy.

8. Deleveraging is the key to turn household finances into better shape.

9. A consumer-driven recovery in America will eventually lead to higher interest rates.

10. The increase in life expectancy has raised the desired stock of savings.

11. American stagnationists believe that a lower equilibrium rate implies a sign that growth will secularly fall below past averages.

12. The authors of the Chicago paper believe that the Fed will soon raise rates for the risk of secular stagnation is overdone.

III. Questions for discussion

1. Today, even the U.S, the world's only superpower, suffers from economic woes at times. What do you think are the possible reasons that lead to this phenomenon?

2. What do you learn about the international financial situation in the 2000s?

3. In America, there are two opposing attitudes towards whether the economy will be "secularly stagnant" or not. Could you provide evidence for the different ideas respectively?

4. If you were the next chairman of the Federal Reserve, how would you promote economic growth of America?

5. Have you heard of "baby boomers"? What do you know about this generation?

6. On today's world stage, China is rising as a new power. What role do you think China should play for a healthier world economic situation in the future? Please illustrate your ideas.

《华盛顿邮报》简介

《华盛顿邮报》（*The Washington Post*），1877 年由斯蒂尔森·哈钦斯（Stilson Hutchins）创办，1880 年成为首家在华盛顿哥伦比亚特区每日出版的报纸，是美国首都规模最大、历史最悠久的报刊。

20 世纪 60 年代以来，《华盛顿邮报》在前总编本·布莱德利（Ben Bradlee）的带领下，开发了新闻调查的新思路，创立了新闻报道的新模式，先后斩获 18 项普利策奖（Pulitzer Prizes）。20 世纪 70 年代初，通过揭露"水门事件"，迫使美国时任总统理查德·尼克松（Richard Nixon）辞职下台，该报获得了国际威望。此后，在关于"五角大楼事件"的报道中，面对政府高压，该报不卑不亢地还以颜色，改写了美国的历史。

据 2003 年 9 月的统计数据显示，《华盛顿邮报》的日平均发行量为 768,023 份，位列全国第五名，已成为美国发行量最大的报纸之一。

《华盛顿邮报》尤其擅长报道美国国内政治动态，注重报道国会消息，号称"美国国会议员与政府官员早餐桌上少不了的一份报纸"。如今，华盛顿邮报公司旗下拥有《新闻周刊》、斯坦利·卡普兰教育服务中心、六家电视台、一个有线电视网和电子媒体、健康保险等宽领域、多层次业务，员工近两万名。2013 年 8 月，华盛顿邮报公司宣布将旗下包括《华盛顿邮报》在内的报纸业务及资产以 2.5 亿美元转让美国亚马逊公司 CEO 杰夫·贝索斯（Jeff Bezos）。

登录《华盛顿邮报》的官方网站，可以阅读该报刊的电子版。

Unit Three Technology

英语报刊文章标题的特点

报刊标题是新闻的"眼睛"（陈明瑶、卢彩虹，2006:42），好的标题能够以新颖的创意、精炼的语言和独特的形式吸引读者去进一步发掘文章内涵，领悟报道主题，选择阅读相关内容。然而有时标新立异、凝练浓缩的标题也会给读者在理解上造成一定困难，因此，认识和学习英语报刊标题的特点，将有助于准确理解新闻重点，提高报刊阅读水平。

第二单元就标题的特点做过简要说明，本单元将再从词汇、句法和修辞的角度对英文报刊标题的文体特征进行分析和概述，从而进一步增强英语理解能力，同时了解欧美社会文化。

1 词汇特点

限于篇幅，英文报刊标题力求短小精悍、简明扼要，通常采用省略形式、缩略语、简单词、短小词等词形，第二单元已经有所提及，本节将主要从外来词和新词两个方面进行概括。

（一）外来词

随着世界各国间的交往日益频繁，英语作为世界语言，不断从各国语言中借用独具特色的词语，展现新闻英语的时代性、趣味性和可读性。英文标题中经常使用外来词，凸显异域特色，其中有些词语保留了源语格式和特征，如：tsunami [日] 海啸；attaché [法] 使馆随员；maskirovka [俄] 军事欺骗；*yin yang* [中] 阴阳等等。而有些外来词经常使用，已经完全英语化，如：percent [拉丁] 百分比；tea [中] 茶；visa [法] 签证等等。

（二）新词

科技发展与进步是新闻英语中新词的来源之一，新鲜事物层出不穷，英文报刊中经常出现临时拼造的新词，并逐渐为人们所接受，如: netizen（网民）；test-tube baby（试管婴儿）；

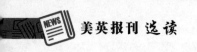

e-Post project（电子邮政项目）等。

　　一个典型例子是 Taikonaut，由汉语拼音"*taikong*"和英语"宇航员（astronaut）"拼缀而成，特指"中国宇航员，中国太空人"。蓬勃发展的中国航天事业赋予了该词稳定使用的生命力。Taikonaut 一词最早出现在 1999 年中国成功发射"神舟一号"无人宇宙飞船之时；当 2005 年首次成功发射神州五号载人飞船后，知名媒体均使用了 Taikonaut 进行报道；直到 2016 年 10 月 17 日中国成功发射神州十一号载人飞船，还在继续沿用，如：

　　Taikonauts Jing Haipeng and Chen Dong attend the see-off ceremony of the Shenzhou-11 manned space mission at the Jiuquan Satellite Launch Center in Jiuquan, northwest China's Gansu province, Oct. 17, 2016.

　　此外，政治、经济、社会的发展也使得新词不断涌现。如：Watergate（水门事件）是 1974 年美国总统尼克松丑闻时出现的，之后 -gate 就用来表达有关丑闻的词语，如 Zippergate（拉链门事件），以及 2016 年希拉里竞选美国总统的 Emailgate（邮件门事件）。在经济领域中出现 Euro（欧元）、dehiring（裁员）、soft-landing economy（软着陆经济）等新词；社会领域有 outplacement（转岗）、home school（家庭学校）等等。

　　所有这些外来词及新词都使得报刊标题富有时代气息，新颖独到，构成了标题特有的表达方式。只有熟悉并掌握这些特点，才能读懂标题，了解新闻内容，提高报刊英语阅读能力。

⒉ 句法特点

（一）省略

　　标题英语为了节省篇幅、突出重点，经常会省略诸如冠词、介词、连词、助动词、代词等具有语法功能的虚词，以强调名词、形容词和动词等关键性词语，使标题内容紧凑、言简意赅，在尽可能精简的版面中提供最大量的信息（陈明瑶、卢彩虹，2006：29）。其中省略最多的是冠词和系动词 be。

　　1. 3-year-old killed in fire found huddled with dog (*USA Today*, Oct. 23, 2016)

　　该标题中省略了不定冠词 a，关系代词 who，系动词 was，人称代词 his，完整的句子为：A 3-year-old who had been killed in a fire was found huddled with his dog.

　　2. Police search for teen who may have fallen down storm drain in N. H. (*USA Today*, Oct. 23, 2016)

　　该标题中省略了定冠词 the 和不定冠词 a，完整的句子为：The police search for a teen who may have fallen down a storm drain in N. H.

（二）一般现在时

一般现在时主要用来表示现在或与现在时间相关的动作或状态。而英语报刊上的新闻报道一般都是新近发生的事实，如果使用过去时态会给读者一种陈旧感，因此为保持新鲜感与现实感，报刊标题常常会使用一般现在时。另外，一般现在时还可以替代进行时或将来时表示目前正在进行或将要发生的事情。

1. Penn State <u>knocks</u> off No. 2 Ohio State 24-21 (= knocked) (*USA Today*, Oct. 23, 2016)

2. New Facebook Feature <u>Allows</u> Users to Order Food and Movie Tickets (= will allow) (*Newsweek*, Oct. 19, 2016)

3. Chinese firm <u>issues</u> U.S. recall after massive cyber attack (= has issued) (*USA Today*, Oct. 25, 2016)

4. Police <u>search for</u> teen who may have fallen down storm drain in N. H. (= are searching for) (*USA Today*, Oct. 23, 2016)

（三）动词的非谓语形式

不定式、现在分词、过去分词等动词的非谓语形式也常常出现在报刊标题中，分别用来表示即将发生、正在进行的动作，以及被动语态，使标题简单明了，主题突出。

1. 使用不定式表示按时间或计划进行的事件。例如：

NBA <u>to honor</u> Craig Sager in opening night ceremonies (= will honor) (*USA Today*, Oct. 24, 2016)

AT & T <u>to buy</u> Time Warner for $85.4 billion (= is to buy) (*The Washington Post*, Oct. 23, 2016)

2. 使用现在分词表示正在进行的动作或是正在变化发展的事态。例如：

Trump chatter <u>breaking</u> all records on Facebook (= is breaking) (*USA Today*, Oct. 19, 2016)

<u>Liberating</u> women from the elliptical (= A campus fitness club is liberating women from the elliptical trainer) (*The Washington Post*, Oct. 25, 2016)

3. 使用过去分词表示被动语态。例如：

Tree impersonator <u>nabbed</u> in Portland, Maine (= was nabbed) (*The Washington Post*, Oct. 25, 2016)

Theresa May <u>Warned</u> Against 'Reckless' Brexit Approach to Scotland, Wales and Northern Ireland (= has been warned) (*Newsweek*, Oct. 24, 2016)

3 修辞特点

报刊标题除了在词汇和句法方面求新求简，通常还会注意使用修辞手法，使标题简明洗练，形象生动。本节主要介绍较为常用的修辞手段：比喻、双关和引用。

（一）比喻

比喻（metaphor）在英文报刊中广泛使用，旨在使报道更加生动活泼，韵味无穷。如：在标题 Chinese economic engines lose steam; heading for slower growth 中，"engines lose steam"表示"发动机失去动力"。此处用 economic engines 比喻推动经济前进的因素，说明中国经济增长势头放缓的态势，具体形象，令人回味。标题 Swimming with bigger fish 将商界大小企业比喻成大鱼和小鱼，将其间的激烈竞争描述成大小鱼之间的生存之战，形象生动，幽默风趣（肖小月，2013）。

（二）双关

双关（pun）是指同音/近音异义或一词二义的词语的诙谐用法，可分为谐音双关和语义双关。报刊标题中常会巧妙地利用英语双关语，同时表达深浅两层不同的含义。谐音双关的例子如 Damon is Bourne again，其中 Bourne（伯恩）读作 [bɔn]，发音与 born[bɔːn]（出生）接近。报道讲述伯恩的扮演者马特·达蒙（Matt Damon）重返环球影业拍摄《谍影重重 5》的经历过程。标题包含两层意义，一是说明马特·达蒙再次出演伯恩这个角色；二是马特·达蒙回归伯恩系列影片拍摄犹如再生一般，经历过痛苦和煎熬，寓意深刻。语义双关可以表现在 Yao Ming: NBA Giant is Big in U.S., Bigger in China 这个标题里，"big"就是一个双关词，在口语中 big 可以表示"受欢迎的（popular）"，表示姚明在美国 NBA 篮球界取得的巨大成功，同时也暗示姚明 2.26 米的"巨人"身高，使得整个标题形象鲜明，活泼有趣。

（三）引用

英文标题常常引用典故谚语、名著名篇或名人名言，增强语言的趣味性，引人注目。如：Farewell to Arms 一文直接引用美国著名作家海明威的小说题目《永别了武器》（*A Farewell to Arms*），报道了美国 20 世纪 90 年代的枪支回收运动，标题和内容十分贴切。再如：In Rome, Using '*Roman Holiday*' as a Guide 介绍意大利首都罗马的游览路线，标题引用美国著名影片《罗马假日》（*Roman Holiday*）的片名，文章则按照影片中奥黛丽·赫本（Audrey Hepburn）饰演的安妮公主在罗马的一天中所到访过的地方安排行程，介绍景点，勾起人们的美好回忆，激发起浓厚的阅读兴趣。

Text A

导读

现代生活中，汽车为人们提供了极大的便利，对汽车技术的研发也是日新月异。新能源汽车和无人驾驶汽车可减缓能源消耗，降低环境污染，避免人为失误，提高出行安全，因此，越来越受到人们的追捧。

美国特斯拉汽车公司 (Tesla Motors) 生产纯电动汽车，并推出了自动辅助驾驶模式 (Autopilot)，使无人驾驶技术真正进入了人们的生活。但是，一起因特斯拉 Model 5 使用 Autopilot 致命的事故引发了对无人驾驶汽车安全性的质疑。本文就这起事故进行分析，从不同角度对无人驾驶汽车的发展和应用提出了意见和看法。

What Tesla Autopilot crash means for self-driving cars

By Greg Gardner

This summer, autonomous cars collided with reality.

All those sensors and cameras and spinning cylinders of laser beams don't know as much as we thought they did. At least not yet.

Sure, Tesla Motors[1] is taking the brunt of the public relations and political damage. To be fair, we don't yet know whether and to what extent the upstart electric vehicle maker's Autopilot[2] feature contributed to a series of recent crashes, including one fatality.

But Karl Benz[3] (the Benz in Mercedes-Benz) and Henry Ford[4] (of well...you know) had setbacks too. Billy Durant, who assembled what would become the empire of General Motors[5], was ousted from the company twice before winding up running a bowling alley.

Don't expect development to stop driver-assist technologies or the search for the holy grail[6] of full self-driving autonomy.

But still, it's time to ask what we can learn from recent events. Here are a few lessons to draw from Tesla's recent stumbles:

• **Roads.** In a country that has neglected its roadways so badly for so long, our infrastructure makes autonomous driving riskier.

• **Communication Tech.** Autonomous vehicles will depend on a much more extensive

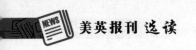

network of what is called vehicle-to-vehicle communication. Southeast Michigan is lucky to be the nation's first test-bed for this type of technology, but extending it to the rest of the country could take decades and major public spending.

•**Man vs. machine.** We must get over the notion that sensors and cameras can replace humans as vehicle operators, at least for the foreseeable future. Humans are imperfect drivers who make mistakes. Technology and humans together can save lives.

•**Tuning out.** The more we see autonomous vehicles as a way to "free" us to work, entertain ourselves or tune out, the longer this evolution will take.

"Everyone in the autonomous vehicle industry understands consumer over-trust is a significant problem," said John Maddox, CEO[7] of the American Center for Mobility[8], the proposed proving ground for connected and automated vehicles under development on 335 acres at Willow Run, where the U.S. produced B-24 bombers during World War II. "No one has an answer to that problem yet, to be perfectly blunt."

At the heart of the recent Tesla crashes is the question of how engaged or disengaged was the driver when things went wrong. Josh Brown, the 40-year-old who died in Williston, Fla., on May 7 when his Tesla Model S ran into a tractor-trailer turning left in front of him, was playing a Harry Potter DVD when the crash occurred.

"It's a human nature that when we're bored with a given task we find something else to occupy our minds. There are ways the industry can look at to maintain driver interest," Maddox said.

Later this summer, the National Highway Traffic Safety Administration[9] is expected to release its federal guidelines for autonomous vehicles.

Though Michigan is known for being home to the nation's traditional auto industry, it could play an outsized role in development of self-driving cars. Michigan wants to be a leader in the research and development of self-driving vehicles. That goal must be balanced against MDOT's[10] mission to maximize traffic safety.

"These technologies will be significantly better when the vehicles can 'talk' to each other and to signals in traffic lights and elsewhere," says Kirk Steudle, director of the Michigan Department of Transportation.

MDOT is working with General Motors, Ford and the University of Michigan to deploy vehicle-to-infrastructure communication technology on more than 120 miles of metro Detroit roadway.

The technology uses a Wi-Fi derivative called "dedicated short-range communication." The system can configure stoplights or alert drivers to adjust speeds in order to smooth traffic flows during rush hours.

To be effective in the long term, projects like this depend on a much higher penetration of technology within the vehicle population. In the shorter term, automakers, suppliers and technology companies are making important strides on their own.

Yet with every step forward there is a growing awareness of autonomous driving's limits.

Steudle said the owner of a Tesla with Autopilot offered him a test drive recently.

"We came up to a busy intersection with a traffic light and there were one or two cars ahead of me, and the car stopped on its own," Steudle said. "But if there had been no other car ahead of us I would have had to pump the brakes myself at the traffic light."

Michigan alone has 122,000 miles of public roads, Steudle said. Half of those will never have a paint line on them because they are either dirt or subdivision streets. Paint lines are part of the language that sensors, cameras, and LiDAR[11], an acronym for Light Detection and Ranging, can interpret in such a way that lets them guide the vehicle.

Self-driving advocates contend that when this technology is perfected we can save 35,200 lives a year—the number of auto-related traffic deaths last year in the U.S.—because many of us are bad drivers.

"The argument goes that human error causes 90% of all accidents, so let's get rid of the human driver," said Maddox of the American Center for Mobility. "But that overlooks that we drive 100 million miles between fatal accidents. We overestimate the shortcomings of human drivers."

Early next year General Motors will launch its Super Cruise[12] feature on the Cadillac CT6. As described by GM executives, it is similar to Tesla's Autopilot, but the company declined to comment on what it has learned from Tesla's recent incidents.

Google also declined to comment. Most of the pod-like self-driving cars Google tests[13] on public roads in northern California operate at speeds of under 35 miles per hour. Often a Google employee is on board and knows how to respond if something out of the ordinary happens.

Consumers also have much to learn. Tesla's owners manuals make clear that drivers must be prepared to take the steering wheel[14] if Autopilot acts unpredictably or can't process a traffic situation. But not all Tesla owners, like customers of every other automaker, read their manuals.

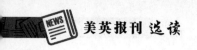

"An informed consumer is the best consumer," MDOT's Steudle said. "They really need to understand the limitations of what the technology can do currently. There's a lot of information out there about where it can take us. But it's not there yet."

(From *USA Today*, July 17, 2016.)

NOTES

1. Tesla Motors 特斯拉汽车公司，美国一家生产和销售纯电动汽车的公司，于 2003 年在加州硅谷成立。2008 年，特斯拉推出第一款纯电动汽车 Tesla Roadster，使用锂离子电池提供动力，2015 年，该公司在全球的交货量超过 5 万辆。现在所有车型均配备具有全自动驾驶功能的硬件，并可以随技术发展提供系统升级服务，提高驾驶安全性。

2. Autopilot feature 自动辅助驾驶模式。根据美国国家公路交通安全管理局（NHTSA）的分类，特斯拉汽车的自动驾驶功能属于第 2 级半自动驾驶，驾驶员双手应该放在方向盘上，以便于必要时操控汽车。特斯拉增强版自动辅助驾驶的软件将使特斯拉能够根据交通状况调整车速；保持在车道内行驶；自动变换车道；在接近目的地时驶出高速；在接近停车场时自动泊车；在车库内听候车主的"召唤"等。

3. Karl Benz 卡尔·本茨（1844-1929），德国著名汽车公司梅赛德斯 - 奔驰汽车公司（Mercedes-Benz）的创始人之一，被认为是现代汽车工业的先驱者。1984 年入选美国汽车名人纪念堂（The Automotive Hall of Fame）以表彰其在汽车制造领域的突出贡献。

4. Henry Ford 亨利·福特（1863-1947），美国汽车工程师与企业家，福特汽车公司（Ford Motor Company）的创始人。他是世界上第一位使用流水线进行汽车批量生产的汽车制造者。1999 年，福特被《财富》（*Fortune*）杂志评为"20 世纪最伟大的企业家"，以表彰他以及福特汽车公司对人类发展所做出的贡献。2005 年《福布斯》(*Forbes*)杂志公布了有史以来最有影响力的 20 位企业家，亨利·福特位居榜首。

5. General Motors 美国通用汽车公司（简称：GM），成立于 1908 年，由威廉·杜兰特（William Durant）创建，全球总部设在美国底特律（Detroit），旗下拥有雪佛兰（Chevrolet）、别克（Buick）、GMC 商用车、凯迪拉克（Cadillac）、霍顿（Holden）、欧宝（Opel）、沃克斯豪尔（Vauxhall）等品牌。

6. holy grail 也作 Holy Grail，圣杯，据说是耶稣基督在最后的晚餐中饮用葡萄酒的酒杯，后来不知所踪，为此引出许多以寻找圣杯为题材的故事。现在常用来指渴望而不可及的东西；努力追求但不可能实现的目标（或理想）。

7. CEO 首席执行官，总裁（Chief Executive Officer）。

8. The American Center for Mobility 美国车辆测试中心（简称 ACM），是美国密歇根州在建的一处车辆驾驶测试场，位于密歇根州伊普斯兰提小镇。它是非盈利性的未来车辆的测试和研发场所，旨在实现车联网技术和自动车辆技术的安全验证。

9. The National Highway Traffic Safety Administration 美国国家公路交通安全管理局（简称：NHTSA），隶属于美国交通部（U.S. Department of Transportation, DOT），是根据 1970 年道路交通法案设立的有关机动车辆和道路安全的机构，致力于通过教育、研究、安全标准制定与实施来拯救生命、防止受伤并减少由道路交通事故造成的经济损失。

10. MDOT 密歇根州交通部（Michigan Department of Transportation），负责管理密歇根州公路系统，同时也负责管理其他州和联邦航空运输方案、城际客运服务、铁路运输、当地公共交通服务、交通运输经济发展基金（TEDF），以及其他服务。

11. LiDAR 激光雷达（Light Detection and Ranging），本文是指一种安装在汽车上的激光探测和测距系统，通过激光的反射波来测量汽车和其周围物体的距离，是自动驾驶模式的重要组成部分。

12. Super Cruise 超级巡航系统，美国通用汽车公司（GM）将搭载于凯迪拉克 CT6 上的自动驾驶系统，能够让车辆在高速公路上保持安全速度与既定车道。

13. Google 谷歌公司，1998 年由 Larry Page 和 Sergey Brin 创建，总部设在美国加利福尼亚州山景城，提供互联网搜索、电邮、博客等网络信息服务。谷歌也涉足无人驾驶领域，已推出全自动驾驶汽车，不设方向盘和刹车，能够自行启动、行驶以及停止，现处于测试阶段。出于安全考虑，无人驾驶汽车测试的全程都有驾驶员在车上。

14. steering wheel （汽车）方向盘。

📰 USEFUL WORDS

advocate	['ædvəkeɪt] *n.*	a person who supports or speaks in favour of sb or of a public plan or action 拥护者；支持者；提倡者
autonomous	[ɔːˈtɑːnəməs] *adj.*	(of a person) able to do things and make decisions without help from anyone else （人）自主的；有自主权的
brunt	[brʌnt] *n.*	the main force of something unpleasant 主要力量，撞击，冲击
configure	[kənˈfɪgjər] *v.*	to set up for a particular purpose 配置；设定
deploy	[dɪˈplɔɪ] *v.*	(formal) to use sth effectively 有效地利用；调动
engaged	[ɪnˈgeɪdʒd] *adj.*	(formal) busy doing sth 忙于；从事于
evolution	[ˌiːvəˈluːʃn] *n.*	the gradual development of sth 演变；发展；渐进
fatality	[fəˈtæləti] *n.*	a death that is caused in an accident or a war, or by violence or disease（事故、战争、疾病等中的）死亡
infrastructure	[ˈɪnfrəstrʌktʃər] *n.*	the basic systems and services that are necessary for a country or an organization to run smoothly, for example buildings, transport and water and power supplies （国家或机构的）基础设施；基础建设
manual	[ˈmænjuəl] *n.*	a book that tells you how to do or operate sth, especially one that comes with a machine, etc. when you buy it 使用手册；说明书；指南
oust	[aʊst] *v.*	~ sb (from sth/as sth) to force sb out of a job or position of power, especially in order to take their place 剥夺；罢免；革职

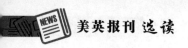
outsized	['aʊtsaɪz] *adj.*	larger than normal for its kind 特大的；特大号的
overestimate	[ˌoʊvər'estɪmeɪt] *v.*	to estimate sth to be larger, better, more important, etc. than it really is 高估
penetration	[ˌpenə'treɪʃn] *n.*	the act or process of making a way into or through sth 穿透；渗透；进入
setback	['setbæk] *n.*	a difficulty or problem that delays or prevents sth, or makes a situation worse 挫折；阻碍
stride	[straɪd] *n.*	an improvement in the way sth is developing 进展；进步；发展
stumble	['stʌmbl] *n.*	an unintentional but embarrassing blunder 差错；失误；过失
upstart	['ʌpstɑːt] *adj.*	characteristic of someone who has risen economically or socially but lacks the social skills appropriate for this new position 自命不凡的；狂妄自大的

EXERCISES

I. Vocabulary

Choose among the four alternatives one word or phrase that is closest in meaning to the underlined part in each statement.

1. This summer, autonomous cars underline{collide with} reality.

   A. crash into   B. cross into   C. conflict with   D. converse with

2. Tesla Motors is underline{taking the brunt of} the public relations and political damage.

   A. suffering from   B. dealing with

   C. worried about   D. concerned about

3. The more we see autonomous vehicles as a way to "free" us to work, entertain ourselves or underline{tune out}, the longer this evolution will take.

   A. turn out   B. turn off   C. shut off   D. zone out

4. At the heart of the recent Tesla crashes is the question of how engaged or underline{disengaged} was the driver when things went wrong.

   A. free   B. distracted   C. isolated   D. indifferent

5. Later this summer, the National Highway Traffic Safety Administration is expected to underline{release} its federal guidelines for autonomous vehicles.

   A. issue   B. deliver   C. express   D. relieve

6. The system can underline{configure} stoplights or alert drivers to adjust speeds in order to smooth traffic flows during rush hours.

   A. assemble   B. form   C. arrange   D. design

7. To be effective in the long term, projects like this depend on a much higher underline{penetration} of technology within the vehicle population.

   A. attack   B. perception   C. intrusion   D. breakthrough

8. We came up to a busy underline{intersection} with a traffic light and there were one or two cars ahead of me, and the car stopped on its own.

   A. mixture   B. crossroad   C. juncture   D. connection

9. Self-driving advocates <u>contend</u> that when this technology is perfected we can save 35,200 lives a year.

A. compete   B. fight   C. maintain   D. debate

10. An <u>informed</u> consumer is the best consumer.

A. wise   B. resourceful   C. reliable   D. knowledgeable

II. Comprehension

Decide whether the following statements are true or false according to the information given in the press clipping. Mark T or F to each statement.

1. We know clearly how Tesla's Autopilot feature results in the recent accidents.

2. In spite of the car crashes, the research of self-driving technology will continue.

3. Since humans are imperfect drivers, sensors and cameras can replace human as vehicle operators, at least for the foreseeable future.

4. Consumer over-trust in technology is a significant problem, which does not have a solution yet.

5. In the research and development of self-driving vehicles, traffic safety should be the most important mission to fulfil.

6. Michigan, as the home to American traditional auto industry, plays a leading role in developing self-driving technology.

7. With Autopilot feature, the driver would not have to brake the car at the traffic light.

8. In Michigan, most of the public roads have paint lines to provide signals for sensors, cameras and LiDAR to guide the cars.

9. According to the report, General Motors has learned much from Tesla's recent incidents.

10. Tesla's owner manuals clearly state what the drivers ought to do if Autopilot does not act properly, but not all Tesla owners read their manuals.

III. Questions for discussion

1. According to the analysis of Tesla's fatal crash, there are four aspects to consider: roads, communication technology, relation between man and machine, and tuning out. Are there any other aspects to consider? Please discuss with your partners.

2. With the improvement of technology, do you believe that self-driving devices can replace human drivers? Why or why not?

3. In face of all the setbacks and accidents in autonomous vehicles, why do the major automobile manufacturers keep on the research of self-driving technology?

4. "An informed consumer is the best consumer." How do you interpret this statement?

5. Suppose you are a driver, which one will you choose, a traditional car or a self-driving car?

源于美国的第三次科技革命

　　美国经济趋势基金会主席，经济社会评论家里夫金（Rifkin, 2011）认为第三次工业革命的标志是互联网和可再生能源的结合，提出互联网、绿色能源、3D打印技术将开启第三次工业革命的大门。但是，关于第三次工业革命的起讫时间众说纷纭，为避免混淆，此处采用"第三次科技革命"的说法。第三次科技革命是在第二次世界大战后起源于美国的科技领域的重大革命[1]，是人类文明史上继蒸汽技术革命和电力技术革命之后科技领域里的又一次重大飞跃。它以原子能、电子计算机、空间技术和生物工程的研发应用为主要标志，涉及信息技术、新能源技术、新材料技术、生物技术、空间技术和海洋技术等诸多领域（邓友平，2014），产生了大批新型工业，开辟了信息时代，催生了知识经济，出现了一大批科技新成果：

　　（1）空间技术的利用和发展。继苏联于1957年成功发射第一颗人造地球卫星以后，美苏展开了长达数十年的太空竞赛。为此，美国于20世纪60年代就制定了登月计划，并于1969年成功登月。20世纪70年代后，空间技术领域从近地空间发展为超越太阳系的技术研发。

　　（2）原子能技术的利用和发展。1945年美国成功地试制原子弹后，1952年又成功试制氢弹。1949年至1964年期间，苏、英、法、中四国相继成功研制核武器。除了军事领域，原子能技术在其他工业领域的和平利用也有了较大发展。

　　（3）电子计算机技术的利用和发展。1946年，第一台电子计算机（ENIAC）在美国诞生。20世纪50年代，贝尔实验室成功研制晶体管计算机（TRADIC），运算速度每秒在100万次以上。20世纪60年代至70年代，相继出现了小规模、中规模、大规模和超大规模的集成电路（英文简称分别为SSI、MSI、LSI、VLSI），极大地提高了计算机的性能。1978年，计算机的运算速度可达1.5亿次每秒。20世纪80年代，出现了智能计算机（intelligent computer）。20世纪90年代起，出现了光子计算机（photon computer）、生物计算机（biological computer）等。计算机在速度提高、体积减小、成本降低方面发展迅速。20世纪80年代起，微机（microcomputer）迅速发展。电子计算机技术以及互联网技术在世界范围内的广泛应用，

1　也有观点认为第三次科技革命发生于20世纪40至60年代，20世纪70年代以后的科技革命是第四次科技革命（或称"新科技革命"）。

极大提高了生产生活的自动化和现代化水平，使人们之间的物理距离不再成为障碍。

科技革命和科技创新是国际竞争的决定性实力，加剧了各国发展的不平衡，使国家之间的国际地位发生了新变化（王长勤、纪海涛，2015）。同时，第三次科技革命对现行经济带来了较大影响：

一、科技成果转化得到重视

在发达国家，企业具有较高的科技成果研发的自觉意识和责任意识，是科技研发的投资主体，占科技研发（R&D）经费总投入的 60-70%，特别在高新技术产业方面投入巨大（李孔岳，2006）。以美国为例，各行业研发资金的投入在产品的销售收入中所占比例存在较大差异，其中生物技术类产品为 55%、医药类产品为 20%、软件技术类产品为 11%、汽车产品为 8~12%、电子技术类产品为 8%、石油类产品为 5%、纺织类产品为 1%。据统计，第三次科技革命中的科技成果转化周期大为缩短，一般在 10 年内就能完成投入应用，如雷达原理从发现到制造用时 10 年；原子能用时 6 年；晶体管用时 4 年；移动电话用时 4 年；激光用时不足 2 年。

二、科技进步因素占 GNP（国民生产总值）的比例增大

在两次世界大战期间，西方国家工业生产的年均增长率为 1.7%，在 1950 年至 1972 年增至 6.1%。在世界范围内，1953 年至 1973 年的工业产量，与 1800 年以后 150 年工业产量总和大致相当。发达国家科技进步因素带来的产值占 GNP 比重由最初的 5% ~ 10%，增至20 世纪 70 年代的 60%，21 世纪以来已增至 80%。

三、科学分化与综合的双向发展

从单一技术到高科技群，自然科学已成为多层次、综合性的学科统一体，学科之间的交叉与融合不断加深，联系日益密切，各学科之间的空隙得到了有效弥补。

四、发达国家的经济结构变化较大

随着新一轮科技革命的推进，西方发达国家不同部门经济结构也发生了新的变化。首先，第一、二产业的 GDP 占值以及从业人数比重均有所下降。美国的农业人口在 1970 年占总人口 5%，1979 年降为 3%；制造业从业人口在 1970 年占 30%，1979 年降为 13%。其次，新旧工业发生了分化。由劳动和资本密集的传统工业转为技术与知识密集的新兴工业，如电子科技、激光技术、合成材料、遗传工程等主导的工业部门长足发展，钢铁、纺织、采矿等工业部门缓慢发展，占比逐渐下降。

第三次科技革命将促使健康的绿色能源和新型能源系统的形成，以改变社会发展的动

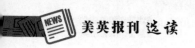

力，同时将促使计算机技术、互联网技术和新型的通讯系统的形成，以改良整个社会生产过程和生活方式（刘燕华、王文涛，2013）。可以说，科技革命不仅极大地推动了人类社会经济、政治、文化领域的变革，而且也影响了人类生活方式和思维方式，随着科技的不断进步，人类的衣、食、住、行、用等日常生活的各个方面必将发生重大变革。

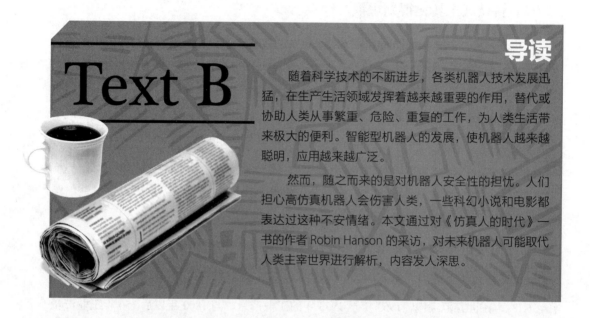

导读

随着科学技术的不断进步，各类机器人技术发展迅猛，在生产生活领域发挥着越来越重要的作用，替代或协助人类从事繁重、危险、重复的工作，为人类生活带来极大的便利。智能型机器人的发展，使机器人越来越聪明，应用越来越广泛。

然而，随之而来的是对机器人安全性的担忧。人们担心高仿真机器人会伤害人类，一些科幻小说和电影都表达过这种不安情绪。本文通过对《仿真人的时代》一书的作者 Robin Hanson 的采访，对未来机器人可能取代人类主宰世界进行解析，内容发人深思。

If robots are the future of work, where do humans fit in?
We need to rethink our view of jobs and leisure—and quickly, if we are to avoid becoming obsolete

By Zoe Williams

Robin Hanson thinks the robot takeover, when it comes, will be in the form of emulations. In his new book, *The Age of Em*[1], the economist explains: you take the best and brightest 200 human beings on the planet, you scan their brains and you get robots that to all intents and purposes are indivisible from the humans on which they are based, except a thousand times faster and better.

For some reason, conversationally, Hanson repeatedly calls these 200 human prototypes "the billionaires", even though having a billion in any currency would be strong evidence against your being the brightest, since you have no sense of how much is enough. But that's just a natural difference of opinion between an economist and a mediocre person who is now afraid of the future.

These Ems, being superior at everything and having no material needs that couldn't be satisfied virtually, will undercut humans in the labour market, and render us totally unnecessary.

We will all effectively be retired. Whether or not we are put out to a pleasant pasture or brutally exterminated will depend upon how we behave towards the Ems at their incipience.

When Hanson presents his forecast in public, one question always comes up: what's to stop the Ems killing us off? "Well, why don't we exterminate retirees at the moment?" he asks, rhetorically, before answering: some combination of gratitude, empathy and affection between individuals, which the Ems, being modelled on us precisely, will share (unless we use real billionaires for the model).

Opinion on the precise shape of the robot future remains divided: the historian Yuval Noah Harari argues, in *Homo Deus: A Brief History of Tomorrow*[2], that artificial intelligence robots will be the first to achieve world domination. This future is bleaker than Hanson's—lacking empathy, those robots wouldn't have a sentimental affection for us as their progenitors—but essentially the same. Harari predicts the rise of the useless class: humans who don't know what to study because they have no idea what skills will be needed by the time they finish, who can't work because there's always a cheaper and better robot, and spend their time taking drugs and staring at screens.

These intricacies, AI[3] versus Ems, AI versus IA (intelligence amplification, where humans aren't superseded by our technological advances but enhanced by them) fascinate futurologists. Hanson argues that AI is moving too slowly, while only three technologies need coincide to make an Em possible: faster and cheaper computers, which the world has in hand; brain scanning, which is being worked on by a much smaller but active biological community; and the modelling of the human mind, "which is harder to predict".

But all the predictions lead to the same place: the obsolescence of human labour. Even if a robot takeover is some way away, this idea has already become pressing in specific sectors. Driverless cars are forecast to make up 75% of all traffic by 2040, raising the spectre not just of leagues of unemployed drivers, but also of the transformation of all the infrastructure around the job, from training to petrol stations.

There is always a voice in the debate saying, we don't have to surrender to our own innovation: we don't have to automate everything just because we can. Yet history teaches us that we will, and teaches us, furthermore, that resisting invention is its own kind of failure. Fundamentally, if the big idea of a progressive future is to cling on to work for the avoidance of worklessness, we could dream up jobs that were bolder and much more fulfilling than driving.

There are two big threats posed by an automated future. The first—that we will irritate the robots and they will dominate and swiftly obliterate us—is for Hollywood[4] to worry about. There

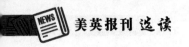

is not much apparatus we can build in advance to make ourselves less annoying. There will undoubtedly be those who believe our obliteration is so inevitable that every other anxiety is a sideshow.

If you can hold your nerve against that, the critical question becomes: in a world without work, how do we distribute resources? It is a question articulated precisely by Stephen Hawking[5] last year, when he noted: "Everyone can enjoy a life of luxurious leisure if the machine-produced wealth is shared, or most people can end up miserably poor if the machine owners successfully lobby against wealth redistribution."

Like so many things, from debt cancellation to climate change, the reality of the situation is easily understood by scientists, academics, philosophers from the left and right, activists from within and without the establishment; and the only people who staunchly resist it are the self-styled political "realists".

The question of how to distribute wealth in the future curves back round to meet a conundrum raised by the past: how do we remake the social safety net so that it embodies solidarity, generosity and trust, rather than the welfare state of the present, rickety with the woodworm of mutual suspicion.

The idea of a universal basic income is generally framed as a way to "shift from the Beveridge principle of national insurance[6] based on contributions and the sharing of risk, to a system of income as of right" (as described in a Compass paper by Howard Reed and Stewart Lansley[7]). In its simplest iteration, all citizens receive the same income. There is work to be done on the numbers—whether this income needs to be supplemented for housing, in what form it has its most progressive effect, whether and how it is taxed back in the higher deciles, how it can be affordable at the same time as genuinely livable.

There is also work to be done on the surrounding incentives, whether a basic income would capsize the work ethic and leave the world understaffed while we await the robot takeover (a pilot scheme in Canada concluded the only groups who worked less with an income were mothers of young babies and teenagers still in education; other pilots are under way in Kenya and across Europe).

Enter the future, with its possibility that many vocations will be unnecessary, and we face more existential questions: how do we find meaning without work? How do we find fellowship without status? How do we fill leisure intelligently? These mysteries possessed Bertrand Russell[8] and John Maynard Keynes[9], then fell out of currency as we realised we could consume our way out of futility, and ignite our urge to earn by spending it before it arrived.

Even absenting the constraints of the globe, that plan has failed. Consumption may have lent necessity to work, but it didn't confer meaning upon it. And perhaps the most profound accommodation we have to make with the future isn't whether or not we are capable of sharing, but where we will find our impetus.

"Can you just write," Hanson asked at the end of our conversation, "that even though I'm talking about dire and dramatic things, I'm a friendly guy who smiles a lot?" I'm not sure how much this helps. Some of his predictions are only bearable if you assume that you'll have died before they come to pass.

Hanson doesn't insist that his is the only possible outcome. Rather, "you should expect that, whatever change is going to happen, it's going to happen pretty fast. Like, five years from nothing different that you'd notice to a completely different world. What I want is to have people understand how urgent it is, when this thing shows up, to have made a plan."

(From *The Guardian*, May 24, 2016)

NOTES

1. *The Age of EM*《仿真人的时代》，由美国乔治·梅森大学 (George Mason University) 经济学教授 Robin Hanson 创作，2016 年 5 月由牛津大学出版社出版。该书预测了模拟人脑形成的机器人未来会取代人类，并对世界产生巨大影响。

2. *Homo Deus: A Brief History of Tomorrow*《未来简史：从智人到智神》，由以色列希伯来大学历史系教授尤瓦尔·赫拉利（Yuval Noah Harari）创作，描述未来人类的生存状态。此书是继作者畅销书《人类简史：从动物到上帝》（*Sapiens: A Brief History of Humankind*，2014）之后的又一力作。

3. AI 人工智能（artificial intelligence），是指一种新型科学技术，通过对模仿和扩展人类智能的理论、方法、技术及应用的研究，从事机器人制造、语言和图像识别、自然语言处理等领域的开发应用。

4. Hollywood 好莱坞，位于美国加利福尼亚州洛杉矶市西北郊（Los Angeles，California），是世界影视业的中心，聚集着美国六百多家影视公司，如梦工厂、迪士尼、20 世纪福克斯、索尼公司、环球公司、WB（华纳兄弟）、派拉蒙等电影巨头。好莱坞制作过不少关于机器人的科幻大片，如《人工智能》（*AI*，2001）、《我，机器人》（*I, Robot*，2004）、《机器人启示录》（*Robopocalypse*，2015）等，对未来机器人对人类生活生存的影响进行思考。

5. Stephen Hawking 史蒂芬·霍金（1942-），英国著名物理学家和宇宙学家。他患有肌肉萎缩性侧索硬化症（渐冻症，ALS），全身瘫痪，不能发音。霍金主要研究宇宙理论和黑洞理论。他的主要科普作品包括《时间简史》（*A Brief History of Time*，1988），《果壳中的宇宙》（*The Universe in a Nutshell*，2001）等。本文提到的霍金教授关于资源分配的说法源于他通过 Reddit AMA 对人工智能领域问题的回答。

6. Beveridge principle of national insurance 是指英国经济学家威廉·贝弗里奇爵士 1942 年提交的《社会保险和相关服务》[*Social Insurance and Allied Services*，也称作 *The Beveridge Report*（《贝弗里奇报告》）] 中的社会保障原则和计划。这份报告对全世界社会保障制度发展产生了深远影响，是社会保障发展史上具有划时代意义的著作。

7. a Compass paper by Howard Reed and Stewart Lansley 是指由英国 Compass 出版社 2016 年 5 月出版的由 Howard Reed 和 Stewart Lansley 撰写的论文 *Universal Basic Income: An idea whose time has come?* 文章对全民基本收入计划（universal basic income）的可行性及实施进行分析论证。

8. Bertrand Russell 伯特兰·罗素（1872-1970），是二十世纪英国哲学家、数学家、逻辑学家、历史学家，无神论者或者不可知论者，也是二十世纪西方最著名、影响最大的学者及和平主义社会活动家之一。1950 年，伯特兰·罗素被授予诺贝尔文学奖。他的代表作品有《数学原理》[*Principia Mathematica*，与怀特海（Alfred North Whitehead）合作，1910-1913]、《物的分析》（*The Analysis of Matter*，1927）、《幸福之路》（*The Conquest of Happiness*，1930）、《西方哲学史》（*A History of Western Philosophy*，1945）等。

9. John Maynard Keynes 约翰·梅纳德·凯恩斯（1883-1946），英国经济学家，是现代西方经济学最有影响的经济学家之一，创立了宏观经济学。其代表作品为《就业、利息和货币通论》（*The General Theory of Employment, Interest and Money*，1936）。书中第一次提出国家政府可以干预经济，强调贸易顺差影响国民收入，利于提高投资水平和扩大就业，使国家经济走向繁荣昌盛，该书为宏观经济学的确立和发展做出了突出贡献。

USEFUL WORDS

capsize	['kæpsaɪz]	*v.*	(a boat) to turn over in the water（船）翻；倾覆
conundrum	[kə'nʌndrəm]	*n.*	a confusing problem or question that is very difficult to solve 令人迷惑的难题；复杂难解的问题
empathy	['empəθi]	*n.*	the ability to understand another person's feelings, experience, etc. 同感；共鸣；同情
emulation	[ˌemju'leɪʃn]	*n.*	the act of emulating or imitating 仿真；模仿
emulate	['emjuleɪt]	*v.*	(of a computer program, etc.) to work in the same way as another computer, etc. and perform the same tasks（计算机程序等）仿真；模仿
exterminate	[ɪk'stɜːrmɪneɪt]	*v.*	to kill all the members of a group of people or animals 灭绝；根除；消灭；毁灭
futility	[fjuː'tɪləti]	*n.*	uselessness as a consequence of having no practical result 无益；无用；徒劳；白费
impetus	['ɪmpɪtəs]	*n.*	something that encourages a process or activity to develop more quickly 动力；推动；促进；刺激
incipience	[ɪn'sɪpɪrns]	*n.*	beginning to exist or to be apparent 开始；早期

iteration	[ˌɪtəˈreɪʃn] *n.*	doing or saying again; a repeated performance 反复；重述
mediocre	[ˌmiːdiˈoʊkər] *adj.*	(disapproving) not very good; of only average standard 平庸的；普通的；平常的
obliterate	[əˈblɪtəreɪt] *v.*	to remove all signs of sth, either by destroying or covering it completely 毁掉，覆盖；清除
obsolescence	[ˌɑːbsəˈlesns] *n.*	(formal) the state of becoming old-fashioned and no longer useful 过时；陈旧；淘汰
progenitor	[proʊˈdʒenɪtər] *n.*	(formal) a person or thing from the past that a person, animal or plant that is alive now is related to（人或动、植物等的）祖先；祖代
rickety	[ˈrɪkəti] *adj.*	not strong or well made; likely to break 不结实的；不稳固的；易折断的
solidarity	[ˌsɑːlɪˈdærəti] *n.*	support by one person or group of people for another because they share feelings, opinions, aims, etc. 团结；齐心协力；同心同德；相互支持
spectre	[ˈspektər] *n.*	something unpleasant that people are afraid might happen in the future 恐惧；恐慌；忧虑
staunchly	[ˈstɔːntʃli] *adv.*	in a staunch way; firmly, surely 坚定地；忠实地
staunch	[stɔːntʃ] *adj.*	strong and loyal in one's opinions and attitude 忠实的；坚定的
supersede	[ˌsjuːpəˈsiːd] *v.*	to take the place of sth/sb that is considered to be old-fashioned or no longer the best available 取代；替代（已非最佳选择或已过时的事物）
undercut	[ˌʌndəˈkʌt] *v.*	to sell goods or services at a lower price than your competitors 削价竞争；以低于（竞争对手）的价格做生意
understaffed	[ˌʌndəˈstɑːft] *adj.*	not having enough people working and therefore not able to function well 人员不足；人手太少

EXERCISES

I. Vocabulary

Choose among the four alternatives one word or phrase that is closest in meaning to the underlined part in each statement.

1. But that's just a natural difference of opinion between an economist and a <u>mediocre</u> person who is now afraid of the future.

   A. inferior   B. poor   C. average   D. timid

2. These Ems, being superior at everything and having no material needs that couldn't be satisfied virtually, will <u>undercut</u> humans in the labour market, and render us totally unnecessary.

   A. prevent   B. beat   C. defeat   D. be cheaper than

3. Whether or not we are <u>put out to a pleasant pasture</u> or brutally exterminated will depend upon how we behave towards the Ems at their incipience.

   A. retired   B. sent to a good place

   C. troubled   D. defeated

4. Even if a robot takeover is some way away, this idea has already become <u>pressing</u> in specific sectors.

    A. important   B. urgent   C. critical   D. necessary

5. There is always a voice in the debate saying, we don't have to <u>surrender</u> to our own innovation: we don't have to automate everything just because we can.

    A. yield   B. abandon   C. show   D. relinquish

6. There will undoubtedly be those who believe our obliteration is so inevitable that every other anxiety is <u>a sideshow</u>.

    A. unpleasant   B. additional   C. accompanying   D. less important

7. If you can <u>hold your nerve against that</u>, the critical question becomes: in a world without work, how do we distribute resources?

    A. become nervous   B. feel frightened   C. keep calm   D. feel worried

8. There is also work to be done on the surrounding <u>incentives</u>, whether a basic income would capsize the work ethic and leave the world understaffed while we await the robot takeover.

    A. rewards   B. stimuli   C. occasions   D. payments

9. Consumption may have lent necessity to work, but it didn't <u>confer</u> meaning upon it.

    A. consult   B. give   C. discuss   D. exchange

10. Some of his predictions are only <u>bearable</u> if you assume that you'll have died before they come to pass.

    A. disposable   B. lasting   C. passable   D. tolerable

II. Comprehension

Decide whether the following statements are true or false according to the information given in the press clipping. Mark T or F to each statement.

1. In *The Age of Em*, the robots are based on humans and faster and better than humans.

2. Hanson calls the 200 human prototypes "the billionaires" because they are wealthy men.

3. The Ems not only imitate the human brains, but also share the human emotions.

4. In the future, it is predicted that humans do not need to work for there is no work to do.

5. Humans will automate everything in the future.

6. According to Stephen Hawking, everyone can enjoy a life of luxurious leisure on the basis of wealth distribution.

7. At present, our social safety net embodies solidarity, generosity and trust.

8. The idea of universal basic income advocates that all citizens receive the same income.

9. In the future when many vocations disappear, the ability of sharing will become the most profound accommodation we have to make.

10. Robin Hanson attempts to remind people to make full preparations as soon as possible for the future which he describes in his book *The Age of Ems*.

III. Questions for discussion

1. Robin Hanson thinks that in the future, robots will dominate the world in place of human beings. Do you agree with him? Why?

2. Hanson calls the human prototypes "the billionaires" for the Ems, but he makes the Ems share human emotions of gratitude, empathy and affection "unless we use real billionaires for the model". How do you understand "real billionaires"?

3. The historian Harari predicts in his book that humans will turn into "a useless class who don't know what to study because they have no idea what skills will be needed by the time they finish, who can't work because there's always a cheaper and better robot, and spend their time taking drugs and staring at screens." What does the author try to tell us about human beings in the future?

4. In order to avoid worklessness in the automated future, this article makes a suggestion that "we could dream up jobs that were bolder and much more fulfilling than driving". What kind of jobs could meet such a need?

5. Work is of great significance in human life, without which life may become meaningless. Do you agree with this statement? Please elaborate your opinion with examples.

《今日美国》简介

　　《今日美国》（*USA Today*）是美国唯一的一份全国性综合日报，由美国最大的甘尼特报业集团（Gannett Co., Inc.）总裁艾伦·纽哈斯（Al Neuharth）于 1982 年 9 月创办，总部设在弗吉尼亚州的麦克莱恩（McLean, Virginia）。报纸创办之初，并未被寄予厚望。经过多年的努力，《今日美国》作为美国大报中最年轻的一份报纸，发行量已连续多年名列前茅，如今已与百年老报《华尔街日报》（*The Wall Street Journal*）和《纽约时报》（*The New York Times*）并驾齐驱。据其官网 2016 年数据，《今日美国》读者人数每日达到约七百万人，创造了美国报业的奇迹。

　　该报利用彩色的版面、及时的消息、丰富的图表和内容、大量的体育报道等特色来吸引读者。报纸设有两个版面——国内版和国际版，分别在国内和国外多个印刷点印刷发行，以满足美国各地及亚欧等大洲人们的阅读需求。2012 年，《今日美国》重新设计报标和版面，用一个蓝色圆圈替代原来的蓝色地球标识，且圆圈会根据版面内容变换颜色和版面名字。

《今日美国》虽然办报时间不长，但特色鲜明。首先，报纸版面固定清晰，内容丰富，阅读一份报纸即可了解美国各地及世界的重大新闻。其次，语言简洁明快，报道突出新闻内容，篇幅较短，以便刊登更多信息，适应人们快节奏忙碌的生活方式。再次，图片色彩鲜艳，图表数据丰富，使报纸版面图文并茂、生动活泼、形象醒目，迎合读者通过形象方式获取信息的习惯。该报还有整版的色彩绚丽的气象地图，股市行情和各州体育赛事成绩等等。最后，内容大多积极、正面。该报奉行"希望新闻学"，注重"新闻平衡"，让读者看到希望和光明（端木义万，2005:26）。

登录《今日美国》的官方网站，可以阅读该报刊的电子版。

Unit Four Lifestyle

报刊英语的构词特点

作为大众媒体，新闻报刊写作需要迎合广大读者的水平，语言应通俗易懂，用词往往简单而具体。同时新闻传播又十分强调时效性，以体现特有的新闻价值。新闻报道在提供最新消息的同时也传播了相关的新词（端木义万，2005:9）。记者们通过不断创造出新式词语，以反映社会生活日新月异的变化，并增加文章的新鲜感和吸引力，达到出奇制胜的效果。如此，就不难理解为何新词往往首先出现在报纸杂志等新闻媒体上了。

新词的产生，有的是通过词类转化、派生、拼缀、复合、省略等构词法构成的，有的是旧词赋予新义，也有临时更换词素仿造的（陈明瑶、卢彩虹，2006:62）。

本节将从词类转化、派生词、拼缀词、缩略词、截短词和复合词等几个方面来探讨报刊英语的构词特点。

1 词类转化

词类转化（conversion）是指不需要改变形态就可以从一种词类转化为另一种词类的构词法，无需借助词缀即可实现词性转化，使其产生新的意义和作用，成为新词。在报刊英语中，词类转化经常使用，可以节省篇幅，并使句子变得生动有力。常见的词类转化类型有名词转动词、动词转名词、形容词转动词或名词等（端木义万，2005: 212）。

1. 名词转化成动词

He mouthed fine words about friendship. 他满口是友谊。

2. 动词转化成名词

Like today's haves and havenots, we will have a society of the knows and knownots. 就像今天社会上有富人和穷人一样，将来社会上会出现有知识的人和无知识的人。

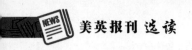

3. 形容词转化成动词或名词

The leaders, who exchanged views without aids for an hour today, will brief newsmen after a second round of talks tomorrow. 今天，领导人在没有助手出席的情况下交换了一个小时意见，他们准备在明天第二轮谈判后向新闻记者做简要的介绍。（形容词 brief 转化成动词"简要介绍 / 汇报"）

形容词修饰语用作名词的例子也有不少，如：undesirables 不受欢迎的人；the young marrieds 新婚的年轻人

2 派生词

派生法（derivation）是用词根 (root) 加上词缀（affix）组合后形成的新词。派生法是现代英语运用最多的构词法，所构成的词占新词总数的 30%-34%（端木义万，2005:101）。语言中词缀可分为三类：前缀（prefix）、中缀（infix）和后缀（suffix）。英语主要以前缀和后缀为主，通常前缀改变词义，后缀改变词性。在报刊英语中，通过添加前后词缀合成新词的方式比较常见，可以快捷地发布消息，感受到词义与词性的变化。

新闻中比较活跃的前缀有 anti-，eco-，inter-，mini-，non-，out-，over-，pro- 等，比如 anti-tank weapons（反坦克武器）；anticlimax（扫兴的结局）；eco-friendly（环保的）；eco-tourism（生态旅游）；inter-city（市际的）；Internet（互联网）；minicam（微型照相机）；miniboom（短暂繁荣）；non-governmental organization （NGO，非政府间组织）；non-interference（不干涉）；outnumber（数量上压倒）；outpatient（门诊病人）；overproduction（生产过剩）；overload（超载）；pro-European（亲欧的）；pro-democracy（拥护民主）。

另外，比较常见的后缀有名词后缀 -in，-ism，-speak，-wise 等，例如 sit-in（静坐抗议）；phone-in（电话抗议）；ageism（年龄歧视）；sexism（性别歧视）；bizspeak（商业语言）；White-House-speak（按白宫的说法）；educationwise（在教育方面）；securitywise（在安全方面）。还有形容词后缀，environment-friendly（利于环保的）；user-friendly（用户友好的 / 为用户考虑的）；和动词后缀 modernize（现代化）；computerize（计算机化）等。

此外，科学技术的发展催生了不少派生词语，比如，由于信息技术的革命，使得前缀 cyber-（网络……）构成了许多新词，如 cybercafé（网吧），Cyber Monday（网购星期一，指感恩节假期过后的第一个星期一之疯狂网购），cyber love/romance（网恋）等。

3 拼缀词

拼缀词（blending）是将两个词语进行剪裁之后复合而成的新词，如：motel（motor+hotel 汽车旅馆）。在现代英语中，这类拼缀词越来越多，可使文字新颖活泼，又节省空间，符

合新闻英语节俭性的需求。根据端木义万（2005）说明，就混合的方式而言，拼缀词大体可分为以下四类：

1. 前词首部 + 后词尾部：

stagflation (stagnation + inflation 滞胀)，medicide (medical+suicide 医助安乐死)

2. 前词全部 + 后词尾部：

screenager (screen + teenager 屏幕青少年，从小就看电视，玩电脑的青少年)

Obamacare (Obama + medicare 奥巴马医改计划)

3. 前词首部 + 后词全部：

exerhead (exercise + head 运动狂)，e-journal (electronic + journal 电子刊物)

4. 前词首部 + 后词首部：

interpol (international + police 国际警察)，hi-tech (high + technology 高科技)

📰4 缩略词

缩略词（abbreviations）是可以使新闻报道经济简洁的办法，因此新闻报道使用缩略词的频率很高。缩略词的形式主要有首字母缩略词 (alphabetism) 和首字母缩拼词 (acronym)。

1. 首字母缩略词：由词组每个词的第一个字母组成并按字母发音，如：GM (genetically modified 转基因的)；WTO (World Trade Organization 世贸组织)。

2. 首字母缩拼词：由词组中每个词第一个字母组成并拼读为一个词，如：APEC (Asia-Pacific Economic Cooperation 亚洲和太平洋经济合作组织)，FAST (Five-hundred-meter Aperture Spherical Telescope 500 米口径球面射电望远镜)。

📰5 截短词

截短词（clipping）是把原来词的某一或某些部分截除而得的词。这类词在英语报刊中较为常见，可以节约篇幅，精炼语言。截短词可分为以下五类：

1. 截去后面部分，只留词头。如：pop (popular 流行的)，celeb (celebrity 名流)。

2. 截去前面部分，只留词尾。如：copter (helicopter 直升飞机)，Net (Internet 因特网)。

3. 截去首尾部分，只留中间。如：flu (influenza 流行性感冒)，tec (detective 侦探)。

4. 截去中部，保留头尾。如：int'l (international 国际的)，Cwealth (Commonwealth 英联邦)

5. 截去词组中的一个词，只留另一词。如：seniors (senior citizens 老年人)，tabloids (tabloid newspapers 小报)。

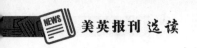

6 复合词

复合词（compounds）是把两个或两个以上的词结合在一起构成新词的方法。在整个英语发展过程中，复合法在构词方面起着积极作用，它构成的新词数量仅次于派生法（端木义万，2005:125）。复合词可以使意图表达得简洁有效，使读者能够根据旧词或背景猜出词义。数量较多的复合词有复合名词、复合形容词、复合动词。

1. 复合名词: letter bomb（书信炸弹）、moonwalk（月亮上行走）、watergate（水门事件）。

2. 复合形容词：freezing-cold（冰冷的）、top-heavy（头重脚轻的）、war-weary（厌倦战争的）。

3. 复合动词：fast-talk（花言巧语企图说服），green wash（绿刷洗，指塑造关于环境保护的形象），wallet X-ray（钱袋透视，指收治病人前对其经济支付能力的审查）。

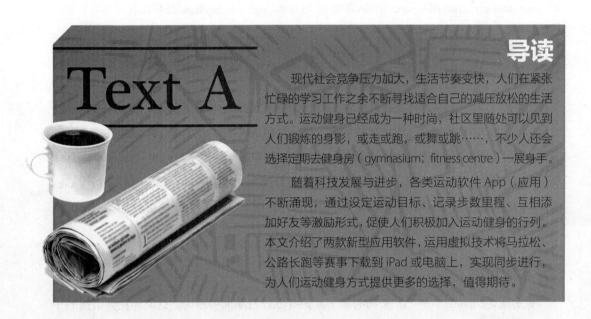

Text A

导读

现代社会竞争压力加大，生活节奏变快，人们在紧张忙碌的学习工作之余不断寻找适合自己的减压放松的生活方式。运动健身已经成为一种时尚，社区里随处可以见到人们锻炼的身影，或走或跑，或舞或跳……，不少人还会选择定期去健身房（gymnasium; fitness centre）一展身手。

随着科技发展与进步，各类运动软件 App（应用）不断涌现，通过设定运动目标、记录步数里程、互相添加好友等激励形式，促使人们积极加入运动健身的行列。本文介绍了两款新型应用软件，运用虚拟技术将马拉松、公路长跑等赛事下载到 iPad 或电脑上，实现同步进行，为人们运动健身方式提供更多的选择，值得期待。

New running apps blur the line between virtual reality and real life

By Mike Plunkett

During the extreme winter of 2009-2010, Gary McNamee relied on his treadmill to train for the Boston Marathon[1]. McNamee lives in Hopkinton, where the race starts, but the weather stymied his attempts to go out for a long run.

"I'm in my basement thinking, 'Jeez, the course is right up the road. I can go out there and film it and watch it while I was on the treadmill,'" McNamee said.

So he did—and realized that he could market a video simulation of the famed course to other runners.

Thus he began Outside Interactive[2], a company that, along with others, is merging fitness with high-definition virtual technology.

Runners log in to the Outside Interactive app and pay for videos of routes, which they watch on their iPad or Android tablet or on an HD television. While running, they can manually select the pace or sync their tracking device to the app. The video will speed up and slow down as the runners change speed. In a bit of surreality, the crowds and fellow racers in the video will run and cheer in proportion to the speed of the real runners.

Taking it a stride further, RunSocial[3], a company based in Singapore that launched its running app last year, uses augmented reality technology[4], where the app overlays the runner's virtual presence via an avatar with a video of a real-world route (a la Pokémon Go[5]). The avatar's speed is determined by the company's TreadTracker foot pod[6] or can be set manually.

"We had this idea of a mixed-reality concept, where basically we wanted to run real-world routes but didn't want computer graphics, but also would love to see others in these routes while we run," said Marc Hardy, RunSocial's co-founder and chief executive.

Hardy, who describes himself as a regular runner, saw an opportunity for treadmill users who struggle with boredom and motivation to enhance their running experience.

Although RunSocial's main products are virtual running apps for indoors, Hardy said the company is focusing more on the sociability factor. Both the virtual running app and RunSocial GPS, an outdoor tracking system that the company just launched, feature ways for participants to race one another, complete with a countdown clock and a leader board.

"Everybody, everywhere can run together, virtually," Hardy said.

Both Outside Interactive and RunSocial offer what McNamee calls the "holy grail"—the ability to sync with smart treadmills to adjust the incline levels to match the flat and hilly sections of each of the recorded courses.

Real Collaborations

Some real-life races are working with Outside Interactive and RunSocial to expand and enhance their own efforts.

Earlier this year, RunSocial launched a digital version of the Prague Marathon[7] and also offered a digital version of the Virgin Money London Marathon[8] for a second year. The digital

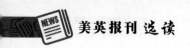
London Marathon featured astronaut Tim Peake[9], who ran the course on a treadmill aboard the International Space Station. Hardy said RunSocial is looking to make inroads in the U.S. market with future partnerships and more U.S.-based video routes.

In 2015, Outside Interactive collaborated with the New Balance Falmouth Road Race[10], a seven-mile course on Cape Cod, Mass. Jennifer Edwards, Falmouth's general manager, said the race organizers were hesitant at first when they heard McNamee's pitch but saw the opportunity to give those who couldn't run the live race—because of scheduling or geography—a chance to participate.

Edwards said Falmouth's goal was "not to add to the race day experience but add another opportunity to be a part of the experience."

In 2015, Outside Interactive collaborated with the New Balance Falmouth Road Race, a seven-mile course in Cape Cod. Forty finishers completed the virtual race, which was held at the same time as the actual Falmouth race. (Outside Interactive)

Edwards said 40 finishers completed the virtual race, which was held at the same time as the actual race. Each was given a bib and a finisher's certificate, as well as guaranteed entry to the 2016 Falmouth. Edwards said the field included competitors from as far away as California, Florida, Texas and Oregon.

It also included Kara Salvagno, a longtime Connecticut resident who relocated to Scottsdale, Ariz., last year. She has competed in the Falmouth Road Race almost every year since 1993.

"I thought, 'This is fabulous! I have so many friends who still run the race, but I can't do it this year," she said.

Salvagno said she made the virtual run a full event. She asked her home gym to open at 6 a.m. so she could start racing at the same time the race began on Cape Cod.

She also FaceTimed[11] with a friend who was running seven miles at their favorite running spot in Connecticut at the same time Salvagno ran the virtual Falmouth.

"It was a waltz down memory lane, really," Salvagno said. "We just laughed the entire time. It didn't feel like we were running."

The Peachtree Road Race[12] in Atlanta, the world's biggest 10k race with more than 60,000 participants, allowed Outside Interactive to film its course this past Fourth of July before the actual race.

Rich Kenah, the president of the Atlanta Track Club, which operates the race, said the success of the Falmouth led his team to use the app as a way to promote the Peachtree Race. That event usually draws 90 percent of its participants from Georgia.

"As we look toward the future of the race, we want to attract more people from out of state. So this partnership gives us the opportunity to showcase the race to those unfamiliar with Atlanta, Peachtree Road and what the race looks like and feels like," Kenah said.

Virtual racing's future

Outside Interactive and RunSocial hope that interest eventually will match the opportunity, especially in generating revenue.

"Can you imagine in the future a million people literally running, walking or crawling the virtual Boston Marathon on a global scale? I mean, it's kind of a mind-blower," McNamee said.

For now, McNamee and Hardy said their goal is to find pioneers who are technologically savvy and receptive to the concept. Although questions remain about the value of virtual racing, McNamee said that the app isn't meant to replace an actual race. He added that some experience of racing is better than no experience at all.

Hardy said that although he is invested in what the next level of virtual technology will bring, he is more intrigued by the shifting definitions of shared experiences.

"When you're doing an event, you're not having a chat with everyone, right? But you are sharing an experience together, and that's more motivating than a regular run on your own. That doesn't mean you want to talk to everyone, but you're still sharing an experience together, and that's interesting."(1088)

Both apps are free, and users pay per video, starting at $3.99. Real-life races such as Falmouth incorporate the price of the video route into the overall race package, which can include a bib, swag and a finisher's certificate. Visit runsocial.com or outsideinteractive.com for more information.

(From *The Washington Post*, July 19, 2016)

NOTES

1. The Boston Marathon 波士顿马拉松赛，作为全球首个城市马拉松比赛于 1897 年开始举办。迄今为止，波士顿马拉松通常每年 4 月中旬举行。整个路线的起伏较大，有超过一万人参加。

2. Outside Interactive 这是由美国人 Gary McNamee 2011 年创办的公司，开发出以著名公路长跑赛事为基础的虚拟视频路线应用软件 Virtual Runner，在跑步机上实现与真实比赛同步进行。

3. RunSocial 这是总部设在新加坡的公司，使用增强现实技术开发出跑步应用软件，实现在跑步机上与著名马拉松赛事同步比赛。

4. augmented reality technology 增强现实技术（简称：AR），利用计算机生成一种逼真的虚拟环境，通过各种传感设备让用户的视、听、触和动等感觉都沉浸到这个虚拟环境中，实现用户和环境直接进行自然交互，是一项能"把现实带入虚拟，让虚拟增强现实"的应用技术。

5. Pokémon Go 《口袋妖怪 GO》，由 Pokémon 公司、任天堂（Nintendo）、和谷歌的 Niantic Labs 公司在 2016 年合作开发的一款现实增强手游，属于饲养宠物精灵进行对战的游戏，可以将虚拟世界和现实世界联系起来，玩家可以通过智能手机在现实世界里寻找发现精灵，进行抓捕和战斗。

6. foot pod 计步器或步感器，具有测量速度、步幅、距离等功能的传感器，固定在鞋上，可以记录跑步者脚部运动，帮助跑步者分析其跑步特性以改进表现等等。

7. The Prague Marathon 布拉格马拉松赛，始于 1995 年，每年 5 月举行，属于国际田联路跑金标赛事，是世界上沿途风景最美丽的马拉松比赛之一。2016 年 5 月 8 日第 22 届布拉格国际马拉松比赛中，来自 116 个国家和地区的一万多名选手参加了比赛，其中中国选手超过 550 人。

8. The Virgin Money London Marathon 伦敦马拉松赛在 1981 年开始举行，比赛每年 4 月下旬进行。比赛出发点在伦敦西南的布莱克希思格林尼治公园，途经议会大厦和白金汉宫，终点靠近圣琼斯公园。参赛选手超过三万人，沿途可以欣赏到伦敦许多历史名胜。

9. Tim Peake 蒂姆·皮克，英国陆军航空队少校，欧洲航天局宇航员，于 2015 年 12 月至 2016 年 6 月作为首位英籍宇航员进入国际空间站（International Space Station，简称 ISS）执行任务。2016 年 4 月在国际空间站跑步机上通过 RunSocial 虚拟视频软件参加了 2016 伦敦马拉松比赛。

10. The New Balance Falmouth Road Race 马塞诸塞州法尔茅斯公路赛，始于 1973 年，2011 年由纽柏伦公司（New Balance）冠名赞助，每年举办一次，全程 7 英里。

11. FaceTime 是苹果 iPhone 手机的一款免费视频聊天软件，通过接入互联网，装有 FaceTime 软件的设备之间可进行视频通话。该词可作动词使用，表示视频聊天、视频通话。

12. The Peachtree Road Race 佐治亚州亚特兰大 Peachtree 公路赛，始于 1970 年 7 月 4 日，每年举办一次，全程 10 公里，约有 6 万人参加。

USEFUL WORDS

augment	[ɔːgˈment]	*v.*	(formal) to increase the amount, value, size, etc. of sth 增加；提高；扩大
avatar	[ˈævətɑːr]	*n.*	a picture of a person or an animal which represents a person, on a computer screen, especially in a computer game or chat room（尤指电脑游戏或聊天室中代表使用者的）化身；头像
bib	[bɪb]	*n.*	(especially British English) a piece of cloth or plastic with a number or special colours on it that people wear on their chests and backs when they are taking part in a sport, so that people know who they are（运动员佩戴的）号码布；彩色身份标记
blur	[blɜːr]	*v.*	to become or make sth become difficult to distinguish clearly（使）难以区分
enhance	[ɪnˈhɑːns]	*v.*	to increase or further improve the good quality, value or status of sb/sth 提高；增强；增进
fabulous	[ˈfæbjələs]	*adj.*	(informal) extremely good 极好的；绝妙的
high-definition	[haɪ ˌdɛfəˈnɪʃən]	*adj.*	(technical 术语) using or produced by a system that gives very clear detailed images 高清晰度的；高分辨率的
incline	[ɪnˈklaɪn]	*n.*	(formal) a slope 斜坡；倾斜；斜度
intrigue	[ɪnˈtriːg]	*v.*	to make sb very interested and want to know more about sth 激起……的兴趣；引发……的好奇心
proportion	[prəˈpɔːʃn]	*n.*	the relationship of one thing to another in size, amount, etc. 比例；倍数关系
revenue	[ˈrevənjuː]	*n.*	the money that a government receives from taxes or that an organization, etc. receives from its business 财政收入；税收收入；收益
savvy	[ˈsævi]	*adj.*	(informal, especially North American English) having practical knowledge and understanding of sth; having common sense 有见识的；懂实际知识的；通情达理的
showcase	[ˈʃəʊkeɪs]	*v.*	to display or present to the best advantage 展示
stymy	[sˈtaɪmɪ]	*v.*	to hinder or prevent the progress or accomplishment of 从中作乱；完全妨碍
surreality	[səˈriːəlɪtɪ]	*n.*	noun form of surreal 离奇；超现实主义
surreal	[səˈriːəl]	*adj.*	very strange; more like a dream than reality, with ideas and images mixed together in a strange way 离奇的；怪诞的；梦幻般的；超现实的
sync	[sɪŋk]	*v.*	to make synchronous or adjust in time or manner 同时；同步
treadmill	[ˈtredmɪl]	*n.*	an exercise machine that has a moving surface that you can walk or run on while remaining in the same place（锻炼身体的）跑步机；走步机
virtual	[ˈvɜːtʃuəl]	*adj.*	made to appear to exist by the use of computer software, for example on the Internet（通过计算机软件，如在互联网上）模拟的；虚拟的

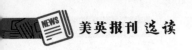

EXERCISES

I. Vocabulary

Choose among the four alternatives one word or phrase that is closest in meaning to the underlined part in each statement.

1. Thus he began Outside Interactive, a company that, along with others, is <u>merging</u> fitness <u>with</u> high-definition virtual technology.

   A. combining ...with
   B. changing ...into
   C. turning ...into
   D. separating ...with

2. In a bit of surreality, the crowds and fellow racers in the video will run and cheer <u>in proportion to</u> the speed of the real runners.

   A. in spite of   B. due to   C. in line with   D. in relation to

3. Both the virtual running app and RunSocial GPS, an outdoor tracking system that the company just launched, <u>feature</u> ways for participants to race one another, complete with a countdown clock and a leader board.

   A. include   B. display   C. find   D. explain

4. Hardy said RunSocial is looking to <u>make inroads in</u> the U.S. market with future partnerships and more U.S.-based video routes.

   A. enter into   B. invade into   C. march towards   D. head for

5. Mass. Jennifer Edwards, Falmouth's general manager, said the race organizers were hesitant at first when they heard McNamee's <u>pitch</u> but saw the opportunity to give those who couldn't run the live race—because of scheduling or geography—a chance to participate.

   A. sound   B. strength   C. promotion   D. degree

6. It also included Kara Salvagno, a longtime Connecticut <u>resident</u> who relocated to Scottsdale, Ariz., last year.

   A. physician   B. immigrant   C. guest   D. inhabitant

7. That event usually <u>draws</u> 90 percent of its participants from Georgia.

   A. moves   B. attracts   C. pulls   D. takes

8. Outside Interactive and RunSocial hope that <u>interest</u> eventually will match the opportunity, especially in generating revenue.

   A. attraction   B. hobby   C. concern   D. benefit

9. I mean, it's kind of <u>a mind-blower</u>.

   A. a drug   B. a shock   C. an excitement   D. a surprise

10. Hardy said that although he is invested in what the next level of virtual technology will bring, he is more <u>intrigued by</u> the shifting definitions of shared experiences.

    A. interested in
    B. affected by
    C. startled by
    D. amazed by

II. Comprehension

Decide whether the following statements are true or false according to the information given in the press clipping. Mark T or F to each statement.

1. Gary McNamee did not take part in the Boston Marathon in 2010 due to the extreme cold weather.

2. Runners can log on to the Outside Interactive app and watch the videos of routes free of charge.

3. Using running apps, the runners cannot select their speed on their own.

4. The routes in the Outside Interactive or RunSocial apps are from real-world races.

5. RunSocial virtual running apps cover the race routes both indoors and outdoors.

6. Both RunSocial and Outside Interactive have collaborated with the real-life long-distance races in the United States.

7. Virtual running apps can provide those who cannot run the actual race with an opportunity to participate.

8. The Peachtree Road Race is the world's biggest 10km race with more than 60,000 participants mainly from Atlanta.

9. Both Outside Interactive and RunSocial have obtained great benefits from the virtual running apps.

10. According to Marc Hardy, it is interesting to share experience with others through virtual races.

III. Questions for discussion

1. What do you think are the advantages of virtual running apps developed by Outside Interactive and RunSocial?

2. Suppose you were a regular runner, would you like to try a virtual race if you were unable to take part in the real life race? Please state your reasons.

3. Both RunSocial and Outside Interactive offer free apps, but you need to pay for the videos of virtual routes. How would you comment on this charging policy?

4. According to McNamee, the virtual running app is not meant to replace an actual race. Do you agree with him? What do you think is the relation between the virtual race and the actual one?

5. Both Outside Interactive and RunSocial hope they will make profits on their virtual apps and find investors to support their projects. How do you think of the future of the virtual races?

美英国家的饮食文化简介

　　运动与饮食同人们的生活方式密切相关。在人们的生活中，饮食是不可或缺的部分，不同国家地区拥有不同的饮食文化。所谓饮食文化，是指附着在饮食上并在饮食过程中体现出来的文化意义（隗静秋，2010）。美英国家的饮食文化体现着美英国家的生活方式、价值观以及文化传统。因此，在美英报刊中，通常会有关于美食的专栏。比如《华盛顿邮报》中的 Lifestyle 栏目里，就开辟了 Food 专栏，分成 Recipe Finder；Going Out Guide；Tom Sietsema；$20 Diner；Nourish；Dinner in Minutes；Wine；Spirits 等若干主题模块。

一、日常饮食

　　和我们一样，美英国家正常情况下每天有三顿饭——早餐、午餐和晚餐。通常早上七点半至八点半是早餐时间，中午十二点至两点为午餐时间，晚上七点至九点为晚餐时间。除此之外，下午四、五点钟是英国人下午茶时间，除了喝热茶或咖啡之外，通常配有蛋糕、饼干等茶点。下午茶起源于 19 世纪英国上层社会，最初是由于晚餐时间要等到晚上八点之后，午餐后至下午四五点钟，人们会感觉饥肠辘辘，于是就会准备些面包、松饼等点心，同时配上上等红茶。渐渐地这就演变成一种礼仪，形成英国独有的下午茶文化。

　　传统的英式早餐比较丰盛，包括煎培根、香肠、炒蛋、烤番茄、茄汁黄豆、烤面包等主食，还有麦片粥或麦片玉米片搭配牛奶或酸奶，并可以加入干果或水果；饮料包括红茶、咖啡或果汁。美式传统早餐基本上汇集了英式早餐和欧洲大陆各国的早餐内容，营养齐全，种类丰富，涵盖燕麦、玉米片等谷类；煎蛋、水煮蛋、炒蛋等蛋类；吐司、法式牛角面包、丹麦甜面包等面包；水果或果汁；以及红茶、咖啡、牛奶等饮料。

　　午餐通常比较简单，多数人选择三明治或汉堡、烤马铃薯或炸薯条，基本以快餐为主。

　　晚餐则是一天中最重要的一餐，也称正餐，一般饭前先喝汤，饭后上水果。正餐顺序大致包括开胃饮料或酒、汤（浓汤为主，有时会配有面包）、主菜（牛排、火腿等肉类或鱼类、蔬菜沙拉、土豆等）、餐后甜品（点心、水果、冰激凌等）、最后是咖啡，在英国喝咖啡前还会吃些饼干和乳酪。

　　从上述日常饮食中可以看出，美英人士饮食主要以丰富的肉类食品和奶制食品为主，以蔬菜为辅。这主要与美英国家农业以畜牧业为主的产业结构有关。他们采用简单的烹饪方式，主要以煎、煮、炖、炸、拌为主，讲求食物的营养和搭配，注重选取新鲜的食材和原料，菜肴主要讲求原汁原味，强调在烹调过程中保持食物原有的营养成分和味道。美国人追求食物的营养，讲求食物的营养成分，会考虑蛋白质、脂肪、碳水化合物等元素的组成是否能为人们所吸收（赵敬，2010）。

二、就餐礼仪

美英国家所代表的西餐非常讲究礼仪，主要包括入座方式、餐具使用、用餐规矩等等。

首先，从左侧入座是最得体的入座方式。在西餐厅，就坐前先靠近桌子站直，等餐厅领位者把椅子拉出再推进来，腿弯碰到椅子时，就可以坐下。就座时，端正坐好，双手自然下垂放在腿上，双腿平放，与餐桌的距离以便于使用餐具为佳。将餐巾对折放在膝上准备用餐，不宜随意摆弄餐桌上已摆好的餐具。

其次，西餐中餐具的布置和摆放十分讲究。通常是有几道菜摆放几副刀叉，吃一道菜换一副刀叉，如吃主菜用主餐刀和主刀叉，饭后甜品也有其专门的刀叉使用。使用刀叉进餐时，按照摆放顺序从外侧往内侧取用，左手持叉，右手持刀。切东西时左手拿叉按住食物，右手执刀将其切成小块，用叉子送入口中。使用刀时，刀刃向内。进餐中放下刀叉时应将刀叉顶端靠拢，摆放在餐盘边上。刀刃朝向自身，表示还要继续使用。每吃完一道菜，则要将刀叉并拢放在盘中。用餐过程中如果要谈话，可以拿着刀叉，无需放下。不用刀时，可用右手持叉。但若需要做手势时，就应放下刀叉，不要手执刀叉在空中挥舞摇晃，也不要一手拿刀或叉，而另一只手拿餐巾擦嘴，也不可一手拿酒杯，另一只手拿叉取菜。

最后，西餐用餐过程中有很多规矩要遵守。用餐时不要弄出声响，喝汤时不要吸啜，吃东西时要闭嘴咀嚼。如果汤菜过热，可待稍凉后再吃，不要用嘴吹。喝汤时，用汤勺从里向外舀，汤盘中的汤快喝完时，用左手将汤盘的外侧稍稍翘起，用汤勺舀净即可。吃完汤菜时，将汤匙留在汤盘（碗）中，匙把指向自己。吃牛排、鸡肉、鱼肉等大块食物，要切一块吃一块，不能切得过大，或一次将肉都切成块。注意嘴里有食物时一般不要开口说话。就餐时宜低声交谈，切勿大声喧哗。另外，使用餐巾也有讲究。不要抖开餐巾再去折叠，也不要在空中挥动餐巾。餐巾应放在大腿上，如果离开餐桌，要将餐巾放在椅子上，并把椅子推近餐桌。用餐结束时将餐巾从中间拿起，轻轻地放在餐桌上盘子的左侧。

餐桌礼仪是随着社会进步与社会交往而逐步形成的规范和礼节，体现着对他人的尊重，是人类文明的表现，从中可以感受美英饮食文化的独特魅力，也是了解学习西方文化的一种真实体验。

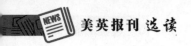

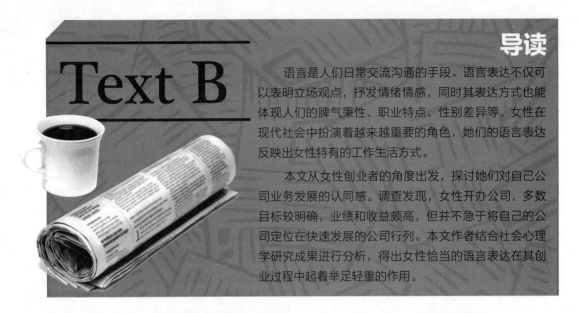

导读

语言是人们日常交流沟通的手段。语言表达不仅可以表明立场观点，抒发情绪情感，同时其表达方式也能体现人们的脾气秉性、职业特点、性别差异等。女性在现代社会中扮演着越来越重要的角色，她们的语言表达反映出女性特有的工作生活方式。

本文从女性创业者的角度出发，探讨她们对自己公司业务发展的认同感。调查发现，女性开办公司，多数目标较明确，业绩和收益颇高，但并不急于将自己的公司定位在快速发展的公司行列。本文作者结合社会心理学研究成果进行分析，得出女性恰当的语言表达在其创业过程中起着举足轻重的作用。

Women's talk: why language matters to female entrepreneurs

When Sue Stockdale set out to find women business-owners with fast-growth companies she found the language we use to offer opportunities to women is key

By Sue Stockdale

"Wanted—successful women entrepreneurs running fast-growing companies". You would think that an advert like this would have hordes of women making contact, wouldn't you? Well, that's not the case.

A few years ago I was involved in an initiative whose target market was women entrepreneurs running fast-growth companies. My role was to find these businesses to see how they could be supported in raising capital, and gaining access to mentors to help them during their growth journey. However, the problem was that we could not find many women who identified with this description. The traditional advertising routes were not working, so I set out to check if the lack of interest meant that they actually didn't exist.

What I discovered surprised me. There were many women who had ambitious growth plans and whose businesses were generating annual revenues well in excess of £250,000—but they did not categorise themselves as a "fast growth company". In fact, it took a little time during the conversations for them to recognise how successful they actually were. I would begin with getting to know them as individuals and find out what their passions were; why they started up their business and what progress they had made to date. Then I would enquire what their future plans were, and what they hoped to gain as a result of that success. In other words, I started with where they were now, and slowly uncovered what they were moving towards.

As a result of these conversations I realised that in every case, the businesses did qualify as fast growth, and the business owner was focused and driven to achieve further success. What I had uncovered was that the women did not identify with the label used and had not come forward as a result. So the language seemed to matter.

More recently I have been delivering a series of talks on the subject of risk, and using the risk type compass[1] as a way to help leaders to appreciate that risk-taking can look quite different depending on your risk disposition. For those that are warier and prudent, or more risk averse; stating ambitious growth aspirations for their company may seem highly uncomfortable. While they are perfectly capable of getting that outcome, how they express their ambitions may be somewhat different to those who are more adventurous and carefree, and more comfortable with risk-taking.

I describe these differences using the story of climbing a mountain. If I was to ask the more risk-averse woman to climb a mountain, their immediate reaction is likely to be, "no that's too difficult, I can't do that—you should ask my friend Jo, she likes adventures".

However, if I said, "let's go out for a walk, and enjoy the fresh air, we can have a chat along the way—it might get a bit uneven under foot, so come prepared" they are likely to turn up with enthusiasm and the correct footwear, then before they know it we have walked half way up the mountain! Two ways to achieve a similar outcome, but different language used to motivate the individual depending on what words resonate with them.

TED[2] talk superstar, Amy Cuddy[3] also talks about how language can have an impact on action in her recent book, *Presence*. She recalls her desire to become a runner and that she repeatedly failed in her New Year resolution[4] because in every run she did, she felt like a failure against her ideal of someone who was self-disciplined, fast and able to complete marathons. Eventually she took a different approach. She just resolved to run once. She dropped the long term, aspirational goals, and just set out to make running a positive experience. Rather than focusing on what she believed she could not do, she focused on what she could do and linked it to something she enjoys, which is travel. So now when she travels for work, so goes for a short run to experience a little more of her new environment in a different way.

Cuddy uses the term "self-nudging" to describe this approach. Along with her Harvard colleague Alison Wood Brooks, they arranged a seminar on the topic, aiming to discover more

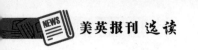

about the psychological hurdles that stop people from performing well. What they learned was that when we reframe anxiety as excitement, the better we are likely to do.

Brooks carried out experiments with people using three different stressful situations and found that those who took a moment to reframe their anxiety as excitement outperformed the others. Self-nudging, is about focusing on each moment in front of you, rather than the end outcome, to slowly nudge yourself towards being bolder.

So what does this mean for those who are working in the field of women's enterprise support? I think it means that language matters. We are so used to talking about aspirational end goals—startup to IPO[5], fast growth to exit, making a million, that maybe some thought should be given to "being the best you can be in your business today" mantra. Reflecting on "what is" as well as "what could be" using real-time feedback as a means of motivating oneself without being pressurised into defining what the end outcome should be.

The UK government formed a behavioural insights team focused on implementing changes in processes and systems to nudge people. They have had successes in the areas of car tax and income tax, so perhaps they should now turn their attention to developing some nudges to encourage more women to start up and grow their businesses, or encourage more diversity in the workplace. We can all think about how to encourage people to make different choices based on how options are presented, so maybe a little more thought about the words you are using can make a big difference.

(From *The Guardian*, June 29, 2016)

NOTES

1. risk type compass 风险承担类型罗盘，是心理学测试工具，用来分析个人承受风险的倾向类型。

2. TED 技术、娱乐、设计（technology, entertainment, design 的缩写），是美国的一家非营利机构。该机构以其组织的 TED 大会著称，大会宗旨是 "值得传播的创意 (ideas worth spreading)"。TED 诞生于 1984 年，其发起人是理查德·沃曼（Richard S. Wurman），2001 年起，克里斯·安德森 (Chris Anderson) 接管 TED，创立了种子基金会 (The Sapling Foundation)，并运营 TED 大会。TED 大会每年举行一次，邀请世界各领域的杰出代表出席大会，进行演讲。内容涉及科学、设计、文学、音乐、宗教、慈善等方方面面，受邀代表同与会者一同思考和探索有关技术、社会和人的关系。TED 大会将演讲做成视频放在互联网上，供全球观众免费分享。

3. Amy Cuddy 艾米·卡迪，美国社会心理学者，哈佛大学商学院副教授。2012 年 6 月在 TED 大会上做了题为 "肢体语言塑造你自己（*Your body language shapes who you are*）" 的演讲，全球观看人数达到 3500 万人，受到广泛好评。这次演讲内容后写入 2015 年出版的《风度》（*Presence*）一书中，该书荣登美国纽约时报畅销书排行榜，在同类图书中排名第三。

4. New Year resolution 新年愿望，通常是在 1 月 1 日新年时许下的心愿清单，希望在新的一年里完成，这是英美人士的一种惯行做法。

5. IPO 首次公开募股或首次公开发行（Initial Public Offerings），是指一家企业或公司（股份有限公司）第一次将它的股份向公众出售，或指股份公司首次向社会公众公开招股的发行方式。

USEFUL WORDS

advert [ˈædvɜːt] *n.* (British English) = advertisement, an announcement in a newspaper, on television, or on a poster about something such as a product, event, or job 广告

ambitious [æmˈbɪʃəs] *adj.* needing a lot of effort, money or time to succeed 规模宏大的；艰巨的；耗资的

aspiration [ˌæspəˈreɪʃn] *n.* ~ (for sth) / ~ (to do sth) a strong desire to have or do sth 渴望；抱负；志向

averse [əˈvɜːrs] [əˈvɜːs] *adj.* (formal) not liking sth or wanting to do sth; opposed to doing sth 不乐意的；反对的

disposition [ˌdɪspəˈzɪʃn] *n.* (formal) a tendency to behave in a particular way 倾向；意向

enthusiasm [ɪnˈθuːziæzəm] *n.* a strong feeling of excitement and interest in sth and a desire to become involved in it 热情；热心；热忱

entrepreneur [ˌɑːntrəprəˈnɜːr] *n.* a person who makes money by starting or running businesses, especially when this involves taking financial risks 创业者；企业家（尤指涉及财务风险的）

horde [hɔːd] *n.* (sometimes disapproving) a large crowd of people 一大群人

hurdle [ˈhɜːdl] *n.* a problem or difficulty that must be solved or dealt with before you can achieve sth 难关；障碍

implement [ˈɪmplɪmənt] *v.* to make sth that has been officially decided start to happen or be used 使生效；贯彻；执行；实施

initiative [ɪˈnɪʃətɪv] *n.* a new plan for dealing with a particular problem or for achieving a particular purpose 倡议；新方案

mantra [ˈmæntrə] *n.* a statement or a principle that people repeat very often because they think it is true, especially when you think that it not true or is only part of the truth（尤指认为并不正确或只是部分正确的）准则；原则；圭臬

mentor [ˈmentɔːr] *n.* an experienced person who advises and helps sb with less experience over a period of time 导师；顾问

nudge [nʌdʒ] *v.* to push sb/sth gently or gradually in a particular direction（朝某方向）轻推；渐渐推动

outperform [ˌaʊtpəˈfɔːm] *v.* to achieve better results than sb/sth（效益上）超过；胜过

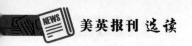

prudent	['pruːdnt] *adj.*	sensible and careful when you make judgments and decisions; avoiding unnecessary risks 谨慎的；慎重的；精明的
resolution	[ˌrezə'luːʃn] *n.*	a firm decision to do or not to do sth 决心；决定
resonate	['rezəneɪt] *v.*	to remind sb of sth; to be similar to what sb thinks or believes 使产生联想；引起共鸣；和……的想法（或观念）类似
wary	['weəri] *adj.*	careful when dealing with sb/sth because you think that there may be a danger or problem （对待人或事物时）小心的；谨慎的；留神的；小心翼翼的

 EXERCISES

I. Vocabulary

Choose among the four alternatives one word or phrase that is closest in meaning to the underlined part in each statement.

1. A few years ago I was involved in <u>an initiative</u> whose target market was women entrepreneurs running fast-growth companies.

    A. a process   B. a plan   C. an action   D. a decision

2. The traditional advertising routes were not working, so I <u>set out</u> to check if the lack of interest meant that they actually didn't exist.

    A. started   B. left   C. arranged   D. explained

3. There were many women who had ambitious growth plans and whose businesses were generating annual revenues well in excess of £250,000—but they did not <u>categorise</u> themselves as a "fast growth company".

    A. place   B. display   C. suggest   D. classify

4. What I had uncovered was that the women did not identify with the label used and had not <u>come forward</u> as a result.

    A. offered help   B. taken action

    C. stood out   D. turned up

5. More recently I have been delivering a series of talks on the subject of risk, and using the risk type compass as a way to help leaders to appreciate that risk-taking can look quite different depending on your risk <u>disposition</u>.

    A. temperament   B. property

    C. tendency   D. arrangement

6. While they are perfectly capable of getting that outcome, how they express their ambitions may be somewhat different to those who are more adventurous and <u>carefree</u>, and more comfortable with risk-taking.

    A. thoughtless   B. irresponsible   C. trouble-free   D. cheerful

7. Two ways to achieve a similar outcome, but different language used to motivate the individual depending on what words <u>resonate</u> with them.

   A. identify   B. resound   C. repeat   D. echo

8. What they learned was that when we <u>reframe</u> anxiety as excitement, the better we are likely to do.

   A. rearrange   B. reorganize   C. redefine   D. reset

9. <u>Reflecting on</u> "what is" as well as "what could be" using real-time feedback as a means of motivating oneself without being pressurised into defining what the end outcome should be.

   A. Remembering   B. Considering   C. Reverberating   D. Indicating

10. We can all think about how to encourage people to make different choices based on how options are presented, so maybe a little more thought about the words you are using can <u>make a big difference</u>.

    A. become quite different   B. draw a clear distinction

    C. turn into different state   D. have an important effect

II. Comprehension

Decide whether the following statements are true or false according to the information given in the press clipping. Mark T or F to each statement.

1. With the advert for successful women entrepreneurs running fast-growing companies, many women came to apply for it.

2. In fact, many successful women did not recognize themselves as running a fast-growth company.

3. One's risk disposition decides what kind of risk one would like to take.

4. The women who are risk averse seem uncomfortable to state their ambition for they are unable to achieve fast-growth in their company.

5. The story of mountain-climbing indicates the effect of language used to motivate the individuals to accomplish their goals.

6. Amy Cuddy failed to become a runner because she did not find the right way to practice.

7. Self-nudging refers to the approach to focus on what one can do for the moment, rather than for the final outcome.

8. The experiment discovered that those who treated anxiety as excitement performed better than others.

9. Proper language has an important influence on helping women entrepreneurs with their aspirational end goals.

10. It is suggested that the words can make a difference if we think about the way we present options for others to choose.

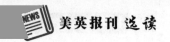
III. Questions for discussion

1. What was the purpose of the initiative Sue Stockdale participated in a few years ago, that is, finding women entrepreneurs running fast-growth companies?

2. Many women entrepreneurs have made great success in their business, but they do not regard their companies as fast-growing ones. How do you explain this phenomenon?

3. As to the subject of risk, one's risk disposition can decide the degree of risk-taking. Those who are warier and prudent may seem different to express their ambitions from those who are more adventurous and carefree. What category do you belong to in terms of risk-taking? Would you like to share your risk-taking experience with your classmates?

4. Amy Cuddy and her colleague have found that self-nudging, focusing on each moment in front rather than the end goal, can push one person towards being braver. What is the significance of this finding to the women entrepreneurs?

5. In this article, it is concluded that language plays an important role in encouraging women to start up and grow their businesses. What do you think are the functions of language?

《华尔街日报》简介

《华尔街日报》（*The Wall Street Journal*）于 1889 年在纽约创刊，由美国道·琼斯公司（Dow Jones & Company）所有，后被新闻集团（News Corp）收购，是侧重于商业和经济新闻的英语国际日报。《华尔街日报》国际影响广泛，日发行量达 200 万份，是美国发行量最大的财经类报纸。同时还出版了亚洲版、欧洲版、网络版，每天大概有 2000 多万人阅读纸质或电子版报纸。《华尔街日报》系列的目标是提供公正、准确、独立的财经新闻给高层管理人员、政府官员以及商界决策者。

作为一家享誉全球一百多年的财经类报纸，保证质量是关键，《华尔街日报》始终不遗余力地追求高质量新闻。该报擅长进行深度报道，谨慎选择适合题材，选题周期较长，通常为一月有余。报社对新闻写作手法历来要求非常严格，逐渐形成了独特的文体——"华尔街日报体"，强调严谨文风，表达明了清晰。在报道抽象枯燥的新闻时，开头通常以与新闻主题有关的感性人物故事入手，层层递进，主题不断得到深化，透过富于人情味的报道，使得非事件性新闻因人物的介入变得鲜明突出、引人注目。

《华尔街日报》的内容主要涵盖美国经济、国际话题以及财经新闻。高度可信的信息源是保证新闻质量的关键因素之一，《华尔街日报》的信息主要来源于美国和世界著名的证券交易机构，权威的政府发布部门或著名信息发布部门，言论分析则来自权威人士。

　　《华尔街日报》报道风格严肃，较少使用新闻图片，报纸主要以文字报道为主。经过改版，报纸与网络形成了更好的融合：纸质版精简记录昨日之报道，网络版则更为详尽。另外，网上还推出一系列免费博客。

　　《华尔街日报》的读者绝大多数属于高收入、高学历、高职位人群，定位较高。为了培养市场，抓住未来的读者，自 1991 年起，该报设立了《华尔街日报》教室版（*The Wall Street Journal* Classroom Edition），每月一期，专门刊登学生感兴趣的文章。同时，美国有些重点商学院会建议 MBA 学生在校期间每人订阅一份《华尔街日报》作为课外阅读的材料。

　　登录《华尔街日报》的官方网站，可以阅读该报刊的电子版。

Unit Five
Sports

报刊英语中动词的应用

报刊内容的经济性要求新闻工作者在有限的篇幅内传达尽量多的信息，以满足读者的阅读需求。就动词的使用而言，报刊英语往往以短小的动词来替换含字母较多的动词。这种趋势在英语报刊的标题中表现尤为明显。

1 短动词

aid=assist 帮助

begin=commence 开始

bilk=cheat 欺骗

grill= investigate 调查

laud=praise 赞扬

lop=diminish 下降，减少

mark=celebrate 庆祝

prompt=cause 引起

rule=decide 裁决，裁定

shun=keep away from 回避

slay=murder 谋杀

soar=skyrocket 急剧上升

stem=prevent 制止，阻挡

sway=influence 影响

allege=declare 宣布

bid=attempt 努力

blast=explode 爆炸

claim=cause the death of... 夺去……的生命

clash=disagree strongly 发生分歧，争议

map=work out 制订

net=tak possession of 捕获，抓获

quiz=question 询问，审问

sack=dismiss 解雇

=search thoroughly and rob 劫掠，洗劫

snub=pay no attention to 冷落，拒绝

spur=encourage 激励，鞭策

swap=exchange 交流，交换

thwart=prevent from being succeful 阻挠

trim=reduce 削减	vie=compete 竞争
vow=determine 决心，发誓	voice=express 表达
void=determine to be invalid 使无效	wed=marry 结婚
weigh=consider 考虑	woo=seek to win 争取，追求

报刊英语中选用短小的动词可节约版面，省去读者的阅读时间。上面列举的便是常见的短动词以及语义对应的长动词，由于在新闻报道中经常使用，这些短动词词汇在一定程度上成了新闻报道中的惯用词汇。

2 说意动词

在新闻报道中，为了使新闻报道具有真实感和生动性，显示客观与公正，需要适时引用有关人士的话语。引语分直接引语与间接引语。直接引语需要将新闻人物所说的话语真实准确、一字不差地记录下来，用引号标识出来。间接引语则是新闻撰稿人对新闻中人物所说的话语进行转述，无需引号，但转述的内容须与新闻中人物的话语一致。无论是转述还是直接引用原话，都有必要用某某人"说"加以交待，以便读者分辨出该部分内容是文章作者自己的观点还是别人的观点。

（一）标识直接引语的说意动词

英语中有大量表示"说"意的动词可用于标识直接引语：

acknowledge 承认	add 又说
admit 承认	affirm 肯定，确认
agree 同意说	air 使公开
allege 断言	analyze 分析道
announce 宣布	argue 争辩，主张
assert 断言	believes 相信，认为
blame 责备	boast 夸口说
cackle 叽叽呱呱地讲，咯咯笑着表示	call 大声说（或读）出，喊，叫
challenge 质疑	caution 告诫说
cheer 喝彩说	claim 声称有
complain 抱怨	commend 表示赞同，称赞
comment 进行评论，发表意见	conclude 断定，下结论

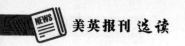
concede 承认

concur 同意，赞同

confess 承认

contend 声称，主张，认为

contradict 反驳说

croak 用低沉而沙哑的声音说出

declare 声明，声称

depict 描绘，描述

deny 否认，拒绝相信

denounce 谴责，宣布

disagree 不同意

disclose 透露

disputes 争论，辩论说，反对，辩驳

doubt 怀疑

inquire 询问

emphasize 强调说

exclaim 大声说

find 发现

fuss 抱怨

explain 解释说

elaborate 详细叙说

go on 继续说

gurgle 以咯咯声表示

hasten 急急忙忙地说

hypothesize 假设，假定

insist 坚持说

infer 推测

hold 认为，想，相信

imply 暗指，暗示

ignore 不理，忽视

illustrate（用图或例子）说明，阐明

indicate 简要地陈述，暗示

joke 开玩笑说

maintain 坚持；断言，主张

mistrust 对……有预感，猜测

note 谈及，表明

object 反驳说

observe 说，评论，评述

persist 坚持说，坚称，坚持问，追问

pledge 保证给予；许诺，保证发誓

point out 指出

proclaim 宣告

propose 提出，提议，建议

protest 抗议

predict 预测

question 疑问

quote 引用

reaffirm 重申

remark 议论

reply 回应说

report 报道说

reveal 透露，泄露

retort 反诘

refute 反驳

shriek 尖声发出，尖声叫喊

suggest 建议说

sing out（大声清晰地）喊出（唱出）

speculate 推测，推断，怀疑，设想

sputter（因激动、愤怒）唾沫飞溅地说   state 声明，声称

stress 着重说   scream 尖声地说，尖叫着发出

shrug 以耸肩表示   sputter 气急败坏地说

stammer 结结巴巴地说   suspect 怀疑

suppose 假定，猜想；认为   summarize 概括，总结

tweet 啾啾地说   urge 敦促

warn 警告   whisper 小声说

write 写到   validate 使生效，批准

verify 证明，证实   vow 郑重地宣告（声明）

voice 说，表达

举例如下：

Insulting political language is nothing new. In the 19th century, Ms. Jamieson <u>notes</u>, such attacks came in printed form, with the posting of "broadsides" that cast aspersions. But "in the mass media age, with a large viewing audience, we have not had anything comparable to the Republican debates," Jamieson <u>says</u>. （*The Christian Science Monitor*,Mar. 4, 2016）

"It's not going to be an easy period," Treasury Secretary Jack Lew said. He <u>added</u> that although the legislation includes a temporary stay on bondholder lawsuits, Puerto Rico would have to negotiate lasting restructuring terms with its creditors on a voluntary basis. (*The Washington Post*, June 30, 2016）

"We should have kept (Lin)," Houston Rockets G.M. Daryl Morey <u>tweeted</u> on 9 February. (*The Independent*, Feb.16, 2012）

"Can you imagine if I was singing about texting?" She <u>cackles</u>. "You would never get me singing about having a drink in the club." （*Time*, Jan. 4, 2016）

"May she burn in hell fires," <u>tweeted</u> George Glloway, who <u>quoted</u> an Elvis Costello protest song, "Tramp the dirt down." (*The Guardian*, Apr. 8, 2013)

上述例子中 notes，says，added，tweeted，cackles，quoted 都是用来表达直接引语的动词。说意动词除了与有明确消息来源的信息结合在一起外，也常与模糊的消息来源一起用于新闻报道之中，例如：authorities say（权威人士讲），a witness said（目击者称），a source close to the Pentagon revealed（一位接近五角大楼的人士披露），foreign radios announced that（外电播报），foreign wire services were quoted as saying（援引外国通讯社的报道称）（周学艺，2010）。

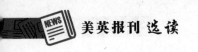

（二）标识间接引语的说意动词

间接引语是文章作者转述新闻中人物的话语，这种转述必须客观。文章作者在转述过程中不能曲解原话的本意，不能添加或减少原话语的意思，这是新闻报道应该遵守的职业道德，也是新闻做到客观公正的底线。用于标识直接引语的动词也都常用于标识间接引语。如：

But Mr. Donney <u>said</u> he's still open to voting for Trump. "It depends on how he acts," he <u>said.</u> That was before Thursday night's debate. (*The Christian Science Monitor*, Mar. 4, 2016)

前一个句子 But Mr. Donney said he's still open to voting for Trump 本身是间接引语，是报道者根据 Mr. Donney 的话语做出的一种合理推论，这种推论当然不可避免地会包含文章作者对原话的评判，当然撰稿人的这种判断在动词 said 一词上的体现是很弱的。随后的直接引语 "It depends on how he acts," 便是报道的写作者做出前面推论的依据。更多的例子如：

In his most popular book, *The God Delusion*, published in 2006, Dawkins <u>contends</u> that a supernatural creator almost certainly does not exist and that religious faith is a delusion. In his 1986 book *The Blind Watchmaker*, he <u>argues</u> against the watchmaker analogy, an argument for the existence of a supernatural creator based upon the complexity of living organisms.

(https://en.wikipedia.org/wiki/Richard_Dawkins)

China, <u>said</u> Simon, sees talent as the next big global race for driving competitiveness and innovation. (*The Washington Post*, Nov. 16, 2011)

Wang also <u>explained</u> that the Chinese see this talent pool as the key to moving from a "made in China" orientation to a "created in China" capability. China's future growth, <u>continued</u> Wang, will rely more on the new talent strategy, even as its past successes were built mainly on its population dividend and investment. (*The Washington Post*, Nov. 16, 2011)

在这三个例子中 contends、argues、said、explained、continued 都是用于间接转述他人的观点或看法的。

可以看到，选取某些动词不可避免会表达出引述者的主观色彩，体现了其主观判断，当新闻报道者选用某个动词或某些动词表达"说"时，实际上已经加入了其自身对被引用者或被转述者语气、态度、情态乃至举止方式等的判断。例如下列动词：admit 承认、assert 断言、believes 相信，认为、boast 夸口说、caution 告诫说、complain 抱怨、concede 承认、confess 承认、contend 争辩、contradict 反驳说、concur 同意，赞同、claim 声称、commend 表示赞同，称赞、doubt 怀疑、hold 怀有（见解）等、insist 坚持，坚决认为；坚决主张，坚决要求、imply 暗含、maintain 坚持，断言，主张、object 反驳说、protest 抗议、pledge 承诺、

question 怀疑，对……提出疑问、warn 警告等。

"It sends a signal to other countries because they're rushing to gain scientific and technological leadership while we're getting distracted with a pseudoscience issue," warned Gerry Wheeler, executive director of the 55,000-member National Science Teachers Association in Arlington, Va. (*Time*, Aug. 15, 2005)

warned 一词的使用体现了文章作者对说话者目的的把握与解读，他把新闻中人物的话语解读为一种警告。实际上读者也应该对文章作者的这种解读进行积极的思考并做出自己正确的解读。又如：

But as William Wohlforth of Dartmouth College reminded the NIC conference in Texas last week, America has been through phases of declinism before. (*Financial Times*, Nov. 24, 2008)

撰稿人是在转述别人的语言，标识间接引语的动词是 reminded，这是撰稿人对被引用的人的话语的一种判断和归类。

Ken Livingstone also offered a critical assessment. He blamed Thatcher for causing unemployment and leaving people dependent on welfare: "She decided when she wrote off our manufacturing industry that she could live with two or three million unemployment," he said (*The Guardian*, Apr. 8, 2013)

在上例中，作者使用的标识间接引语的动词是 blamed，这也是作者对被引用话语的一种"定性"，把后面的话语"定性"为一种"责备"。

'All of these liars will be sued when the election is over': Donald Trump denounces accusers (*Los Angeles Times*, Oct.23, 2016)

选用 denounce（谴责、公开抨击）一词也是出于作者对特朗普说话的内容与态度的判断。

导读

山姆·阿勒代斯（Sam Allardyce，1954—）英格兰籍前足球运动员、足球教练员，常被称为"大山姆"（Big Sam）。曾担任西布罗姆维奇（West Bromwich Albion）俱乐部助理教练职务和博尔顿球队（Bolton Wanderers）经理，2007 年任纽卡斯队（Newcastle United）的主教练，2008 年起执教布莱克本（Blackburn Rovers），2011 年起担任西汉姆联队（West Ham United）的主教练，2016 年 6 月起担任英格兰国家队（England national team）主教练，前后共 67 天。

本文讲的是阿勒代斯竞争英格兰国家队主教练职务一事，文章作者分析了英格兰国家队选择领队时的窘境、球队的弱项和外部形势、阿勒代斯执教的理念与风格、职业经历、个性特点以及其他球队教练对他的评价等。

Sam Allardyce the big man gets the biggest job in football

By Andrew Anthony

England's new manager has long craved the role, despite the vilification that has been the lot of his predecessors since 1966. With a position whose demands change with the nation's mood, we have now gone for no-nonsense, writes Andrew Anthony.

After such a sustained period of disappointment, the level of expectation is at an historical low.

Last week, the worst-kept secret in international football was spilled when Sam Allardyce was announced as the new England manager. Apparently, the FA's[1] first choice was Allardyce's old critic and sparring partner, Arsenal[2] manager Arsene Wenger[3], who once accused the one time Bolton manager of producing "anti-football". Wenger preferred to remain in his current job.

That the Frenchman was first on the FA's list and Allardyce second paints a vivid picture of the confusion that has bedevilled English football at all levels of coaching and administration for at least a generation. It's rather as if a film studio, on finding that the auteur Terrence Malick was unavailable to direct a film, decided to go for Guv Ritchie instead. What kind of film, you would rightly ask, do they have in mind?

By the same token, what kind of football does the FA have in mind? Because there could be no two more divergent philosophies of the game than Wenger's and Allardyce's. If the Arsenal man is all about the aesthetics of possession, intricate passing and swift movement, then the Englishman has built his career on blunt pragmatism that more often than not takes the shape of intimidating physical strength and emphatically direct football.

The new Manchester United[4] manager, Jose Mourinho, who is no martyr to the school of art for art's sake[5], once referred to Allardyce's football as the "19th century". Elsewhere, he has been regularly pilloried for second practicing the crude "long-ball" tactics that held English football in aspic for decades.

In his two biggest jobs, as manager of Newcastle United and then of West Ham United[6], Allardyce was sacked not because of any great failure, but because his style of football was unpopular with the fans. To some extent, these criticisms are unfair. Leicester City[7] played a brand of football to win the Premier League[8] last season very similar to the kind Allardyce preaches and they couldn't have been more adored.

Part of the reason for this inconsistency comes down to personality and appearance. "Big Sam" had the misfortune of looking like the archetype of a manager from another era. He's a large man with a meaty, implacable face and a confidence that borders on the egomaniacal. He can often seem as though he is figuratively clothes in a sheepskin coat.

"Unfortunately, I cannot help the way I were born and the way I look." He told one interviewer. "If people see you skin deep, then they'll make a skin-deep judgment. The 'rugged' perception comes from the past, the career history: not a flamboyant or cultured footballer, a fairly straightforward, basic defender that played in all four divisions of the Football League…But it's never really worried me. I do whatever I think needs to be done."

But in spite his protestation about not caring, there is a sense that the cocksure manner is the product of poorly concealed resentment at not being fully appreciated by the football establishment, the media and the fans. Lesser men would have buckled under the negative reactions that Allardyce has provoked. But his outlook has remained balanced by a chip on both shoulders. He famously said that he would never manage a top-four side because his name wasn't Allardici.

However, he seems to be motivated by an ever-deepening desire to prove the world wrong and gain the acclaim he feels he deserves. And nowhere provides a better opportunity than the England job. Nor does any other position offer a greater chance of personal defeat. If all political careers end in failure, then the England manager's job ends in national humiliation. Only Sir Alf

Ramsey has ever won anything—the World Cup in 1966—and he was sacked and practically erased from public view.

Others have not been treated quite so kindly. Bobby Robson, Graham Talor, Glen Hoddle, Kevin Keegan, Steve McClaren and Roy Hodgson: all of them departed with boos ringing in their ears and vicious lampoons in the newspapers. And that's not to mention the lavishly paid foreign imports Sven-Goran Eriksson and Fabio Capello, whose teams were studies in underachievement.

The only advantage Allardyce has is that, after such a sustained period of disappointment, the level of expectation is at a historical low. Perhaps the position was inadvertently best summed up by the football writer who, recalling the stubbornly defensive performance by Allardyce's West Ham that earned Mourinho's condemnation, asked: "What wouldn't England's supporters have given for such an approach against Iceland."

In other words, so far have national prospects fallen, that our greatest hope is that a team from the wealthiest football nation in the world might set out to gain a 0-0 draw against a sparsely populated volcanic island with a league that is ranked 36th in Europe. In a way, Allardyce's job is to turn England into the new Iceland. His expertise lies with plucky underdogs, making small clubs punch above their weight.

Brought up on a council estate in Dudley in the West Midlands, he enjoyed a journeyman career as an unflinching centre half for unglamourous sides such as Bolton, Millwal and Preston.

Turning to management, he took the Irish side Limerick into Ireland's top flight before making his way back to Bolton. He took the club back into the Premier League and kept them there, finishing as high as sixth place in 2005. He made Bolton into the proverbial location that no one wanted to go to on a wet Tuesday night in November. Particularly Wenger, whose slick Arsenal side were frequently bullied into unlikely defeat.

By his own estimation, his natural position is among the European elite. When he was manager of the Blackburn he suggested he was better suited to Real Madrid[9]. People laughed. Are they laughing now?

In truth, it's hard to think of a better candidate for England than Allardyce. For one thing, he's openly craved the job for a decade and more. For another, there are very few realistic options. Even if Wenger had accepted the offer, he's probably too old now.

Football managers, with only a handful of exceptions, tend to be like rock bands—they have a few golden years, and then repeat themselves with ever dwindling results. Young, hungry managers either don't want the England job or are not sought by the FA, which prefers a proven track record.

And if it comes down to football managers who are English, the list of those who have enjoyed real success is vanishingly short. No English manager, for example, has ever won the Premier League title, let alone the Champions League[10].

It used to be said that English coaches were inward-looking with poor levels of study. In this globalised world of international players and coaches and Uefa badges, that's no longer really true. And indeed Allardyce, who has been willing to learn from abroad, is known for his innovative methods of data collection and fitness analysis. Yet in terms of the weird business of encouraging young talented athletes to pass the ball to each other in an attractive and effective manner, as the French, Germans, Italians and Spanish seem to do, then that's where English football managers go missing.

The closest we've come is getting them to pass the ball in an occasionally attractive but invariably ineffective manner. That's been the story of England in recent years. Lots of possession but no end product. And despite the FA's flirtation with Wenger, it looks as if that experiment has now been put to rest.

"I take great satisfaction from the way I've managed to evolve," Allardyce said a couple of years ago. "I've changed styles, changed methods. I've always had an open mind, always been prepared to listen."

Perhaps, but no one has ever accused one of Allardyce's teams of epitomizing the beautiful game.

And just as Big Sam never minded Arsenal hogging the ball when they played against Bolton, if his side could nick a goal from a set piece in the 87th minute, so we can imagine that he will be more than ready to accept England's inferiority and make a virtue of it against our stronger rivals such as Germany, Brazil, Argentina and, of course, Iceland.

Is this a step backwards? Quite possibly, but given that England has made such a hash of stepping forward and, come to that, sideways, then it's no surprise that new direction might come with a retro feel. The question is, can he take English football back 50 years, to when we last won something?

(From *The Observer*, July 24, 2016)

NOTES

1. FA 英国足联（the English Football Association），英国足球的管理机构，成立于 1863 年，是世界上历史最悠久的足球协会，负责对英国境内足球比赛的所有方面加以监管。英足联在全国范围内对所有足球比赛拥有处罚权，也可通过郡足协在地方做出间接处罚。该组织举办多种比赛，最有名的比赛是英足联杯比赛（FA Cup）。

2. Arsenal 阿森纳足球俱乐部（Arsenal Football Club），职业足球俱乐部，基地在伦敦市，1886 年创立，前身名为迪尔广场（Dial Square），后更名为皇家阿森纳（Royal Arsenal），1893 年更名为沃尔维奇阿森纳（Woolwich Arsenal），1913 年迁往伦敦北部的海布里（Highbury），次年再次更名为阿森纳（Arsenal）。阿森纳在足球场上成绩卓著，2016 年福布斯估价该俱乐部为英国价值第二高的足球俱乐部，估价为 20 亿美元。

3. Arsène Wenger 法国足球教练，阿森纳教父，曾执教过南斯（Nancy-Lorrain）、摩纳哥（AS Monaco）和名古屋鲸八足球俱乐部（Nagoya Grampus Eight），1996 起执教阿森纳足球俱乐部，2003 年被授予大英帝国勋章，曾 11 次并评为英超联赛月度最佳主教练。

4. Manchester United 曼彻斯特联盟足球俱乐部（Manchester United Football Club），英文简称 Man Utd 或 MUFC，中文简称曼联，位于英国英格兰西北区曼彻斯特郡曼彻斯特市，是一家职业足球俱乐部。1878 创立，其前身为牛顿·希斯兰卡夏郡和约克郡铁路足球俱乐部（Newton Heath LYR Football Club）。1893 年从铁路公司独立，名称中的 LYR（Lancashire and Yorkshire Railway）自然也被去掉。1902 年球队正式改组为曼联，现为英格兰足球超级联赛（Premier League）俱乐部，曼联的球队移到老特拉福德（Old Trafford）体育场，一直沿用至今，是英国足球场上的一支劲旅，绰号"红魔"（the Red Devils）。

5. art for art's sake 为艺术而艺术，源自法语"l'art pour l'art"，是 19 世纪早期法国唯美主义诗人和作家泰奥菲尔·戈蒂耶（Théophile Gautier, 1811-1872）倡导并践行的艺术主张，表达的哲学理念是：艺术的内在价值是与教化、道德或实用性分离的。

6. West Ham United 西汉姆联足球俱乐部（West Ham United Football Club），英格兰超级联赛球队之一，英格兰传统足球俱乐部，位于外伦敦东部纽汉区，成立于 1895 年，球队主场是厄普顿公园球场。为各级国家队输送了多名富有才华的青年球员，故有"足球学院"（The Academy of Football）的美称。

7. Leicester City 莱切斯特城足球俱乐部（Leicester City Football Club），位于英国英格兰莱斯特城，现从属于英格兰足球超级联赛。莱斯特城的前身莱斯特福斯（Leicester Fosse）创立于 1884 年，1890 年加入英格兰足球协会。1894 年参加英格兰足球乙级联赛，1919 年一战结束后球队更为现名。

8. Premier League 英格兰足球超级联赛，常简称为"英超"，英国男子足球俱乐部的专业足球联盟，是一家足球公司，股东有 20 支足球俱乐部。执掌英国足球联盟（English Football League）晋降级的具体运作，赛季从头一年的 8 月至第二年的 5 月。英超一直被看作是世界上最好的足球联赛之一，参赛的强队多，节奏快、竞争激烈，声隆誉高。

9. Real Madrid 是皇家马德里（Royal Madrid Football Club）的普通叫法，是一家职业足球俱乐部，总部在马德里。1902 年成立，当时名称为 Madrid Football Club，real 一词在西班牙语里实为 royal，意为"皇室的"。1920 年由国王 Alfonso XIII 赠名与该俱乐部。2009 年，被国际足球历史和统计联合会（IFFHS）评为 20 世纪欧洲最佳俱乐部。

10. The UEFA Champions League 欧洲冠军联赛，简称"欧冠"，是一年一度的欧洲大陆俱乐部间足球比赛，由欧洲足球协会联盟（Union of European Football Associations 简称 UEFA）组织，也是世界上最负盛名的巡回赛，1992 年取代了之前的欧洲冠军俱乐部杯（European Champion Clubs' Cup）。欧洲足球协会联盟赛事的优胜者有资格参加欧洲足球协会联盟超级杯赛（the UEFA Super Cup）和国际足联俱乐部世界杯赛（FIFA Club World Cup）。

USEFUL WORDS

archetype	[ˈɑːkɪtaɪp] *n.*	(written) the most typical or perfect example of a particular kind of person or thing 典型；原型
aspic	[ˈæspɪk] *n.*	[u] clear jelly which food can be put into when it is being served cold 花色肉冻
buckle	[ˈbʌkl] *v.*	to fasten sth or be fastened with a buckle 用搭扣扣紧
bedevil	[bɪˈdevl] *v.*	(formal) to cause a lot of problems for sb/sth over along period of time 长期困扰
conceal	[kənˈsiːl] *v.*	to hide, to keep secret 掩藏；掩盖
dwindle	[ˈdwɪndl] *v.*	to become gradually less or smaller 减少，变小，缩小；衰落，变坏；退化
epitomize	[ɪˈpɪtəmaɪz] *v.*	to make to serve as a model of or perfect example of sth. larger or wider 作……的摘要；成为……的缩影；概括，集中体现
hog	[hɔːg] *v.*	to use or keep most of sth yourself and stop others from using or having it 独占，贪心占取
inadvertently	[ˌɪnədˈvɜːrtəntli] *adv.*	by accident,without intending to 漫不经心地；疏忽地，非故意地
intimidate	[ɪnˈtɪmɪdeɪt] *v.*	to frighten,esp,to influence by threats 恫吓，恐吓，威胁
lampoon	[læmˈpuːn] *n.*	(written) a piece of writing that criticizes sb./sth. and makes them or it look silly 讽刺文章或言辞
lavish	[ˈlævɪʃ] *adj.*	large in amount, or impressive, and usually costing a lot of money 过分丰富的，大量生产的
plucky	[ˈplʌki] *adj.*	(informal) having a lot of courage and determination（尤指成功的希望渺茫时仍）勇敢的；坚决的
slick	[slɪk] *adj.*	(sometimes disapproving) done or made in a way that is clever and efficient but often does not seem to be sincere or lacks important ideas 光滑的；熟练的，灵巧的，机灵的，聪明的；华而不实的
spar	[spɑːr] *v.*	to argue with sb usually in a friendly way 争论，争吵
sparsely	[ˈspɑːrsli] *adv.*	only present in small amounts or numbers and often spread over a large area 稀疏地，稀少地
spill	[spɪl] *v.*	to divulge 泄露（机密）

sustain	[sə'steɪn] *v.*	to make something continue for some time 使保持；使稳定持续
vilify	['vɪlɪfaɪ] *v*	(formal) to say or write unpleasant things about sb/sth so that other people will have a low opinion of them 污蔑，中伤，诽谤 vilification *n.*
unflinching	[ʌn'flɪntʃɪŋ] *adj.*	remaining strong and determined,especially in a difficult or dangerous situation 坚定的；无所畏惧的

EXERCISES

I. Vocabulary

Choose among the four alternatives one word or phrase or paraphrase that is closest in meaning to the underlined part in each statement.

1. Last week, the worst-kept secret in international football was <u>spilled</u> when Sam Allardyce was announced as the new England manager.

    A. emptied   B. diverged   C. disclosed   D. caused to fall

2. Because there could be no two more <u>divergent</u> philosophies of the game than Wenger's and Allardyce's.

    A. different   B. similar   C. difficult   D. diffuse

3. He's openly <u>craved</u> the job for a decade and more.

    A. criticized strongly   B. desired strongly

    C. devoted to   D. applied for

4. His expertise lies with <u>plucky</u> underdogs, making small clubs punch above their weight.

    A. tough   B. coward   C. sturdy   D. encouraged

5. Perhaps the position was <u>inadvertently</u> best summed up by the football writer....

    A. accidentally   B. adequately   C. absolutely   D. inadequately

6. That the Frenchman was first on the FA's list and Allardyce second paints a vivid picture of the confusion that has <u>bedeviled</u> English football at all levels of coaching and administration for at least a generation.

    A. intrigued   B.troubled   C. confused   D. introverted

7. After such a <u>sustained</u> period of disappointment, the level of expectation is at an historical low

    A. maintained   B. kept

    C. provided with nourishment   D. endured

8. The Englishman has built his career on blunt pragmatism that more often than not takes the shape of <u>intimidating</u> physical strength and emphatically direct football.

    A. intriguing   B. frightening

    C. intoxicating   D. exhilarating

9. There is a sense that the cocksure manner is the product of poorly <u>concealed</u> resentment at not being fully appreciated by the football establishment.

A. exposed   B. opened   C. discovered   D.hidden

10. He seems to be motivated by an ever-deepening desire to prove the world wrong and gain the <u>acclaim</u> he feels he deserves.

A. exclamation   B. applause   C. appreciation   D. praise

II. Comprehension

Decide whether the following statements are true or false according to the information given in the press clipping. Mark T or F to each statement.

1. The new Manchester United manager, Jose Mourinho, like Arsène Wenger, also seems to be critical of Sam Allardyce's philosophy of the football game.

2. People's unfair criticism of Allardyce comes only from the fact that they are not pleased with Allardyce's character and what he looked like.

3. Leicester City's victory under the managment of Allardyce in the Premier League is not adored by people at all.

4. According to Sam Allardyce, people's judgment of him is not fair.

5. Sam Allardyce dislikes the negative way people look at him, but he hides his dislike very well.

6. According to the article, Sam Allardyce is a quite confident person.

7. There is a high possibility for Arsène Wenger to be the new England manager.

8. According to the article, Sam Allardyce's strategies can make up what is missing in England football team.

9. According to the article, French and German football teams pay much attention to the skills of passing ball during the competition.

10. The article is not objective because its analysis of the situation where Allardyce and FA stand is biased.

III. Questions for discussion

1. What helps Allardyce get the biggest job in football?

2. Do you like playing football? What benefits can football games bring to people?

3. What risks does a national team manager like Allardyce have to face when the level of national expectation is at a new high or at a historical low?

4. Do strong sports really help exalt the power of country?

5. What do you think of the national football team of China? And what are the problems it has? Do you have any good idea to alter the situation?

美英国家主要体育赛事

一、美国重要的体育赛事

（一）篮球（basketball）

篮球是 1891 年由在美国任体育教师的加拿大人詹姆士·奈史密斯博士（Dr. James Naismith）发明的一项体育运动。美国全国篮球协会（National Basketball Association，简称 NBA）目前被广泛赞誉为世界上专业水平最高的男子篮球联盟，旗下拥有 30 个篮球队（美国 29 个，加拿大 1 个）。NBA 是美国和加拿大四大主要的职业运动联盟之一，其比赛分为：季前赛（NBA Preseason）、常规赛（NBA Regular Season）和季后赛（NBA Playoffs）三大部分。

（二）美式橄榄球或美式足球（American football）

美式橄榄球或美式足球是在英式足球（association football）和英式橄榄球（rugby football，一译"拉格比足球"）的基础上在美国逐渐发展起来的，在美国和加拿大美式橄榄球或美式足球直接被称为足球（football）。自 2012 年起，每年约有 1,100 万高中生和 7 万大学生参与这一体育竞赛。沃尔特·坎普（Walter Camp）对美式橄榄球规则加以改进，使其有别于英式足球，被称为美式橄榄球之父（Father of American Football）。美国国家橄榄球联盟（National Football League，简称 NFL）是北美最大的美式橄榄球组织，成立于 1920 年，其组织的比赛有季前赛，常规赛和季后赛等。

（三）棒球（baseball）

棒球源于 19 世纪的一种儿童游戏，在美国非常普及，早在 1856 年，棒球就被称为美国的"国球"（national pastime）。美国职业棒球大联盟（Major League Baseball，简称 MLB）的赛季是每年的四月至十月，最后的冠军赛称为"世界大赛"（World Series）。

（四）冰球（ice hockey）

冰球是继棒球、橄榄球和篮球后在美国特别是美国北部最受欢迎的体育项目。最重要的组织机构为国家冰球联盟（National Hockey League，简称 NHL），是一个由北美冰球队伍所组成的职业冰球运动联盟。队伍分成东、西两个大区，每个大区各有三个分区。最后产生的 16 个最强队通过淘汰赛的形式产生一个冠军，获得斯坦利杯（Stanley Cup）。

（五）足球（soccer）

足球是继橄榄球、棒球、冰球、篮球之后美国第五个大体育项目，在美国英式足球（association football）被称为 soccer，而 football 一词指的是美式橄榄球或美式足球（American football），全国性的足球组织是"美国足球协会"（United States Soccer Federation，简称 USSF）。美国职业足球大联盟（Major League Soccer，简称 MLS）筹建于 1993 年，自 1996 展开联赛，截至 2016 年，共有 20 支球队，而大联盟中不乏世界知名的足球运动员如戴维·贝克汉姆（David Beckham）和蒂埃里·亨利（Thierry Henry）等。

二、英国重要的体育赛事

（一）网球（tennis）

网球运动最早起源于 12 世纪法国北方，同在法国一样，网球在英国也深受人们的喜爱。温布尔登网球锦标赛（The Championships, Wimbledon）始于 1877 年，是世界上著名的网球赛事之一，在位于伦敦郊区的温布尔登举行。

（二）板球（cricket）

板球运动规则确定于 1787 年，要求选手着装正式，穿白色裤子，比赛一般要持续数天。在 19 世纪，板球运动主要是上层阶级的运动，玩板球的限于在公学就读的男生。国际板球理事会（International Cricket Council）每四年举办一次的板球世界杯（ICC, Cricket World Cup）为一天单局板球比赛（ODI, One Day International cricket）。该项比赛在世界上是拥有观众最多的体育运动之一，板球被英国人看作是一项崇尚体育精神（sportsmanship）和"公平比赛"（fair play）的运动。

（三）高尔夫球（golf）

高尔夫球运动是苏格兰人发明的。截至 16 世纪，高尔夫在苏格兰已经很普及，皇室成员如苏格兰玛丽皇后都对高尔夫有浓厚的兴趣。英国高尔夫球公开赛（The Open Championship，常被称为 the British Open 或 The Open）始于 1860 年，是高尔夫史上最悠久最负盛名的大赛之一，赛事由英国圣安德鲁斯皇家古典高尔夫俱乐部（Royal and Ancient Golf Club of St. Andrews）主办，每年 7 月第三个周末举行。

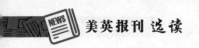

（四）赛马（horse racing）

赛马形式有平地赛（flat racing），越野障碍赛（jump racing），驾辕赛（harness racing）和耐力赛 (endurance racing) 等，在英国广泛开展的有平地赛和全国狩猎赛（National Hunt Racing）。赛马是不列颠第二大观赏性体育项目，比赛规则于 17 至 19 世纪形成，有组织的国家级赛马在全英已有数百年历史。英国最大最重要的赛马赛事是皇家阿斯科特赛马会（the Royal Ascot），每年 6 月在英国伯克郡阿斯科特赛马场（Ascot Racecourse）举行，为期 4 天。阿斯科特赛马场于 1711 年由安妮女王（Queen Anne）创办。看台设有皇家围场（the Royal Enclosure）供国君（如伊丽莎白二世等）和家族成员使用。

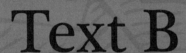

导读

自行车比赛有三大类，分别是场地赛（track cycling）、公路赛（road race）和越野赛（cross country competition），场地赛在赛车场（velodrome）进行。主要的赛事有奥林匹克比赛（Olympic Games）、世界锦标赛（World Championship）和世界杯赛（World Cup）等。奥运会比赛项目有追逐赛（pursuit）、计时赛（time trial）、计分赛（points race）和争先赛（scratch race）、凯琳赛（Keirin）等。追逐赛又分个人（individual pursuit）和团体（team pursuit）项目。场地自行车赛分为两大类：冲刺赛（sprint）和耐力赛（endurance）。冲刺赛有八段和十段赛程（lap）。奥林匹克比赛中共有十项比赛，男女各有五项。

世界锦标赛指的是国际自行车联盟（Union Cycliste Internationale）世界锦标赛（The UCI Track Cycling World Championships），每年举办一次，通常在三月和四月。世界杯赛也是国际自行车联盟组织的赛事，英文全称为 The UCI Track Cycling World Cup。

本文介绍的是英国的自行车团队在 2016 年 8 月里约热内卢举办的奥林匹克运动会上的表现，Sir Bradley Wiggins 是文章的中心，文章还披露了英国自行车团队内部的一些不和谐现象。

Team GB and Sir Bradley Wiggins[1] win Olympic gold in men's team pursuit

Australia beaten in Rio final to give Wiggins a British record eighth medal Ed Clancy, Steven Burke, Owain Doull and Wiggins break world record Sir Bradley Wiggins becomes Great Britain's most successful Olympian.

By Barry Glendenning

So what comes after a knighthood? Great Britain's perfect start to the Olympic track cycling continued as Sir Bradley Wiggins and his team-mates Ed Clancy, Owain Doull and Steven Burke won the men's team pursuit[2] in thrilling style and world record time. They beat Australia in the showdown, reversing the outcome of the corresponding final at the world championships in March. After that reverse, Wiggins advised anyone who'd listen to "put your house" on a British win here.

They were as good as his word, posting a time of 3 min 50.265 sec as they came from behind after 3,500 metres of the 4,000m trip. Even in defeat Wiggins would have become the most decorated Olympian in British history, assured as he was of a medal whatever the outcome. But having stated he had no interest in winning silver or bronze it would have been decidedly anti-climactic if he'd ascended to his new exalted status from anything other than the podium's top step. In a career incorporating five different Olympic Games not to mention assorted outdoor distractions, this was his fifth gold and takes his overall medal tally to eight. "I knew it would be close, so when we crossed the line it was more relief than anything," he said. "I'm just happy to be able to wake up on Monday and not have this. It is a burden. I wanted to go out like this, I wanted it to end like this and not with some crappy little race in the north of France, climbing off at the feed."

How Britain won gold and set a new world record in Olympics team pursuit

Great Britain did it the hard way. Australia led from the gun, with Alexander Edmondson, Jack Bobridge, Michael Hepburn and Sam Wellsford opening a gap of over half a second by halfway, but with eight laps of Siberian pine to negotiate, the eventual winners began to reel them in. Bobridge took a "death pull" for Australia and expended such effort he left his team with just the three men required to post a time. It was a tactic that did not pay off, as the British closed the gap to less than one-hundredth of a second at the 3000m mark and from then the outcome was never in doubt. "It was just about keeping your bottle, it wasn't easy," said Clancy. "We could sense by the crowd we weren't ahead. When we crossed that line a second ahead, I think it was the happiest moment in my life."

Asked about his short and long term plans, Wiggins was in typically forthright mood. "It's

over in a flash and we'll all be hungover tomorrow," he said. "That wasn't my last race, but it was my last Olympic Games. My kids have never known anything other than me being an Olympic athlete and they need me now."

Unused in qualifying on Thursday, Mark Cavendish was once again fifth man but did not turn up at the velodrome[3] to warm up before the day's racing. The Guardian was told he had fallen out with British team pursuit coach Heiko Salzwedel, who Cavendish described as "very stubborn" during the team's training camp in Newport two weeks ago. British Cycling's head coach Iain Dyer described claims Cavendish had refused to attend the velodrome as "bollocks", while Wiggins said his teammate, who will contest the omnium "was hugging me yesterday and telling me he loved me".

On Cavendish's omission from the team, Wiggins said "we gave Mark the opportunity in Newport to come into the squad and he didn't deliver. We saw how close it was and we couldn't afford, having been together for 18 months and it wasn't just me ... I didn't freeze him out or anything like that and he knows that. Ask him about it after the omnium and he'll tell you a totally different story to the one he told Orla [Chennai, from Sky]."

Fresh from winning gold in the men's team sprint the previous day, both Jason Kenny and Callum Skinner followed up with fine performances in qualifying for the individual event. Skinner scorched up the track to set a new Olympic record of 9.703sec in his flying 200m time trial, beaten by Kenny's 9.551 soon after. Kenny went on to ease past Germany's Maximilian Levy in the last 16. Skinner subsequently led from the front to advance to quarter-finals, shutting the door on Australia's Patrick Constable after a two-lap game of cat and mouse. Both men will resume their respective assaults on the competition today [Saturday].

In the day's other final, China won the women's team sprint, beating Russia in the final while Germany bagged bronze in a contest where Great Britain were notable absentees. It was the failure of Jess Varnish and Katy Marchant to qualify that led to the former being dropped from the Team GB "podium programme" and the subsequent row that resulted in the resignation of the team Technical Director Shane Sutton amid allegations of discrimination and bullying, which he strenuously denies.

Two-times Olympic gold medallist Victoria Pendleton said it was "ridiculous" Great Britain were not in the event, stating there is "no way" they are not among the five fastest teams in the world. It seemed something of a rum do that while two of Team GB's fastest women, Marchant and Becky James, were relaxing ahead of the individual competition on Sunday, the lady whose speed either has yet to match was actually in the velodrome providing informative if slightly wistful co-commentary for the BBC.

(From *The Guardian*, Aug. 13, 2016)

📖 NOTES

1. Sir Bradley Wiggins 布拉德利·威金斯爵士（1980 年 4 月 28 日生），英国职业自行车赛手，2001 转为道路自行车专业赛手，2000 年悉尼奥运会上夺得第一枚奥运铜牌，2004 年雅典奥运会上获得 三枚奖牌，其中一枚为金牌，2008 年北京奥运会上获得个人和团体两枚金牌，2009 年环法自行车 大赛分段赛上获得第四名（后由于 Lance Armstrong 的成绩于 2012 年被宣布无效，排名被提到了第 三名）。2014 年道路自行车世界锦标赛计时赛中获得金牌，2016 年里约热内卢奥运会上，他所在 的英国队击败澳大利亚队，他本人从而获得第八块奥运奖牌和第五块奥运金牌。

2. the team pursuit （自行车）团体追逐赛，每队由 4 名运动员组成，第三名运动员很关键，因为计算 成绩是以第三名队员的前轮过终点线为准，每队必须有 3 名运动员到达终点方可计算成绩。现奥 运会比赛项目有男子 4000 米个人追逐赛（1964 年列入）、4000 米团体追逐赛（1920 年列入），
和女子 3000 米个人追逐赛（1992 年列入）。

3. velodrome 场地自行车赛，场地自行车赛包括有争先赛、个人追逐赛、团体追逐赛、记分赛、团体 竞速赛、凯琳赛（Keirin）、麦迪逊赛（Madison）等男、女十个项目。比赛对于自行车的长度、宽度、 重量等规格也都有明确限制。

📰 USEFUL WORDS

allegation	[ˌæləˈgeɪʃn]	*n.*	a public statement that is made without giving proof, aaccusing sb of doing sth that is wrong or illegal 指控；主张，宣称
assault	[əˈsɔːlt]	*n.*	a vigorous armed attack, especially a head-on charge 攻击；冲击
bollock	[bɒlək]	*n.*	nonsense 胡说，废话
exalt	[ɪgˈzɔːlt]	*v.*	to raise up (in position or dignity) 使升高；提升，提拔
crappy	[ˈkræpi]	*adj.*	of very bad quality 劣质的，蹩脚的
hungover	[ˌhʌŋˈoʊvər]	*adj.*	the headache and sick feeling that you have the day after drinking too much alcohol 因余醉未醒感到难受的，心里难受的
incorporate	[ɪnˈkɔːpəreɪt]	*v.*	to uite into a whole, to include 包含
lap	[læp]	*n.*	one journeyfrom the beginning to the end of atrack used for running, etc.（跑 道等的）一圈

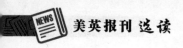
negotiate	[nɪ'goʊʃieɪt] *v.*	to successfully get over or past a difficult part on a path or route 顺利通过，成功越过
omnium	[ɒmnɪrm] *n.*	担保证券的总值
podium	['pəʊdɪəm] *n.*	a small platform that a person stands on when giving a speech or conducting an orchestra, etc. 领奖台；讲台；表演台；乐队指挥台
reel	[riːl] *v.*	to wind on a reel 卷，绕 ~ *sth in/out* to wind sth on/off a reel 往卷轴上绕起，从卷轴上放开
rum	[rʌm] *n.*	a strong alcoholic drink made from the juice of sugar cane 朗姆酒
	adj.	strange 古怪的，奇特的
showdown	['ʃoʊdaʊn] *n.*	[usually sing.] an argument, a fight or a test that will settle a disagreement that has lasted for a longtime[通常用单数] 摊牌；紧要关头；最后一决胜负
scorch	[skɔːrtʃ] *v.*	to burn and slightly damage the surface by making it too hot 烧焦，烤焦
sprint	[sprɪnt] *v.*	to run for a short distance at the greatest speed of which one is capable: 冲刺，用全速跑过
velodrome	['velə.droʊm] *n.*	a track or building used for cycle racing（自行车等的）室内赛车场
wistful	['wɪstfl] *adj.*	thinking sadly about sth that you would like to have, especially sth in the past that you can no longer have 伤感的；徒然神往的

EXERCISES

I. Vocabulary

Choose among the four alternatives one word or phrase that is closest in meaning to the underlined part in each statement.

1. It was a tactic that did not <u>pay off</u>, as the British closed the gap to less than one-hundredth of a second at the 3000m mark and from then the outcome was never in doubt.

    A. pay back   B. pay all the debts

    C. be successful   D. fail

2. But having stated he had no interest in winning silver or bronze it would have been decidedly anti-climactic if he'd ascended to his new <u>exalted</u> status from anything other than the podium's top step.

    A. raised   B. excelled   C. obtained   D. excellent

3. "It's over in a flash and we'll all be <u>hungover</u> tomorrow," he said.

    A. relaxed   B. upset

    C. satisfied   D. happy

4. Australia led from the gun, with Alexander Edmondson, Jack Bobridge, Michael Hepburn and Sam Wellsford opening a gap of over half a second by halfway, but with eight laps of Siberian pine to <u>negotiate</u>.

   A. carry through (a transaction) by discussion

   B. confer

   C. succeed in accomplishing

   D. transfer (a cheque etc.)

5. *The Guardian* was told he had <u>fallen out with</u> British team pursuit coach Heiko Salzwedel.

   A. quarrelled with   B. falled behind

   C. dropped out the line   D. degenerated

6. Both men will resume their respective <u>assaults on</u> the competition today [Saturday].

   A. vigorous armed attacks on

   B. violent critical attacks on

   C. vigorous attacks by armed forces on

   D. the acts of trying to achieve

7. Skinner <u>scorched up</u> the track to set a new Olympic record of 9.703 sec in his flying 200m time trial, beaten by Kenny's 9.551 soon after.

   A. cycled extremely fast along the track   B. burned the track

   C. made the track very hot   D. sped up along the track

8. I didn't <u>freeze him out</u> or anything like that and he knows that.

   A. preserve by refrigeration

   B. get rid of (some objectionable person)

   C. suffer intense cold

   D. fix unchangeably until further adjustment

9. ...and the subsequent <u>row</u> that resulted in the resignation of the team Technical Director Shane Sutton amid allegations of discrimination and bullying, which he strenuously denies.

   A. loud harsh noise   B. quarrel

   C. an orderly line of persons   D. a small street lined with houses

10. It was "<u>ridiculous</u>" Great Britain were not in the event.

   A. laughable   B. funny   C. strange   D. unreasonable

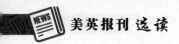

II. Comprehension

Decide whether the following statements are true or false according to the information given in the press clipping. Mark T or F to each statement.

1. After beating Australian in the showdown, Wiggins became very arrogant.

2. Even if Wiggins had not defeated Australian, he was the one who had taken part in Olympic Games and had won the most medals in British history.

3. From Wiggins' words, it can be inferred that he no longer had interest in taking part in cycling race in the north of France.

4. British team had an easy win over Australia.

5. Wiggins, after the Olympic Games, will continue his career as a cyclist.

6. From Wiggin's words, it can be inferred that it was Mark Cavendish's fault not being with the team.

7. Thanks to his higher speed, Callum Skinner made it impossible for Australia's Patrick Constable to advance to quarter-finals.

8. Jason Kenny defeated Germany's Maximilian Levy in the last 16.

9. Skinner and Australia's Patrick Constable play a hide-and-seek game like the one played between a cat and a mouse in the racing.

10. According to Victora Pendleton, there is no possibility for Great Britain to be among the fastest teams in the world.

III. Questions for discussion

1. How would you comment on the opening sentence of the news report, which is "so what comes after a knighthood"? Is it a very good beginning to attract readers to go on reading?

2. Do you like cycling? And what benefits can a cyclist get from cycling?

3. From Wiggins' words, what can you infer about his plan after the Olympic Games?

4. In the sentence "Both men will resume their respective assaults on the competition today" (Line 6, Para. 7), what does the phrase "both men" refer to?

5. What does Wiggins think of Mark Cavendish? What is the most important thing to a team?

《泰晤士报》简介

《泰晤士报》（*The Times*）由约翰·沃尔特（John Walter）于 1785 年在伦敦创刊，原名为《世鉴日报》（*Daily Universal Register*），1788 年起改用现名，是世界上第一张以 "Times" 命名的报纸。该报纸为国家级报纸，总部在英国伦敦。

由于现在有类似于《纽约时报》（*The New York Times*）等的众多时报，使用者有时会称之为《伦敦时报》（*The London Times*）以示区别。《泰晤士报》的英文名称为 *The Times*，中文直译过来应为《时报》，Times 一词与 Thames 一词读音虽然有点接近，但实际上与 the River Thames 毫无关系。由于是约定俗成，人们也就将错就错、不予更改，这个译名沿用至今。

《泰晤士报》是一份在英国发行的综合性日报，在反映和塑造伦敦精英阶层对时事的观点和看法方面起着重要的作用，同时也反映和影响着全世界的政治、经济与文化环境。1981 年《泰晤士报》被属于鲁伯特·默多克（Rupert Murdoch）的新闻集团收购，之后，《泰晤士报》的风格渐趋保守。

《泰晤士报》有一份姊妹报《星期日泰晤士报》（*The Sunday Times*）（1812 年创刊），由泰晤士报出版发行。

登录《泰晤士报》的官方网站，可以阅读该报刊的电子版。

Unit Six
Entertainment

报刊英语的句式特征

新闻稿件具有一定的文学性和艺术性，但是通常受到版面和时间的限制，需要在较短的时间里完成，并在有限的篇幅内融入较多的新闻事实和背景信息，因此，报刊英语中的句型高度扩展，结构非常严谨。

1 省略句式

省略指将句子中一个或多个成分省去以求表达简洁、节省篇幅、突出主要内容。省去的成分往往是人称代词或一些非实义词，如：冠词、介词、助动词等。

（一）省略冠词

Woman tries to teach husband a lesson, wins $1million (=<u>A</u> woman tries to teach her husband a lesson, and wins $1million) (*CNN*, Oct. 31, 2016)

Shots were fired at <u>an</u> officer and <u>a</u> passager during <u>the</u> pursuit (=Shots fired at <u>an</u> officer and <u>a</u> passenger during pursuit) (*CNN*, Oct. 31, 2016)

Mom holds separated twins for first time (=<u>A</u> mom holds her separated twins for <u>the</u> first time (*CNN*, Oct. 31, 2016)

Iraqi special forces enter Mosul over 2 years after Islamic State seized city (=Iraqi special forces enter Mosul over 2 years after Islamic State seized <u>the</u> city)(*The Washington Post*, Nov. 1, 2016)

（二）省略人称代词

Mom holds separated twins for first time (=A mom holds <u>her</u> separated twins for the first time) (*CNN*, Oct. 31, 2016)

（三）省略连系动词

Your tax dollars at work: $5 bribes to take a government survey (=Your tax dollars <u>are</u> at work: $5 bribes to take a government survey)(*The Times*, Oct. 23, 2016)

（四）省略被动语态或进行时态中的助动词

Elite unit fighting human trafficking (=Elite unit <u>is</u> fighting human trafficking) (*CNN*, Oct. 31, 2016)

Suspicious package in Devon linked to device on Tube train (=A suspicious package in Devon <u>is</u> linked to a device on a Tube train) (*The Times*, Oct. 23, 2016)

Bob Dylan branded 'arrogant' over Nobel snub(=Bob Dylan <u>is</u> branded 'arrogant' over Nobel snub) (*The Times*, Oct. 23, 2016)

Thousands of California soldiers forced to repay enlistment bonuses a decade after going to war (=Thousands of California soldiers <u>are</u> forced to repay enlistment bonuses a decade after going to war) (*Los Angeles Times*, Oct. 22, 2016)

Inmate busted with weed(=An inmate <u>is</u> busted with weed) (*The Guardian*, Oct. 13, 2016)

Okla. crime rampage suspect killed in shootout with police (=Okla. a crime rampage suspect <u>is</u> killed in shootout with police) (*The Washington Post*, Oct. 31, 2016)

Trump Revealed: An American Journey of Ambition, Ego, Money, and Power (=Trump <u>is</u> Revealed: An American Journey of Ambition, Ego, Money, and Power) (*The Washington Post*, Oct. 31, 2016)

（五）不定式表示未来动作

Migrants to be removed from Jungle camp in Calais on Monday (=Migrants <u>are going to be</u> removed from Jungle camp in Calais on Monday) (*The Times*, Oct. 23, 2016)

FBI to hunt for secrets on sex pest's computer (=FBI <u>is going to hunt</u> for secrets on sex pest's computer) (*The Times*, Oct. 31, 2016)

Iraqi troops to enter Mosul in 'matter of hours'(=Iraqi troops <u>are going to enter</u> Mosul in 'matter of hours') (*CNN*, Oct. 31, 2016)

2 同位语和解释性结构

同位语和解释性结构在新闻中运用很广，主要是提供背景信息让读者了解新闻中的人

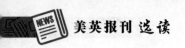

物（官衔、职位、职业范围等）或获得读者应该了解到的其他信息。

Greengrass—who wears Harry Potter glasses, shoulderlength white hair and a mien that in a certain light can make him look like Jay Leno—dedicated much of four years to *The Bourne Supremacy*, sequel to Doug Liman's *The Bourne Identity*, and then *Ultimatum*. (From *Los Angeles Times*, July 26, 2016)

本句的基本句型为 SVOA，who 引导的定语从句里套嵌一个由 that 引导的定语从句，描述了 Greengrass 的穿戴与气质，句子后半部分状语里的 sequel 是 *The Bourne Supremacy* 的同位语。

David Hopper, general secretary of the Durham Miners Association, now a shadow of its once mighty self, in part thanks to Thatcher's defeat of the miners union, spoke for millions—the white-collared teachers and clerical workers, nurses and bus drivers as well as former industrial workers—who blamed Thatcher for the loss of livelihoods that globalization and technology might have taken anyway, but without her blunt coup disgrace. (*The Guardian*, Apr. 8, 2013)

本句的下划线部分提供了新闻中人物的职位等信息。本句的基本句型为 SVA，David Hopper 后面带了两个同位语，millions 之后列举了受撒切尔夫人政策影响的五类人，列举的内容是对 millions 做进一步的更精确的解释。

And Jacquetta Wheeler, one of Britain's established catwalkers, has taken time out from promoting Burberry and Vivienne Westwood to work for Reprieve, a charity which campaigns for prisoners' rights. (*The Economist*, Feb. 11, 2012)

如果不做解释，读者可能根本不知道 Reprieve 是什么，下划线部分对 Reprieve 做了明确的解释说明，填补了读者的知识空白，确保读者对文章的理解。

Denis Fred Simon, author and Vice-Provost for International Affairs at the University of Oregon, was one of the nine foreign experts at the Shenzhen conference. (*The Washington Post*, Nov. 16, 2011)

同理，author and Vice-Provost for International Affairs at the University of Oregon 是 Denis Fred Simon 的同位语，起到进一步解释的作用。

解释性的内容有时被放在两个破折号之间以便提供额外的信息，如：

The authors also found that the sheer number of candidates that some sites provide their love-seeking singles—which can range from dozens to hundreds—can actually undermine the process of finding a suitable mate. （*Time*, Feb. 7, 2012）

3 状语、状语从句、定语从句等

"Crime fiction by women started to ascend post-2008 <u>when the economy crashed, society cracked, people's lives became unmoored and the post-9/11 feeling of togetherness and thinking there could be global order began to crumble</u>," says writer, <u>editor and critic Sarah</u> Weinman. (*The Observer*, July 3, 2016)

when 引导了四个并列的状语从句，第四个状语从句里面嵌进了一个定语从句，句子长但信息量大。列举的这几个并列的状语从句为读者提供了女性作家创作的犯罪小说 2008 年后数量上升的历史背景。词组 editor and critic Sarah Weinman 是 writer 的同位语，同时作者连用三个前置名词 writer, editor and critic 作修饰语修饰 Sarah Weinman，几种方法的综合运用使得这个句子结构紧凑。

Natalie Hand of London's Viva model agency, <u>who represents Ms Campbell</u>, says there has been a shift away from the "very young, impressionable models," <u>who were popular in the past ten years</u>, to "more aspirational young women"(*The Economist*, Feb. 11, 2012)

本句包含两个定语从句，从而使一个简单的 SVO 结构的句子变得很长。两个定语从句对其中的两个名词做出了限定和解释。

It was the failure of Jess Varnish and Katy Marchant to qualify that led to the former being dropped from the Team GB "podium programme" and the subsequent row <u>that resulted in the resignation of the team Technical Director Shane Sutton amid allegations of discrimination and bullying, which he strenuously denies</u>. (*The Guardian*, Aug. 13, 2016)

这句话的逻辑关系是：the failure of Jess Varnish and Katy Marchant to qualify 导致了 the subsequent row，后者又导致了 resignation of the team Technical Director Shane Sutton，而 Shane Sutton 对 allegations of discrimination and bullying 是坚决否认的。从句法结构上来看，强调句型内包含了一个由 that 引导的句子，该句内又包含了一个非限制性定语从句，由 which 引导，从而将一个较为复杂的因果链讲得清清楚楚。这样的句法结构经济且逻辑性强，往往是新闻英语句法特征之一。

4 前置定语

英语报刊经常将通常后置的名词修饰语移到名词前面从而使得句子结构紧凑严密，这是当代英语发展的一种趋势，这种趋势在新闻英语里尤其明显。如：

Britain's round-the-world yachtsmen (=the yachtsmen from Great Britain who plan to go round the world)，其他的例子如：the up-to-the-minute information

这种使英语句子高度浓缩的前置修饰语可以分为带连字符的修饰语和不带连字符的修饰语。

（一）带连字符的前置修饰语

带连字符的前置修饰语有很多种表现形式：

名词 + 名词

billion-dollar deals 十亿美元的交易   supply-demand imbalance 供求关系失衡

north-south dialogue 北南对话   Korea-Japan trade 朝日贸易

snail-pace progress 缓慢的进展   world-class match 世界水准的比赛

year-end report 年终报告   stock-manipulation case 操控股票的案例

shoulder-length hair 披肩发

名词 + 现在分词

cancer-causing drugs 致癌药物   peace-keeping force 维和部队

oil-producing countries 产油国   policy-making body 决策机构

breath-taking scenery 令人赞叹不已的景色

energy-saving device 节能装置   law-abiding resident 守法居民

Pulitzer Prize-winning author 普利策奖获奖者

time-consuming negotiation 耗时的谈判

名词 + 形容词

interest-free loan 无利息贷款   vehicle-free promenade 无机动车场所

hand-free phone 免手提电话   capital-intensive country 资本密集的国家

oil-poor countries 贫油国家   war-weary soldier 厌战的士兵

energy-rich countries 能源丰富的国家

名词 + 过去分词

poverty-stricken areas 贫穷地区   state-owned enterprises 国有企业

bottle-necked road 瓶颈路段   college-bred clerk 受过大学教育的职员

crisis-ridden economy 危机四伏的经济   disaster-hit area 灾区

money-oriented politics 金钱政治   tongue-tied spokesman 张口结舌的发言人

performance-oriented culture 以绩效为主的文化背景

relationship-oriented culture 以人际关系或人情为主的环境

coin-operated washing machine 投币洗衣机

US-led Middle East conference 由美国主导的中东会议

knowledge-based economy 知识经济

名词 + 介词短语

growth-at-all-cost 1970s 不惜一切代价达到经济目标的 20 世纪 70 年代

stay-at-home mother 全职妈妈

形容词 + 过去分词

deep-rooted social and economic problems 根深蒂固的社会与经济问题

quick-frozen food 速冻食品   foreign-owned enterprises 外资企业

clean-cut analysis 明晰的分析   far-fetched explanation 牵强的解释

long-faced job loser 愁眉苦脸的失业者   short-lived coup 短暂政变

形容词 + 名词

open-door policy 门户开放政策   red-carpet welcome 隆重的欢迎

top-level talk 最高级别的会谈   private-eye industry 私家侦探业

long-term low-interest loan 长期低利率贷款

renewable-and-alternative-energy manufacturer 利用可再生和可替代的能源的生产厂商

形容词 + 现在分词

high-ranking official 高级官员   long-standing issue 长期存在的问题

wide-ranging report 内容广泛的报道   wide-spreading AIDS 四处蔓延的艾滋病

easy-going president 待人随和的总统   far-seeing diplomat 卓有远见的外交官

副词 + 过去分词

dimly-lit room 光线昏暗的房间   highly-polished table 擦得铮亮的桌子

hard-won result 艰难赢得的结果   highly-sophisticated technology 高度复杂的技术

newly-found coal mines 新近发现的煤矿   richly-paid job 薪水丰厚的工作

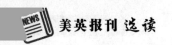

sparsely-populated area 人口稀少的地区　well-informed circles 消息灵通人士

数词 + 名词

100-meter dash100 赛跑　　　　　　one-egg twins 同卵双胎

one-shot criminal 初犯　　　　　　two-party system 两党制

two-way street 双行道路　　　　　　4,000-plus lawsuits 4 千件以上的诉讼案件

one-couple-one-child policy 一对夫妇一个孩子的政策

名词 +to+ 名词

coast-to-coast protest 全国性的抗议　dusk-to-dawn curfew 彻夜宵禁

face-to-face talk 面晤　　　　　　hand-to-hand fighting 白刃战

前后由 and 连接的词组

hit-and-run driver 肇事逃逸司机　　life-and-death experiment 生死攸关的实验

touch-and-go affair 一触即发的局势　wait-and-see policy 坐守观望的政策

up-and-down market 上下起伏的市场　up-and-down relationship 时好时坏的关系

off-and-on war 打打停停的战争

介词 + 名词

on-site service 现场服务　　　　　under-the-counter activities 隐蔽的活动

around-the-clock bombing 昼夜不间断的轰炸

例句如下：

Clinton camp slams FBI over 'jaw-dropping' treatment. (*CNN*, Nov. 1, 2016)

The J-20, a long-range, radar-avoiding stealth combat aircraft, first flew in 2011 but had not been shown to the public until Tuesday. (*CNN*, Nov. 1, 2016)

With the buy-to-let market changing at an alarming rate, here's how to make it work for you, from avoiding voids to cutting your costs and knowing when to spend. (*Reader's Digest*, Nov. 1, 2016)

When your towels wear out, consider replacing them with towels made from environmentally friendly, non-chlorine-bleached materials such as hemp or organic cotton, which are available from specialist shops. (*Reader's Digest*, Nov. 1, 2016)

（二）不带连字符的前置修饰语

"out of the box" thinking 摆脱常规的思维

a "made in China" orientation 中国制造的能力

a study abroad experience 海外留学的经历

a "created in China" capability 中国创造的能力

⑤ 浓缩的后置名词修饰语

除了使用前置修饰语修饰名词之外，新闻报道里总是在可能的情况下将定语从句压缩成由分词短语或不定式短语构成的后置定语。

The woman underline{accused of acting as South Korea's "shadow president"} has been jailed under emergency detention laws, as prosecutors question her about what exact role she played for the real president, Park Geun-hye. (*The Washington Post*, Nov. 1, 2016)

文中 accused of 是 who has been accused of 的浓缩形式。

They were cultural icons, too, underline{celebrated in songs such as Billy Joel's "Uptown girl,"} the video of which starred Christie Brinkley, who became his wife. (*The Economist*, Feb. 1, 2012)

文中 celebrated 是 which were celebrated 的浓缩形式。

⑥ 压缩的状语从句

状语从句常被压缩成由从属连词（after, once, while, although, as, till, lest, if, since, when, whether 等）加分词短语构成的状语以期降低句子长度并使信息得到最大限度的浓缩，有时甚至连从属连词也被省略：

These recent figures are more starling underline{when contrasted} against Gallup polling from the 1970s, when as many as 70 percent of Americans had "trust and confidence" that the government could handle domestic problems. （*The Washington Post*, Jan. 6, 2012 ）

when contrasted 实际上是状语从句的压缩形式，原句是：when they are contrasted...。

Trump bragged about adultery underline{while married} to his adult children's mother (teens at the time). (*The Washington Post*, Nov. 1, 2016)

文中 while married 结构实际上是 while he was 状语从句的压缩形式。

⑦ 被动语态结构

在客观性要求很高的新闻领域，被动语态的使用非常广泛。一是为了显示公正和客观，二是文章的作者确实无法说出行为主体。一些固定的被动语态套语常出现在美英报刊文章里：

It is alleged that ... 据称……

It is argued that ... 有人争论说……

It is asserted that... 有人主张……

It is claimed that ... 据称……；有人宣称……

It was described that ... 据介绍……；有人介绍说……

It is reported that ... 据报道……

It is rumored that... 谣传……；听说……

It is taken that... 人们认为……；有人认为……

It is universally accepted that... 普遍认为……

It is generally recognized that ... 一般认为……；普遍认为……

It can be safely said that ... 可以有把握地说……

It was first intended that... 最初的打算是……

Little was said about... 关于……过去少有谈及

具体例子如下：

It used to be said that English coaches were inward-looking with poor levels of study.(*The Observer*, July 24, 2016)

除了上面所列的一些套用的句型之外，实际上行文过程中被动语态使用的场合和语境也是很多的，如：

The Guardian was told he had fallen out with British team pursuit coach Heiko Salzwedel, who Cavendish described as "very stubborn" during the team's training camp in Newport two weeks ago.（*The Guardian*, Aug. 13, 2016）

不方便讲出受采访的人物身份时，被动语态就成了一个非常有效的语言表达手段，*The Guardian* was told 便是这样的典型例子。

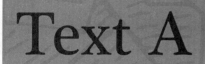

导读

提起悬念、侦探或犯罪主题的小说，读者自然会联想到以下几位著名作家：

阿瑟·柯南·道尔（Sir Arthur Conan Doyle, 1895-1930），英国作家，代表作有《福尔摩斯探案集》等。其笔下的夏洛克·福尔摩斯（Sherlock Holmes）因具有高超的观察力、严密的逻辑推理能力为全世界读者所喜爱。

格雷厄姆·格林（Graham Greene, 1904-1991），英国作家、剧作家、文学评论家，其作品围绕当今世界矛盾交织的政治与道德问题展开探讨，融通俗文学与严肃文学于一体，他的写作手法广受好评。

埃德加·艾伦·坡（Edgar Allen Poe, 1809-1849），美国短篇小说作家，其作品探讨较多的是人的潜意识、非理性或犯罪心理以揭示人性中怪异的一面。

然而近些年来，女性作家的此类作品越来越引起读者关注。本篇文章讨论的是撰写当代犯罪小说的一些女作家，简要概述了女作家的写作动机、心理因素、性别特征、对待暴力犯罪的态度等因素对女性犯罪作品创作的影响以及因此而形成的女性作家作品的特点。

After Agatha[1]... female crime writers delve deep into women's worst fears
As Hollywood brings out two biopics of Agatha Christie, Sarah Hughes examines the rise of 'domestic suspense' thrillers

By Sarah Huhes

From Raymond Chandler's[2] mean streets to Lee Child's[3] hardboiled tales of revenge, crime fiction has often been the preserve of lone men battling betrayal and seeking justice. In recent years, though, the genre has changed with the rise of the "domestic suspense" novel—the many "Girl" books with their unreliable narrators, creeping sense of unease, twisting plots and sly insistence that the home isn't a haven but rather a place where anything and everything can go wrong.

Crime fiction, it seems, is increasingly a woman's game. The year's most eagerly awaited crime novels are written by women—from *You Will Know Me* by Megan Abbott to *The Trespasser* by Tana French; the bestselling debut hardback of 2016 so far is *The Widow* by Fiona Barton; and the forthcoming film adaptation of *The Girl on the Train* by Paula Hawkins, starring Emily Blunt, is one of the most anticipated movies of the year.

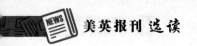

At the same time the grande dame of the genre is being given a fresh Hollywood outing with two rival biopics of Agatha Christie in development, with two of cinema's hottest young talents, Emma Stone and Alicia Vikander, being lined up to star. And after the BBC's adaptation of Christie's *And Then There Were None* proved so successful last Christmas, the team behind that production are reuniting to film her much-loved legal thriller *Witness for the Prosecution*.

"It's certainly a very healthy time for female crime fiction, but it would be wrong to suggest that women writers only discovered their dark side five years ago," says Erin Kelly, author of *The Poison Tree* and co-founder of female crime writing collective Killer Women. "Current stars such as Gillian Flynn and Paula Hawkins have their antecedents in Nicci French in the 1990s. Lois Duncan and PD James in the 1980s, Ruth Rendell in the 1960s and Patricia Highsmith before that."

What's happening now, Kelly argues, is that the publishing world has finally caught on to the idea that female crime sells. It is an argument the industry itself acknowledges.

"Readers of crime fiction are statistically more likely to be female," says Sam Eades, senior commissioning editor at Orion imprint Trapeze. "So it's no surprise that publishers invest heavily in female writers—who is better placed to explore the darkest fears of the female readers?"

Sabine Durrant, whose novel *Lie With Me* is out now, agrees. "When you go to crime festivals or bookshop events there are far more women than men," she says "Roughly 21 billion crime books are sold a year and 80 of those are bought by women."

Yet away from the bottom line something interesting is happening: female led crime fiction is taking the paranoia of our age and applying it to the place we should feel safest, the home.

"Crime fiction by women started to ascend post-2008 when the economy crashed, society cracked, people's lives became unmoored and the post-9/11[4] feeling of togetherness and thinking there could be global order began to crumble," says writer, editor and critic Sarah Weinman. "And I do think it will remain the case, though the psychological suspense stories have to be so outstanding to get attention."

Megan Abbott agrees: "The business answer might be that women buy the most books, but I also think there's a feeling among women that finds its echoes in current crime novels. These books are speaking to a growing refusal to be victimised and a need to explore the politics of the household."

It is also true that the best of the current crop of female crime writers—Abbott, French, Cathi Unsworth, Attica Locke—are adept at creating a sense of unease from the most ordinary of situations. In Abbott's latest novel, *You Will Know Me*, a Hawaiian-themed luau[5] cook-out attended by the local gymnastics club feels pregnant with dread. Unsworth's *Weirdo* taps into a small community's fear of the outsider, while French's *Broken Harbour* spins horror out of an Irish ghost estate, and in Locke's *The Cutting Season* the heroine is haunted by the hungry ghosts of America's slave-owning past.

These are crime novels but in a similar way to Flynn's *Gone Girl* they are also imbued with a strong gothic strain, a sense that nothing can be contained and that horror is bleeding into all walks of the protagonists' lives.

"What you're seeing is a return to the psychological gothic," says Ruth Ware, whose second novel, *The Woman in Cabin 10*, published this month, deliberately nods to Christie and the golden age of crime. "You can see Daphne du Maurier's[6] influence in so many of these novels—the lushness of writing, the emotion, the rollercoaster ride the narrator goes through. That is as much the focus of the novel as the mystery at its heart."

Abbott agrees. "A fan of gothic romances would be entirely at home reading *The Girl on the Train*," she says. "There's an almost nightmarish quality to it. The narrator is so unreliable that everything takes on this strange almost Hitchcockian[7] quality."

There is also, she argues, a sense of an almost uncontrollable anger and fear under the surface. "It's that idea that you feel so trapped you almost cry with frustration and pain."

So do women make such crime writers because their response is so visceral? Laura Lippman, the author of the bestselling Tess Monaghan series, whose latest standalone, *Wilde Lake*, is out this mouth, believes so. "Women think about crime in a very different *way* to men," she says, "Most men don't worry much about being crime victims whereas women think about crime in a very personal way. They know what it's like to walk down a street at night and have to make a snap judgment: am I safe? Thinking about crime is very personal for women because they know what it's like to be prey."

Perhaps because of that, female crime novels are rarely concerned with likeability. "Women don't try to write cool characters,more often than not imperfect characters are what appeal," says Icelandic writer Yrsa Sigurðardottir. It is a sentiment that found its echo in a recent article in the *Atlantic* which argued that women crime writers were successful in part because they had no need of heroes.

Certainly it is true that while even the most stoic male anti-heroes have softness at their core, female crime writers from as far back as Christie have not been bothered by how their leading

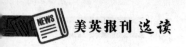

ladies are perceived. Dorothy L Sayers spent much of *Strong Poison* dissecting the likeability or otherwise of her main female character, Harriet Vane, while one of the most striking things about the BBC's adaptation of *And Then There Were None* was the way in which it reminded us that Christie was rarely cosy.

"For a long time it was fashionable to be dismissive of Christie," says Lippman. "That's largely based on a misconception that her stories are1920s and 1930s versions of *Murder, She wrote*. It's a way of suggesting that women write silly, trivial stuff. The reality is that a Christie mystery is extremely difficult to execute well. It's pretty easy to write about a serial killer cutting the left arm of every prostitute on the full moon but a close-circle mystery is much harder because the suspense is not will the killer act again but will they be caught?"

Although psychological thrillers remain in the ascendancy, Eades believes that a return to intricate Christie-style plotting is on its way, having recently signed Lara Dearman whose debut novel *The Devil's Claw* is inspired by the grande dame. "publishers have seen a resurgence of cosy crime novels, in part as a reaction to the popularity of the British Library crime classics series but also perhaps to cater for those readers who are growing tired of psychological suspense," she says. "There's something satisfying and comforting when we recognise the hallmarks of the great Agatha Christie novel. That's why she's endured."

（From *The Observer*, July 3, 2016）

NOTES

1. Agatha Christie（1890-1976）阿加莎·克里斯蒂，英国著名犯罪小说家、短篇小说家和剧作家，推理文学大师之一。多产作家，出版了100多部作品，包括长篇侦探小说、短篇、中篇小说选集、剧本、自传和诗集等，著作译成了44种外语，有"犯罪小说女王"（Queen of Crime fiction）之誉。她的作品反映了人的动机和人性的复杂。代表作品有《东方快车谋杀案》（*Murder on the Orient Express*）和《尼罗河谋杀案》（*Death on the Nile*）等。

2. Raymond Chandler（1888-1959）雷蒙德·钱德勒，美国重要的推理小说作家，被认为是"硬汉派"（hard boiled）风格的侦探小说的缔造者。其笔下的主角菲利普·马洛（Philip Marlowe）成了传统冷硬派私家侦探的同义词，这种硬汉形象对很多后来的侦探小说作家有启发和引领作用。钱德勒发表在《大西洋月刊》上著名的评论《简单的谋杀艺术》（*The Simple Art of Murder*，1944）表达了他对侦探小说的创作理念。其公认的三部代表作为：《再见，吾爱》（*Farewell, My Lovely*，1940），《小妹妹》（*The Little Sister*，1949），以及《漫长的告别》（*The Long Goodbye*，1953）。

3. Lee Child 吉姆·格兰特（Jim Grant 1954-）的笔名，英国惊险小说作家，其风格被人总结为"硬派"（hard-boiled）和商业性（commercial）。作品主要有《索命访客》（*The Visitor* 又被称为 *as*

Running Blind in the US）等。笔下人物杰克·李奇（Jack Reacher）精通各种兵器、近身格斗、法医学以及刑事鉴定学等。

4. The September 11 attacks（9·11 事件）911 事件后美国展开了一系列的反恐战争。

5. luau（常伴有文娱节目的）夏威夷式的宴会。

6. Daphne du Maurier 达夫妮·杜穆里埃（1907-1989），英国悬念与浪漫小说女作家。小说《牙买加客栈》（*Jamaica Inn*）和《吕蓓卡》（*Rebecca*，又译《蝴蝶梦》）均已被电影大师阿尔弗雷德·希区柯克改编成剧本搬上银幕。1952年，她当选英国皇家文学会会员，1969年获大英帝国二级女爵士勋章。

7. Sir Alfred Joseph Hitchcock（1899-1980）阿尔弗雷德·希区柯克，英国杰出的电影导演和制片商，举世公认的"悬念大师"（master of suspense）。拍摄的故事片多达五十多部，许多影片反映了谋杀和其他暴力行为的特点，情节惊悚，结尾曲折。1939年移居好莱坞，1955年成为美国公民。1979年被美国电影艺术与科学学院授予终身成就奖，1980年被英国女王伊丽莎白二世封为爵士。

USEFUL WORDS

adept	['ædept] *adj.*	good at doing sth tha is quite difficult 内行的，熟练地；擅长的
antecedent	[ˌæntɪ'siːdnt] *n.*	[c] a thing or an event that exists or comes before another and my influenced it 前情，前期事件
anticipate	[æn'tɪsɪpeɪt] *v.*	to expect 预感；预见，预料
ascendancy	[ə'sendənsi] *n.*	[u] (formal) the position of having power or influence over sb/sth 优势，支配地位，支配倾向
biopic	['baɪoʊpɪk] *n.*	[c] a film/movie about the life of a person 传记（体影）片
crack	[kræk] *v.*	to break without dividing into separate parts 破裂，裂开，断裂
crash	[kræʃ] *n.*	a sudden serious fall in the price or value of sth; the occasion when a business, etc. fails 暴跌；倒闭；破产；失败
crumble	['krʌmbl] *v.*	to begin to fail or get weaker or to come to an end 衰退；瓦解；消亡
debut	[deɪ'bjuː] *n.*	the first public appearance of a performer or sports player 初次露面，初次表演，处女秀 make one's ~ 初次表演，初次登台
delve	[delv] *v.*	to search for sth inside a bag, container, etc. 翻找
dissect	[dɪ'sekt] *v.*	to study sth closely and/or discuss it in great detail 仔细研究；详细评论；剖析
hardboiled	[haːdbɔɪld] *adj.*	1）boiled until the inside is hard 煮得老的 2）not showing much emotion 不动感情的，强硬的
imbue	[ɪm'bjuː] *v.*	（often passive）to fill sb/sth with strong feelings, opinions or values 使充满，灌输，激发（强烈感情、想法、价值）
outing	['aʊtɪŋ] *n.*	[c] (informal) an occasion when a competitor takes part in a competition 参赛，比赛

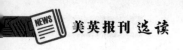

paranoia	[ˌpærəˈnɔɪə] *n.*	1) a mental illness in which a person may wrongly believe that other people are trying to harm them, that they are sb very important, etc. 妄想狂，偏执狂 2) (informal) fear or suspicion of other people when there is no evidence or reason for this（对别人的）无端恐惧，多疑
preserve	[prɪˈzɜːrv] *n.*	[single] an activity, a job, an interest, etc. that is thought to be suitable for one particular person or group of people（某人或群体活动、工作等的）专门领域；独占的事物（或范围）
resurgence	[rɪˈsɜːrdʒəns] *n.*	[u] the return and growth of an activity that had stopped 复苏，中断之后的继续，再起
strain	[streɪn] *n.*	[c] a particular type of plant or animal, or of a disease caused by bacteria, etc.（动、植物的）系，品种；（疾病的）类型
victimise	[ˈvɪktɪmaɪz] *v.*	to make sb suffer unfairly because you do not like them, their opinions, or sth that they have done 责怪或处罚某人不当（使之受冤或代人受过），不正当地使某人受损害或受苦难，欺负某人
visceral	[ˈvɪsərəl] *adj.*	resulting from strong feelings rather than careful thought 出自内心的

EXERCISES

I.　Vocabulary

Choose among the four alternatives one word or phrase that is closest in meaning to the underlined part in each statement.

1. Crime fiction has often been the <u>preserve</u> of lone men battling betrayal and seeking justice.

    A. conservative　　　　　　　　　B. special province

    C. exclusive occupation　　　　　　　D. prodigious

2. The forthcoming film adaptation of *The Girl on the Train* by Paula Hawkins, starring Emily Blunt, is one of the most <u>anticipated</u> movies of the year

    A. participated　　　　　　　　　　B. expected

    C. foreseen　　　　　　　　　　　　D. antecedent

3. It's certainly a very healthy time for female crime fiction, but it would be wrong to suggest that women writers only discovered their <u>dark side</u> five years ago.

    A. the evil nature of women writers unknown to them

    B. the mysterious and hidden area suitable for their detective stories

    C. the bad side of women writers which is unknown to themselves

    D. the bad members among women writers

4. The publishing world has finally <u>caught on to</u> the idea that female crime sells.

    A. caught sth on　　　　　　　　　　B. caught hold on

    C. held on to　　　　　　　　　　　D. understood

5. Current stars such as Gillian Flynn and Paula Hawkins have their <u>antecedents</u> in Nicci French in the 1990s.

    A. the preceding things or events   B. antennae

    C. people engaged in the same job before   D. anticipates

6. At the same time the grande dame of the genre is being given a fresh Hollywood <u>outing</u> with two rival biopics of Agatha Christie in development

    A. competition   B. a trip to Hollywood

    C. a journey to Hollywood   D. equipment

7. Eades believes that a return to <u>intricate</u> Christie-style plotting is on its way.

    A. simplify   B. complicate   C. compound   D. intensive

8. One of the most striking things about the BBC's adaptation of *And Then There Were None* was the way in which it reminded us that <u>Christie was rarely cosy</u>. The underlined clause means:

    A. Christie rarely described warm, comfortable and safe places which are small and enclosed in her stories.

    B. Readers feel that Christie rarely provided warm, comfortable and safe places in her stories because of their simple plots.

    C. Detective stories written by Christie are usually easy for readers to read because their plots are easy.

    D. Detective stories written by Christie are rarely easy for readers to understand because their plots are rarely simple.

9. These are crime novels but in a similar way to Flynn's *Gone Girl* they are also imbued with a strong gothic <u>strain</u>.

    A. characteristics of something   B. act of straining

    C. severe mental or physical demand   D. injury caused by straining a muscle

10. …and the post-9/11 feeling of togetherness and thinking there could be global order began to <u>crumble</u>.

    A. fall down   B. come to an end

    C. break into pieces   D. fall apart

II. Comprehension

Decide whether the following statements are true or false according to the information given in the press clipping. Mark T or F to each statement.

1. According to the article, it seems that more and more women join the ranks of writers writing crime novels.

2. To his/her disappointment, a fan of gothic romances will find that the story *The Girl on the Train* is really a thrilling story.

3. Women writers began to write about the domestic suspense thrillers many years ago.

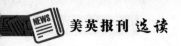
4. According to Lippman, there was a long period of time when it was in a fashion for crime writers to abandon the techniques used by Agatha Christie.

5. Crime fiction written by women is a departure from the conventional way of writing in that they are beginning to describe home as a safe place.

6. Megan Abbot thinks current crime novels reflect a kind of feeling among women that they would not be victims of crimes.

7. In paragraph 11, examples are listed by the author to prove that women crime novel writers are often not good at expressing what they want to express through the description of commonplace events.

8. According to Laura Lippan, the reason for women's success in writing good crime novels is that they have true sense and feelings from the bottom of their hearts.

9. The sentence "Crime fiction, it seems, is increasingly a woman's game" means more and more women do not treat the genre seriously. Instead they play with crime fiction writing.

10. Many crime stories written by women writers have a narrator who narrates what have happened in a trustworthy way.

III. Questions for discussion

1. Do you like thrillers? If so, what is your most favorite one? And what is it that attracts you to read a thriller that always causes fears or anger in you?

2. Have you ever read works of Agatha Christie? What do you think of her skills of writing crime fictions?

3. Do you agree with the view that female writers are better placed to explore the darkest fears of the female readers?

4. Have you ever seen any of the suspense films such as *Rebecca* (adapted from a novel written by Daphne du Maurier) directed by Alfred Hitchcock? What skills are used to create suspense? And what are the functions of suspense? Have you ever used any of the skills consciously or on any purpose in your writing or in your daily life?

5. What are the social and psychological causes that led to the rise of detective stories written by female writers?

美英国家的电影业

一、美国电影的发展历程

（一）美国电影业的起步——从无声到有声

美国电影业是随着爱迪生（Thomas Alva Edison）发明电影视镜（1897年）并创建"囚车"摄影场开始的。早起的主要制片基地在纽约，制片公司有爱迪生公司（Edison Studios）、比沃格拉夫公司（Biograph Company）和维太格拉夫公司（American Vitagraph Company）。在摄制于1903年的《一个美国消防员的生活》（*Life of an American Fireman*）和《火车大劫案》（*The Great Train Robbery*）中，布景呈多样化，电影叙事结构得到探索和发展。自此电影开始发展成为一门艺术，导演鲍特（Edwin S. Porter）用交叉剪辑手法造就戏剧效果，在电影史上具有开创性。

为摆脱由爱迪生1908年成立的电影专利公司在电影制作、发行和放映上的垄断和控制，独立制片商纷纷到自然条件得天独厚的好莱坞去拍片。格里菲斯（David Wark Griffith）1908年起为比沃格拉夫公司导演和摄制了默片《陶丽历险记》（*The Adventures of Dollie*）等多部影片，好莱坞渐渐成为拍摄中心，许多著名演员如吉许姐妹（Lillian Gish 和 Dorothy Gish）等都在电影表演艺术方面得益于格里菲斯的培养。

第一次世界大战前夕，美国电影开始蓬勃发展，其繁荣背后有三大因素：一、爱迪生的电影专利公司1915年解体，位于西海岸的好莱坞成了制片中心。二、第一次世界大战使欧洲电影业受到重创，美国电影则乘虚而入在欧洲建立起霸权地位。三、各大公司都开始实行"明星制"，电影广告等也都以明星招揽观众，这对电影发展起到了很大的推动作用。

截止到1928年美国八大电影公司形成，五家较大的影片公司为派拉蒙（Paramount Pictures, Inc., 组建于1914年）、20世纪福斯（Twentieth Century Fox Corporation，组建于1915年，1935年合并）、米高梅（Metro-Goldwyn-Mayer，于1924年合并）、华纳兄弟（Warner Bros. Entertainment, Inc., 成立于1923年）和雷电华[RKO (Radio-Keith-Orpheum) Pictures 又称 RKO Productions, 等，成立于1928年]，三家较小的公司为环球（Universal Picture Co., 成立于1912年）、哥伦比亚（Columbia Pictures Corp., 成立于1924年）和联美（United Artists 简称 UA，成立于1919年）。

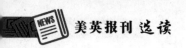

1926年，华纳兄弟影业公司拍摄的由克罗斯兰（Alan Crosland）导演的歌剧片《唐璜》（*Don Juan*）是用唱片来配唱的，1927年，有声故事片《爵士歌手》(*The Jazz Singer*) 放映，1928年福尹（Bryan Foy）的《纽约之光》（*Lights of New York*）诞生，自此，有声电影全面推开。

（二）类型片的发展与繁荣

三四十年代各种类型影片（歌舞片、纪录片、恐怖片、侦探片、故事片等）得以繁荣发展，培根（Lloyd Bacon）导演的《四十二街》（*42nd Street*，1933）等是这一时期的经典作品。在20世纪60年代，优秀歌舞片有顾柯（George Cukor）的《窈窕淑女》（*My Fair Lady*，1964)、怀斯（Robert Earl Wise）的《音乐之声》（*The Sound of Music*，1965）等。浪漫喜剧佳作有卡普拉（Frank Russell Capra）的《一夜风流》（*It happened One Night*，1934）、卓别林（Charlie Chaplin）的《摩登时代》（*Modern Times*，1936）等。反映历史的浪漫影片有弗莱明（Victor Fleming）的《乱世佳人》（*Gone with the Wind*，1939）等。惊悚影片有希区柯克（Alfred Hitchcock）的《蝴蝶梦》（*Rebecca*，1940）、《上海快车》（*Shanghai Express*，1932）和《呼啸山庄》(*Wuthering Heights*，1939) 等。

从20年代末开始美国电影的另一个亮点是动画片。米老鼠（Mickey Mouse）、唐老鸭（Donald Duck）等一系列动画形象被塑造出来，家喻户晓，人人喜爱，影响了整个世界。迪斯尼（Walt Disney Productions）还创造拍摄了《白雪公主和七个小矮人》（*Snow White and the Seven Dwarfs*，1937），《木偶奇遇记》（*Pinocchio*，1940）、《幻想曲》（*Fantasia*，1940，由 Joe Grant 和 Dick Huemer 导演）、《小鹿班比》（*Bambi II*，1942，由 Brian Pimental 导演）等许多脍炙人口的动画长片。

这一时期，威尔斯（Orson Welles）导演的影片《公民凯恩》（*Citizen Kane*，1941）在叙事方式、摄影技术、音乐制作等各方面均有创新，对后来的电影理论研究和拍摄实践影响深远。同时，高质量纪录片也大量问世，如罗伦兹（Pare Lorentz）导演的《开垦平原的犁》（*The Plow That Broke the Plains*，1936）、福特（John Ford）的《中途岛战役》（*The Battle of Midway*，1942），卡普拉（Frank Russell Capra）的《我们为何而战》（*Why We Fight*，1942）等系列堪称长纪录片的经典之作。

除了纪录片之外，故事片也为第二次世界大战期间和20世纪50年代初期的美国影坛做出了很大的贡献，其中有柯蒂斯（Michael Curtiz）的《卡萨布兰卡》（*Casablanca*，1942）、顾柯（George Dewey Cukor）的《费城的故事》（*The Philadelphia Story*，1940）、希区柯克的《破坏者》（*Saboteur*，1942）、李洛埃（Mervyn LeRoy）的《魂断蓝桥》（*Waterloo Bridge*，1940）和《东京上空三十秒》（*Thirty Seconds Over Tokyo*，1944）、舒姆林（Herman Shumlin）的《守望莱茵河》（*Watch on the Rhine*，1943）、伍德（Sam Wood）的《战地钟声》

（*For Whom the Bell Tolls*，1943）、卓别林（Charles Chaplin）的《凡尔杜先生》（*Monsieur Verdoux*，1947）、罗森（Robert Rossen）的《当代奸雄》（*All the King's Men*，1949）、卡善（Elia Kazan）《欲望号街车》（*A Street Car Named Desire*，1951）、惠勒（William Wyler）的《罗马假日》（*Roman Holiday*，1953）等。

20 世纪 50 年代中期，美国电影遇到三个方面的挑战。首先，根据反托拉斯法，美国最高法院在 1948 年对"派拉蒙案"做出裁决，判定大公司垄断为非法，判决要求制片公司放弃发行和经营电影院的业务，影片生产大幅度减少（赵起，2008）。其次，电视迅速普及，电影观众人数大减。再次，自 1947 年起一批好莱坞进步人士受到"非美活动调查委员会"的政治迫害，美国电影的创作元气遭受大伤。但尽管如此，由比伯曼（Herbert J. Biberman）导演的描写锌矿工人罢工的影片《社会中坚》（*Salt of the Earth*，1954）还是被拍摄了出来，该片至今仍受到电影研究人员的重视。

在这一背景下，海斯法典（The Motion Picture Production Code，俗称 Hays Code）被废止，微型影院（micro theatre）、艺术影院（art theatre）、汽车影院（drive-in theatre），独立制片（independent filmmaking）及实验电影（experimental film）得以发展，传统的类型片在继续保持繁荣和传统的基础上渐渐有了新的内容变化。美国青年在 20 世纪 50 年代表现出对社会现实不满，蔑视传统观念，在服饰和行为方面摒弃常规，追求个性的特点。反映这个时期青年人思想和行为的影片有雷伊（Nicholas Ray）的《无因的反抗》（*Rebel Without a Cause*，1955），尼科尔斯（Mike Nichols）的《毕业生》（*Graduate*，1967）等。

其他突出的影片还有：阿尔特曼（Robert Bernard Altman）的《陆军野战医院》（*MASH*，1970），尼科尔斯（Mike Nichols）的《第二十二条军规》（*Catch-22*，1970），沙夫纳（Franklin J. Schaffner）的《巴顿将军》（*Patton*，1970），怀尔德（Billy Wilder）的《热情似火》（*Some Like It Hot*，1959），希区柯克的《后窗》（*Rear Window*，1954）、《玛尔妮》（*Marnie*，1964）等。

美国黑人演员在电影中开始扮演正面角色，如：克雷默（Stanley Kramer）导演的《挣脱锁链》（*The Defiant Ones*，1958）等。刚大学毕业的导演崭露头角，如科波拉（Francis Ford Coppola）的《教父》（*The Godfather*，1972）、卢卡斯（George Lucas）的《美国风情画》（*American Graffiti*，1973）等影片显示出青年导演的创新精神。

（三）类型片的发展与变化

电影领域从来没有停止创新，早在 20 世纪 30 年代"黑色电影"（film noir）就出现了。通常是黑白影片，反映的主题往往带有神秘色彩或与犯罪相关。《吓呆了的森林》（*The Petrified Forest*，1936）为这类影片的先锋之作，怀尔德（Billy Wilder）的《加倍赔款》（*Double*

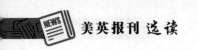

Indemnity，1944）便是四五十年代比较具有代表性的一部。

西部片发生了变化，在福特（John Ford）的《搜索者》（*The Searchers*，1956）、希尔（George Roy Hill）的《虎豹小霸王》（*Butch Cassidy and the Sundance Kid*，1969）等电影中群体取代了单枪匹马的英雄。在韦登（Joss Whedon）的《复仇者联盟》（*Marvel's The Avengers*，2012）里单打独斗的超级英雄变成了一股力量，这与过去的西部片很不同。正反面角色甚至开始发生倒置，李安（Ang Lee）的《断背山》（*Brokeback Mountain*，2005)里的主人公不再是惩恶扬善的英雄，而是在对社会准则采取抵制态度的人物。西部电影涉及的范围也一直在演进和变化，其早已延伸到了太空与外星人，如波顿（Tim Burton）执导的《火星人玩转地球》（*Mars Attacks*，1996）等。

类型混搭杂糅是当今美国电影的另一个特点。

20世纪70年代至20世纪末，美国电影在形式和内容上标新立异。科幻片、灾难片、冒险片更贴近现实，更直面未来，更令人震撼，《弗兰肯斯坦》（*Frankenstein*，1931）等为科幻恐怖影片的先驱。后来经典的有斯皮尔伯格（Steven Spielberg）导演的《第三类接触》（*Close Encounters of the Third Kind*，1977）、《外星人》（*E.T.*，1982）、《侏罗纪公园》（*Jurassic Park*，1993）、艾默里奇（Roland Emmerich）2009年执导的《2012》（2012）等。这些电影既巧妙地宣扬了美国的个人主义和英雄观，树立了美国作为世界救世主的形象，又把严肃的世界问题、社会问题、科技带来的伦理道德问题推送给了观众，引发思考。同样地，科幻片也有了反类型的电影，特兰克（Josh Trank）执导的《超能失控》（*Chronicle*，2012）是以纪录片的方式拍摄的科幻片，其叙事方式颠覆了科幻电影的叙事方式。

类型片杂糅在动画电影中也很明显。在当代的动画电影中动画形象远不如在传统动画中那么明朗，而是充满了"恐怖"。吸血鬼、幽灵、僵尸、亡魂、女巫、狼人等成了动画电影里的重要角色，但狰狞的背后似乎仍留存着些许的善良。塞利克（Henry Selick）执导的《圣诞夜惊魂》（*The Nightmare Before Christmas*，1993），索尼公司制作的《精灵旅社》（*Hotel Transylvania*，2012)和迪斯尼公司的《科学怪狗》（*Frankenweenie*，2012）等都是这方面的代表。

影片里的对立面也起了变化，例如政府的形象与以往有所不同，惊险电影如《绿区》（*Green Zone*，2010）表现了美国政府及情报部门捏造伊拉克存在大规模杀伤性武器的历史事实。本单元选取的文章讨论的是《谍影重重5》，它所反映的不再是传统间谍片中美国与外在敌人的矛盾与斗争，在某种意义上反映的是美国的敌人就是美国本身。

（四）美国电影学术研究与奖励

美国电影学术研究在20世纪六七十年代就已经有了很大的发展，建立于1927年的美国电影艺术与科学学院加强了它的电影学术研究。1967年，在华盛顿和洛杉矶两地分别成立了美国电影研究院。纽约现代艺术博物馆（The Museum of Modern Art）、罗切斯特的伊斯曼电影资料馆（The George Eastman Museum）、华盛顿国会图书馆（Library of Congress）、伯克利太平洋电影资料馆（Berkeley Art Museum and Pacific Film Archive）等对电影资料进行了收集、分类、整理和研究。

电影学院、电影系或专业也陆续在美国许多综合大学设立起来，如：南加利福尼亚大学的电影艺术专业（Cinematic Arts），加利福尼亚艺术学院 (The California Institute of the Arts)，美国电影学院（American Film Institute），加利福尼亚大学 (洛杉矶) 的影剧系和纽约大学的电影制作、电影理论、影剧剧作 3 个系。各种电影理论研究机构和学会的发展，各种电影学术性刊物如《好莱坞记者报》(*Hollywood Reporter*)、《电影季刊》（*Film Quarterly*）、《电影评论》（*Film Comment*）等刊物的繁荣为美国电影研究提供了条件。

美国电影评奖活动有奥斯卡金像奖（Oscars）、美国影评人学会奖（National Society of Film Critics）等。有影响的国际电影节，包括芝加哥国际电影节（Chicago International Film Festival）、洛杉矶国际文化电影节（Los Angeles International Culture Film Festival，简称 LAICFF）、纽约国际儿童电影节（New York International Children's Film Festival，简称 NYICFF) 和旧金山国际电影节（San Francisco International Film Festival，简称 SFIFF) 等。

凭借着雄厚的资金支持、强大的科技力量、一批技艺精湛、对社会问题极其敏感、对世界和未来具有敏锐洞察力的导演、数量庞大演技非凡的演员以及卓有成效的营销策划和商业运作，美国电影不仅是能给美国带来巨大利润的文化产业，同时也充当了向全世界展示和宣扬其文化理念和价值观念的一个重要平台。

二、英国电影的发展历程

（一）英国电影的起步

英国是电影业起步较早的国家，早在 1889 年就制造出了摄影机、转动架等。保罗（RobertW. Paul）1896 年 3 月 26 日放映了由他自己拍摄的《多佛海的狂浪》（*Rough Sea at Dover*），这是电影的首次商业性映出。

英国人不仅参与了早期的电影器材的发明创造，而且英国的电影艺术家和技术革新家们对电影的拍摄技巧也做出了多方面的研究和探索。史密斯（George Albert Smith）采用特大特写镜头拍摄《祖母的放大镜》（*Grandma's Reading Glass*，1900）。赫普沃思（Cecil Hepworth）撰写的《活动摄影术—或电影摄影入门》（1897）是世界上最早的电影论著之一。

但自 1909 年起，美、法两国影片占领英国市场，第一次世界大战爆发和国内加征娱乐税使英国电影变得更加糟糕。1927 年有利于英国电影产业的电影法案正式通过，英国影片的上映比率逐年好转，戈蒙特公司、英国国际影片公司和英狮公司等新的制片厂等先后成立。

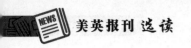

（二）英国电影的发展与繁荣

20 世纪 20 年代末，英国摄制的一批影片使英国电影出现了一番兴旺发达的繁荣景象，阿斯奎斯摄制（Anthony Asquith）的《地下》（*Underground*，1928）、杜邦（E. A. Dupont）的《皮卡迪利大街》（*Piccadilly*，1929）便是其中的两部。

1929 年，有声影片问世。由希区柯克（Alfred Hitchcock）导演的《讹诈》（*Blackmail*），声音效果匠心独运，阿斯奎斯（Anthony Asquith）的《逃出达特穆尔》（*A Cottage on Dartmoor*，1930），福特（Walter Forde）的《罗马快车》（*Rome Express*，1932）等都属于上乘之作。

20 世纪 30 年代，英国电影经历了短暂的繁荣，由柯达（Sir Alexander Korda）导演的《英宫艳史》（*The Private Life of Henry VIII*，1933）最为有名。该片是第一部非好莱坞拍摄的获得学院奖（Academy Award）的影片。

二战间，英国主流电影为爱国电影，代表作有《48 小时》（*Went the Day Well?*，1942）、《与祖国同在》（*In Which We Serve*，1942）等。一批优秀的纪录片也及时问世，鼓舞了英国民众。其他题材的影片较突出的有柯达（Sir Alexander Korda）的《巴格达窃贼》（*The Thief of Bagdad*，1940）、迪克森（Thorold Dickinson）的《煤气灯》（*Gaslight*，1940）和《首相》（*The Prime Minister*，1941）、迪安（Basil Dean）的《二十一天》（*21 Days*，1940）、豪华历史剧《恺撒和克列奥帕特拉》（*Caesar and Cleopatra*，1945）、利恩（David Lean）的浪漫戏剧影片《相见恨晚》（*Brief Encounter*，1945）等。

20 世纪 50 年代晚期，"英国新浪潮"（British "New Wave"）和"自由电影运动"（Free Cinema Movement）蓬勃发展，特点是反映社会现状，重视劳动阶级，强调自由和人的重要性，注重日常生活的意义等。代表作有安德森（Lindsay Anderson）执导的影片《如此运动生涯》（*This Sporting Life*，1961）和理查德森（Tony Richardson）的《蜜的滋味》（*A Taste of Honey*，1961）等。

20 世纪 60 年代英国电影进入多元化时期，经典硬汉角色出现在荧屏上，代表作是电影系列《继续》（*Carry On*）和詹姆斯·邦德（James Bond）系列等。

20 世纪 70 年代为英国电影的困顿期，20 世纪 80 年代重新振作，赫德森（Hugh Hudson）执导的《烈火战车》（*Chariots of Fire*，1981），艾登保禄（Richard Attenborough）执导的《甘地传》（*Gandhi*，1985）一举获得 8 项奥斯卡奖，其他如艾非里的（James Ivory）《看得见风景的房间》（*A Room With A View*，1986）和《尘与热》（*Heat and Dust*，1983）等也都获得了广泛的国际声誉。

20 世纪 90 年代英国电影继续辉煌，李（Mike Leigh）导演的《秘密与谎言》（*Secrets and Lies*，1996）、罗斯（Bernard Rose）导演的《安娜·卡列尼娜》（*Anna Karenina*,

1997）、沃东聂（Damien O'Donnell）导演的《东就是东》（*East Is East*, 1999）、罗杰·米歇尔（Roger Michell）导演的《诺丁山》（*Notting Hill*, 1999）、柯蒂斯（Richard Curtis）导演的《真爱至上》（*Love Actually*, 2003）等都获得了成功。

（三）新世纪的英国电影

进入 21 世纪，奇幻类和传记类电影是英国电影的亮点。前者代表有《哈利·波特》（*Harry Potter*, 2001）系列和根据英国作家托尔金（J. R. R. Tolkien）作品改编的电影《魔戒》（*Lord of the Rings*, 2001-2003）达到了迄今为止的最高峰，影响当今一代人的成长，后者的代表作有《伊丽莎白：黄金时代》（*Elizabeth: The Golden Age*, 2007）、《女王》（*The Queen*, 2006）以及《铁娘子》（*The Iron Lady*, 2011）等。

（四）英国电影的学术研究

英国大电影制片厂有"松木"（Pinewood Studios）、"爱尔斯垂"（Elstree Studios）等。主要电影教育机构有伦敦电影学校（The London Film School）和皇家艺术学院（Royal College of Art）等。主要电影研究机构为英国电影学院（British Film Institute 简称 BFI）（建于 1933 年）。四年一度的伦敦国际电影节（London Film Festival）是国际著名电影节。主要电影出版物有《画面与音响》（*Sight & Sound*, 1932 年创刊）和《银幕》（*Screen*, 1959 年创刊）。

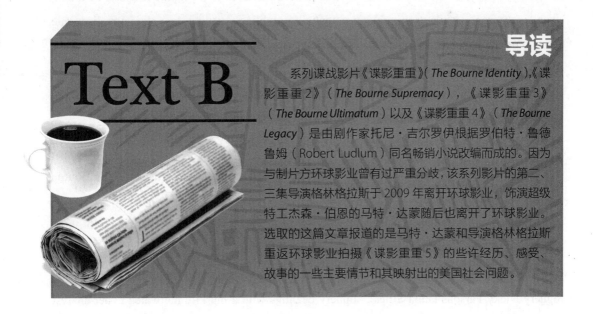

Text B

导读

系列谍战影片《谍影重重》（*The Bourne Identity*），《谍影重重 2》（*The Bourne Supremacy*），《谍影重重 3》（*The Bourne Ultimatum*）以及《谍影重重 4》（*The Bourne Legacy*）是由剧作家托尼·吉尔罗伊根据罗伯特·鲁德鲁姆（Robert Ludlum）同名畅销小说改编而成的。因为与制片方环球影业曾有过严重分歧，该系列影片的第二、三集导演格林格拉斯于 2009 年离开环球影业，饰演超级特工杰森·伯恩的马特·达蒙随后也离开了环球影业。选取的这篇文章报道的是马特·达蒙和导演格林格拉斯重返环球影业拍摄《谍影重重 5》的些许经历、感受、故事的一些主要情节和其映射出的美国社会问题。

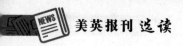

Damon is Bourne again

Spy thriller franchise back with more political intrigue, ampedup action

By Steven Zeitchik

Las Vegas[1]—On a trip to Los Angeles about 18 months ago, the London-based filmmaker Paul Greengrass sat down to lunch with Matt Damon and editor Christopher Rouse.

The latter two had come with stealth mission. Greengrass had long been unwilling to make his third Jason Bourne movie and for a time was even burned up about a spinoff done without him. But with the director wandering in a kind of decade-long exile making globalization cautionary tales, they thought it was time for him, in Bourne-ian terms, "to come in" and direct a new movie about Robert Ludlum's amnesiac assassin.

"I was skeptical there was one to be done, I was skeptical I wanted to do it and I was skeptical it would hold up with the others," recalled Greengrass, 60. "But Matt said, 'We're really lucky to have an audience that loves this character.' Chris said, 'the world has really changed since *The Bourne Ultimatum* in 2007. I thought, 'Maybe I've been too negative to an old friend.'"

Greengrass told this story in Las Vegas, where his new movie Jason Bourne—starring and produced by Damon; edited by and co-written with Rouse-would later that day make its debut.

The figurative distance covered by the director is even greater. When the new Bourne arrives in theatres, Friday, it will land the one-time documentarian back in a tentpole fishbowl he'd long swum away from—while excitingly but potentially troublingly upping the political-realism ante above most Hollywood blockbusters. Jason Bourne expands the possibilities of—and tests the appetite for—serious issues in escapist cinema.

And it wasn't even supposed to exist—not after Universal[2] upset Greengrass by making 2012's *The Bourne Legacy* with rival director Tony Gilroy.

"I had," Damon said, "given up hope that we would get here."

With its trademark handheld cameras and edits faster than a croupier's fingers. Jason Bourne vibrates with the momentum fans know well. From its early set piece at an austerity riot in Athens to its fiery third-act car chase shot practically on the Vegas Strip, Bourne keeps the plot turns coming.

There's the ex-agent's new discoveries about his past, a fresh chapter with his comrade—roguery Nicky Parsons (Julia Stiles), slippery dealings with a murkily motivated cyber-analyst (Alicia Vicander) and a fraught relationship between new CIA[3] director Robert Dewey (Tommy

Lee Jones) and Aaron Kalloor (Riz Ahmed), a Silicon Valley[4] mogul whose user database holds the key to Dewey's intelligence ambitions.

And yes, Bourne is again on the run from shadowy bosses as he tries to learn what brought him here. But you assumed all that. More novel are the social issues: The film's Athens-to-Vegas arc, for instance, which by going from a flailing economy to capitalist excess puts a spotlight on economic disenfranchisement. Or the privacy debate—when Kalloor and Dewey tensely hash out whether a tech company should give the government a backdoor, it so closely echoes the recent Apple-FBI controversy[5] over a terrorist's iPhone you'd think Greengrass shot it last month. [He didn't]

"We looked at the differences from *Bourne Ultimatum* and it was shocking," Damon said. "We thought, If Jason was on the run, why not run him through today's landscape?"

Also, because Bourne now remembers what he's done, moral questions enter. Does he want to use his lethal skills to serve his country or does he refrain out of guilt—patriotism or conscience?

Crucially, every enemy and good guy is firmly within the U.S. government. This is a far cry from all other 21st-century thrillers and even from past Bourne movies (though Ultimatum gets close). No longer is the story about the U.S versus its enemies. It's about the U.S. versus itself.

"In a sense all these films are anchored in identity, because Jason Bourne is trying to find out who he is. But with this one I think we're also asking how we want to define ourselves as a country." Rouse said.

Greengrass—who wears Harry Potter[6] glasses, shoulderlength white hair and a mien that in a certain light can make him look like Jay Leno—dedicated much of four years to *The Bourne Supremacy*, sequel to Doug Liman's *The Bourne Identity*, and then *Ultimatum*.

He imported his style of current-events research (he is known for being moved to direct films by seemingly unrelated writings; Paul Mason's global–uprising study why It's Kicking Off Everywhere and a wired article about hacker recruitment in Vegas were the impetus for this one).

But his first two Bourne movies were, Greengrass admits, "painful in their processes. "Because his spontaneity often led to key moments being omitted, he and a crew would be forced to return to various cities for reshoots, sometimes more than once.

Deciding in 2008—after Bourne scored three Oscars and global success—that he didn't want more stress, Greengrass walked away. He went off to make smaller-scale films. Damon, close with Greengrass, also stayed away.

But universal, short on franchises and not wanting the rights to revert to the Ludlum estate, needed a movie. Soon Gilroy—who had written all three Bourne films but whose *Ultimatum* script Greengrass had almost entirely rewritten—was on board for a spinoff with Jeremy Renner, *The Bourne Legacy*.

Legacy performed modestly, but well enough to keep the franchise alive. Donna Langley, chairman of the Universal, said that she was proud of the movie and believed it had a beneficial effect on the public. She also hoped, soon after, that Greengrass might come back. And he did. The issues in Bourne are timely. Combine that with a documentary-style shoot and you're left with a movie of far more realism than most summer action film.

(From *Los Angeles Times*, July 26, 2016)

NOTES

1. Las Vegas 拉斯维加斯，美国内华达州最大的城市，1905 年 5 月 15 日建市，位于沙漠边缘，全年高温。1931 年在美国大萧条时期，为了度过经济难关，内华达州议会通过了赌博合法的议案，经济因此迅速崛起。现居世界四大赌城之首，是一座以赌博业为中心的旅游、购物的世界知名度假城市。

2. Universal 此处指 Universal Picture，环球影片公司，简称"环球影业"，成立于 1912 年 6 月 8 日。数十年来与斯皮尔伯格（Steven Spielberg）等著名导演合作，发行了《大白鲨》（*Jaws*）、《外星人》（*E.T.*）、《侏罗纪公园》（*Jurassic Park*）、《谍影重重》（*Jason Bourne*）、《速度与激情》（*Fast & Furious*）等影片，进入 21 世纪，环球影业成为好莱坞最擅长开发续集电影和喜剧片的大公司。

3. CIA（美国）中央情报局（Central Intelligence Agency），1947 年成立，美国情报机构之一，负责公开和秘密地收集和分析关于国外政府、公司、恐怖组织、个人、政治、文化、科技等方面的情报。总部在弗吉尼亚州的兰利（Langley），其地位和功能相当于英国的军情六处（MI6）、前苏联克格勃 (KGB) 和以色列的摩萨德 (Mossad)，在美国情报体系中是一个独立的情报部门。

4. Silicon Valley 硅谷，美国电子工业重要基地，位于美国加利福尼亚州的旧金山经圣塔克拉拉（Santa Clara）至圣何塞（San Jose）近 50 公里的一条狭长地带。这是一个在 20 世纪 60 年代中期以后微电子技术高速发展的基础上逐渐形成的基地，硅谷依托斯坦福大学、加州大学伯克利分校、加州理工学院等，既有思科（Cisco Systems, Inc.）、英特尔（Intel Corporation）、惠普（The Hewlett-Packard Company）、朗讯（Lucent Technologies, Inc.）、苹果（Apple Inc.）等大公司，也汇聚着一大批拥有高新技术的中小公司，是一个融产、学、研为一体的基地。

5. Apple-FBI controversy，2016 年 2 月路透社有报道说，美国加利福尼亚中央区地方法院法官 Sheri Pym 要求苹果公司帮助联邦调查局 (FBI) 对枪击案凶手 Syed Rizwan Farook 曾拥有的 5c 苹果手机加以解锁，但苹果总执行官库克（Cook）予以拒绝。苹果公司拒绝为政府在手机上预先设计一个后门（back door），苹果与 FBI 的纷争实际上涉及到的是技术与政治的纷争，其焦点是智能手机该是一个值得公民信赖的通讯手段还是应该成为政府探知公民隐私的某种工具。

FBI（美国）联邦调查局（Federal Bureau of Investigation），成立于 1908 年，由美国司法部管辖。初期主要任务是调查违反联邦法律的犯罪行为，比如偷盗、抢劫等，为地方、国家和国际机构提供帮助，同时在响应公众需要和忠实于美国宪法的前提下履行职责。FBI 曾对持不同政见者如马丁·路德·金、卓别林、爱因斯坦等开展过调查行动。2001 年 9 月 11 日的恐怖袭击后，FBI 将打击恐怖主义列为其首要任务。

6. *Harry Potter*《哈利·波特》，7 卷本系列魔幻小说，为英国作家罗琳（J. K. Rowling）所著，创作时间为 1997 ~ 2007 年。前六部情节围绕霍格沃茨魔法学校（Hogwarts School of Witchcraft and Wizardry）展开，讲述的是小说主人公——巫师学生哈利·波特六年的学习情况和冒险经历，第七卷是关于哈利·波特在第二次巫界大战中如何寻找魂器并消灭伏地魔（Lord Voldemort）的故事。主题涉及到"偏见"、"腐败"、"发疯"，但中心主题是"死亡"。该系列小说被翻译成 73 种语言，成为全世界最畅销的小说系列。该系列小说由华纳电影公司 2001 年起逐渐被搬上银幕，广受观众喜爱。

USEFUL WORDS

amnesiac	[æmˈniːʒiæk] *adj.*	of a medical condition in which sb partly or completely loses their memory 记忆缺失的，遗忘的
anchor	[ˈæŋkər] *v.*	to firmly base sth on sth else 使扎根；使基于
austerity	[ɔːˈsterəti] *n.*	a situation when people do not have much money to spend because there are bad economic conditions 苦行，朴素，节衣缩食
blockbusters	[ˈblɒkbʌstə(r)] *n.*	(informal) sth. very successful, especially a very successful book or film/movie 大片；了不起的人或事；风靡一时的事物
croupier	[ˈkruːpieɪ] *n.*	a person whose job is to be in charge of a gambling table and collect and pay out money, give out cards, etc. 赌台主持人；收付赌注之人
documentarian	[ˌdɒkjəmenˈterɪrn] *n.*	someone who makes documentaries 记实小说作者；记录影片导演（或制片人）
figurative	[ˈfɪɡərətɪv] *adj.*	(of language, words, phrases, etc.) used in a way that is different from the usual meanin, in order to create a particular mental image. 比喻的，象征的，呈现的
haunt	[hɔːnt] *v.*	to be always present as a nagging anxiety in the mind of 萦绕在……心头；缠绕，使苦恼
lethal	[ˈliːθl] *adj.*	causing or able to cause death 致死的，致命的，能致命的 (informal) causing or able to causea lot of harm or damage 破坏性的，有害的
mogul	[ˈməʊɡl] *n.*	a very rich, important and powerful person 有权势的人，大人物，富豪
momentum	[moʊˈmentəm] *n.*	the ability to keep increasing or developing 势头；动力，推动力
refrain	[rɪˈfreɪn] *v.*	(formal) to stop oneself from doing sth, especially sth that you want to do 抑制，克制

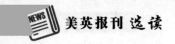

revert	[rɪ'vɜːrt] *v.*	(of property, rights, etc.) to return to the original owner again（财产、权利等）归还；归属
roguery	[rougərɪ] *n.*	roguish behaviour 无赖行为，流氓行为；欺诈
score	[skɔːr] *v.*	to win points, goal, etc. in a game or competition（在游戏或比赛中）得分
sequel	['siːkwəl] *n.*	continuation (especially of a story) 续集，续篇
skeptical	[skeptɪkəl] *adj.*	having doubts that a claim or statement is true or that sth will happen 怀疑性的，好怀疑的
spinoff	['spɪnˌɒf] *n.*	a book, a film/movie, a television programme, or an object that is based on a book, film/movie or television series that has been very successful（根据成功的书籍、电影或电视系列剧制作的）派生作品、搭车产品
spontaneity	[ˌspɒntə'neɪəti] *n.*	the quality of being spontaneous 自发性，自然

EXERCISES

I.　Vocabulary

Choose among the four alternatives one word or phrase that is closest in meaning to the underlined part in each statement.

1. "I was <u>skeptical</u> there was one to be done. I was skeptical I wanted to do it and I was skeptical it would hold up with the others," recalled Greengoass, 60.

   A. doubtful　　　　B. unbelievable　　　C. suspecious　　　D. thoughtful

2. Greengrass had long been unwilling to make his third Jason Bourne movie and for a time was even <u>burned up</u> about a spinoff done without him.

   A. deeply hurt　　　　　　　　　B. completely stimulated

   C. made very angry　　　　　　　D. excited by fire

3. Deciding in 2008—after Bourne <u>scored</u> three Oscars and global success—that he didn't want more stress, Greengrass walked away.

   A. marked　　　　　　B. obtained　　　　C. got　　　　　D. awarded

4. Does he want to use his lethal skills to serve his country or does he <u>refrain</u> out of guilt—patriotism or conscience?

   A. abstain　　　　　　B. sustain　　　　C. obtain　　　　D. ascertain

5. Because his <u>spontaneity</u> often led to key moments being omitted, he and a crew would be forced to return to various cities for reshoots, sometimes more than once

   A. involuntary action　　　　　　B. voluntary action

   C. premeditated action　　　　　　D. impulsive action

6. But universal, short on franchises and not wanting the rights to <u>revert</u> to the Ludlum estate, needed a movie.

   A. reverse　　　　　　　　　　　B. return to a former owner

C. return to a topic   D. return to a former belief

7. In a sense all these films are <u>anchored</u> in identity, because Jason Bourne is trying to find out who he is.

A. firmly secured   B. firmly based on   C. conducted   D. fastened

8. Greengrass—who wears Harry Potter glasses, shoulderlength white hair and a mien that in a certain light can make him look like Jay Leno—dedicated much of four years to *The Bourne Supremacy*, <u>sequel</u> to Doug Liman's *The Bourne Identity*, and then Ultimatum.

A. something that proceeds other things

B. a series of some published materials

C. a book that continues the story of an earlier one

D. a film that continues the story of an earlier one

9. ...a <u>fraught</u> relationship between new CIA director Robert Dewey (Tommy Lee Jones) and Aaron Kalloor (Riz Ahmed).

A. worrying   B. troublesome   C. worried   D. false

10. There's the ex-agent's new discoveries about his past, a fresh chapter with his comrade— roguery Nicky Parsons (Julia Stiles), <u>slippery</u> dealings with a murkily motivated cyber-analyst (Alicia Vicander)...

A. difficult to stand   B. difficult to handle

C. not trustworthy   D. very smooth

II. Comprehension

Decide whether the following statements are true or false according to the information given in the press clipping. Mark T or F to each statement.

1. Matt Damon and Christopher Rouse's purpose of visiting Greengrass is to persuade him to direct another film with Bourne again as the hero.

2. Greengrass is reluctant to direct another film about Ludlum's assassin even though persuaded by Matt Damon and Christopher Rouse.

3. Tony Gilroy was a rival director of Greengrass.

4. The hero Jason Bourne and his extremely exciting actions are well known to the audience who love the series of the films.

5. Aaron Kalloor's user database is crucial to Dewey's intelligence scheme.

6. There is a far cry between the issues touched by the film and the issues which actually exist in American society.

7. Compared with the preceding ones, the plot of the new Bourne movie is closer to social issues.

8. "But with this one I think we're also asking how we want to define ourselves as a country." Rouse said. This sentence means that the film is an attempt to lead its audience to thinking about what a country the U.S. should be.

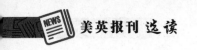
9. The reason Universal had the intention to shoot another film of Bourne is that Donna Langley, chairman of the Universal, was not satisfied with *The Bourne Legacy*, which was not directed by Greengrass

10. Donna Langley, chairman of the Universal, welcomed the return of Greengrass.

III. Questions for discussion

1. Spy thrillers are always exciting. What qualities make the genre so popular?

2. Have you ever seen any of the Bourne series? If so, what interests you most? And why?

3. Do you think it is a far cry between espionage illustrated by the Bournes series and the real life?

4. Edward Joseph Snowden (born June 21, 1983) is an American computer professional, former Central Intelligence Agency (CIA) employee and former contractor for the United States government who copied and leaked classified information from the National Security Agency (NSA) in 2013 without prior authorization. If you put yourself in an ordinary American's shoes, do you think he is right or wrong?

5. Have you ever seen any of the films starring Arnold Schwarzenegger? Can you make a comparison between the styles of Arnold Schwarzenegger and Matt Damon?

《读者文摘》简介

《读者文摘》（*Reader's Digest*）由德威特·华莱士（DeWitt Wallace）和丽拉·贝尔·华莱士（Lila Bell Wallace）于1922年创刊，总部在纽约，是美国最普及的家庭阅读杂志。该杂志小巧紧凑，纸张大小为大多数美国杂志的一半左右，2005年编辑采用的口号就是"你口袋里的美国"（America in your pocket），每年出版10期，读者有7亿之多，遍及70多个国家和地区，语种多达21种，在全球的销售达1,700万册。

几十年来，该杂志每期都由30篇文章构成，此外有词汇页和轶事页等页面。近些年，该杂志还配上了色彩华丽、吸人眼球的图形图画，完整的文章间会插入其他精短的信息。

《读者文摘》国际版占到该杂志发行量的百分之五十，文章由各地的编辑委员会选取，内容与美国和其他地方的版本分享，文章由当地译员翻译并由本族语编辑审稿，以便与美国版"受过良好教育的、非正式的"（well-educated informal）风格保持一致。

登录《读者文摘》的官方网站，可以了解该报的相关信息。

Unit Seven
Artists

 ## 报刊英语中的习语

  习语指的是某一语言长期使用过程中形成的独特的、固定的表达法，其意义比较固定，但不是表达法中每个词意义的简单叠加。习语是语言的精华，文化承载量最为丰富，其结构和含义都不能随意改变。从广义上讲，习语还包括格言、谚语、俚语、行话等。世界上历史悠久的语言都存在大量形式多样、比喻深刻的习语，英语也不例外。英语习语用词精简形象，但能深刻地反映社会现象和习俗。一个民族的社会习俗、思维方式无不在习语中得到淋漓尽致的体现。

  报刊作为一种传播文字资料的工具，早已成为人们认识社会的一个重要窗口，在人们生活中起着举足轻重的作用，是人们生活必不可少的一部分。英语新闻报刊通常力求报道内容的准确性、语言的简洁度和文章结构条理上的清晰感。这种准确、简洁的要求不可避免地会使用到习语；而且有些报刊为了满足不同读者水平需求，文字表达更加多样化，更加贴近读者，也会使用习语。比如在第八单元 Text A 中出现了 "fox guarding the hen house"（狐狸守鸡舍）这一习语，形象生动地指出了当今美国高校教育质量评价体系中的问题。

  对于习语的理解学习，只能通过大量的阅读和平时的积累掌握，不能在文中进行随意猜测。英语报刊中经常出现的习语大致可以分为以下几类：

📖1 比喻性成语（figurative idioms）

  学习任何一门语言，最困难的方面之一，就是理解并运用大量成语。同汉语成语一样，英语成语也是颇具色彩的语言形式。英语有15000多个成语，其中占多数的是比喻性成语。比喻性成语指的是借助某一具体形象来表达意义的固定表达方式。严格意义上讲，只有包含比喻的固定词组才是真正意义上的成语，否则只能称之为固定搭配（徐明初，2002）。所以，比喻性成语是英语成语的核心部分，生动鲜明的形象往往会使人产生丰富的联想。

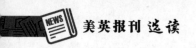

例如:

"On Charter's results and that it would go down as a 'storm in a teacup' for the engineering group". (*Financial Times*, Feb. 15, 2010)

既是风暴,必然狂风肆虐,来势汹涌。但是"在茶杯中的风暴",只能是夸张有余,掀不起波浪。因此本习语比作有些人不恰当地把小事情当作大事来处理,有故意夸张的意思,可对应汉语中的"小题大做"。

"We're ready," Rtskhiladze said. "We're waiting for them to give us the green light." (*The Washington Post*, Nov. 25, 2016)

无论是在中国文化,还是西方文化中,绿灯都是可以通行的意思,所以用"give sb the green light"给某人开绿灯,来比作允许某工程或计划的启动,在此是指在格鲁吉亚的巴统(Batumi)建立特朗普大厦的工程。

2 谚语(proverbs)

谚语类似于成语,都是语言整体中的一部分。谚语大部分来源于劳动人民的生活实践经验,所以表达的是朴素而真实的哲理。其流传途径通常是口头为主,所以口语性强,更加通俗易懂,形式上差不多都是一两个短句或韵语。不同国家的谚语反映不同国家民族的性格。英语谚语是西方民众丰富智慧和普遍经验的规律性总结,正确地使用英语谚语,可以增加英语表达的鲜明性和生动性。在当代美英报刊中,作者大量引用谚语,使文章增辉添色,更贴近生活,同时也能拉近和读者之间的距离。

例如:

But callers on conservative host Dich Farrel's show think Democrats are just crying over spilt milk. (*Forbes*, Nov.11, 2000)

Cry over spilt milk 本意为"对着打翻的牛奶哭也没用",用此谚语形象地说明"民主党已是覆水难收"。寥寥数语表明了迪克·法雷尔秀(Dich Farrel's show)的听众对民主党的态度。

以下列出美英报刊中频繁出现的部分常见谚语:

A chain is no stronger than its weakest link.	一着不慎,满盘皆输。
All is not gold that glitters.	闪光的未必都是金子。
Although the sun shine, leave not your cloak at home.	未雨绸缪。
All covet, all lose.	贪多嚼不烂。
All rivers run into the sea.	殊途同归。
A baker's wife may bite of a bun, a brewer's wife may bite of a tun.	近水楼台先得月。

A staff is quickly found to beat a dog with.	欲加之罪，何患无辞。
All feet tread not in one shoe.	众口难调。
A young idler, an old beggar.	少壮不努力，老大徒伤悲。
A crow is never the whiter for washing herself often.	江山易改，本性难移。
Bread is the staff of life.	民以食为天。
Behind the mountains there are people to be found.	天外有天，山外有山。
Cats hide their claws.	知人知面不知心。
Diamond cut diamond.	棋逢对手。
Do not teach fish to swim.	不要班门弄斧。
Experience is the best teacher.	实践出真知。
Every bean has its black.	金无足赤，人无完人。
Even woods have ears.	隔墙有耳。
Every tub must stand on its own bottom.	人贵自立。
Experience teaches.	吃一堑，长一智。
Full vessels sound least.	大智若愚。
First impressions are half the battle.	先入为主。
Go while the going is good.	三十六计，走为上计。
Good wine needs no bush	酒香不怕巷子深。
Go to the sea, if you would fish well.	不入虎穴，焉得虎子。
He travels the fastest who travels alone.	曲高和寡。
Heaven helps those who help themselves.	求人不如求己。
It is a silly fish that is caught twice with the same bait.	智者不上两次当。
He that runs fastest gets the ring.	捷足先登。
It is a poor mouse that has only one hole.	狡兔三窟。
Keeping is harder than winning.	创业不易，守业更难。
Kill two birds with one stone.	一箭双雕。
Merry meet, merry part.	好聚好散。
No work, no money.	不劳无获。
No fire without smoke.	无风不起浪。
The battle is to the strong.	两强相遇勇者胜。
The best of friends must part.	天下没有不散的宴席。
Unpleasant advice is a good medicine.	忠言逆耳利于行。
You cannot have your cake and eat it.	事难两全其美。

3 典故（allusions）

根据《韦氏》词典（*Merriam-Webster*）的解释，典故是指文学里间接含蓄的引用。英语典故的理解要难于以上提及的成语和谚语，因为英语典故多来自古希腊罗马神话传说和西方重要的宗教和文学作品。

比如 Pandora's Box（潘多拉魔盒）就出自古希腊神话。据说普罗米修斯（Prometheus）盗取天火，造福人类，主神宙斯（Zeus）十分恼怒。他命令儿子火神赫淮斯托斯（Hephaestus）用粘土制作了一个女人，取名潘多拉（Pandora），并令诸神赋予她一切天赋。然后宙斯将潘多拉许给普罗米修斯的弟弟厄庇墨透斯（Epimetheus）为妻，嫁妆是一个密封的盒子，里面装满了各种灾难、祸患和瘟疫。潘多拉出于好奇私自打开了盒子，疾病、罪恶、嫉妒、偷窃、贪婪等一切祸害从盒子里飞出，散落到人间。据此英语常借用 Pandora's box 一语喻指"灾祸之源"。

西方最重要的文学作品当属《圣经》，其地位至高无上，它里边的典故，在西方家喻户晓。比如 Moses' rod（摩西的杖），典出《出埃及记》（*Exodus*）第 4-10 章，指"克敌制胜法宝"。

莎士比亚作品也是英语典故的重要源头之一，比如成语 much ado about nothing（无事生非）就来自于莎士比亚的同名剧作。该剧是一出闹剧，讲述的是少年贵族克劳狄奥（Claudio）在结婚前夕听说未婚妻希罗（Hero）不贞的消息，气愤难当，于是在婚礼上当众羞辱她。不久又得知那原来不过是小人作恶捏造的谣言而已，于是两人和好如初，重新举行了婚礼。

在当今的美英报刊中，合理运用典故会使文章读来回味无穷，因此其使用是非常普遍的。例如：

...but last week Senator Barack Obama was hit below the belt with a cruel new allegation: he may be too skinny to win the White House. (*The Times*, Mar. 18, 2008)

"hit below the belt"原指拳击比赛时打对方腰带以下部位的犯规行为，在此指"暗箭伤人"。

4 俚语（slangs）

根据《牛津词典》（*Oxford English Dictionary*）的解释，俚语是一种高度口语化的语言，包含一些新词或者流行词语。可以说，英文俚语是英语语言中最活跃的部分。新闻报刊作为大众传媒，必须适合广大读者的阅读水平，语言简洁精炼的同时，还要通俗易懂，加上报刊面临着电视、广播、网络等传媒的挑战，还要兼顾生动有趣。所以报纸杂志中常会使用俚语，使文章活泼、幽默、自然。

最早，俚语被认为是军队、黑社会、牛仔、水手等亚文化群所讲的一种"粗俗的语言"，但随着社会的发展，人们生活节奏日益加快，英语语言本身日趋通俗化和口语化。

尤其近年来互联网的迅猛普及，网络用语也成为英语俚语的一大来源，比如，CU（再见），cyberpunk（网友），lady-killer（帅哥）等等；与此同时，创造和使用俚语的人文化层次也在不断提高，俚语这种非标准英语也逐渐从难登大雅之堂的尴尬地位逐渐移步到公众认可的主流地带。有时，俚语的正确使用还属时髦之举。美英新闻报刊作为求新求快的媒介和社会风尚的导向标，当然会不可避免地使用俚语。

英语俚语的构成和变化一方面来自新创词，另一方面来自词语的转义。比如 The Bitch America Needs (*The New York Times*, Sept. 10, 2016)，此标题中的"Bitch"指的是希拉里。不熟悉俚语的读者看到这个标题，会对像《纽约时报》这样的严肃报纸竟公然使用 bitch 一词感到不可思议，但是如果了解了该词在俚语中已经从最初的粗鄙之义进化为"指那些为理念而战、不受淑女规范束缚的新时代女性"，就会领悟到该词的妙用了。文章指出希拉里铁腕强势的形象彻底颠覆了传统女性柔弱的形象，而这恰是一个国家领导人所必备的素质。女权主义的发展使独立自强的女性从男人手中夺回话语权，赋予其新的意义。

俚语虽然能使报刊文章更加新潮时髦，拉进作者与读者之间的距离，但是不宜在报刊文章中大量使用，否则会破坏报刊英语的文体。只有正确地使用俚语，才能起到锦上添花的作用。

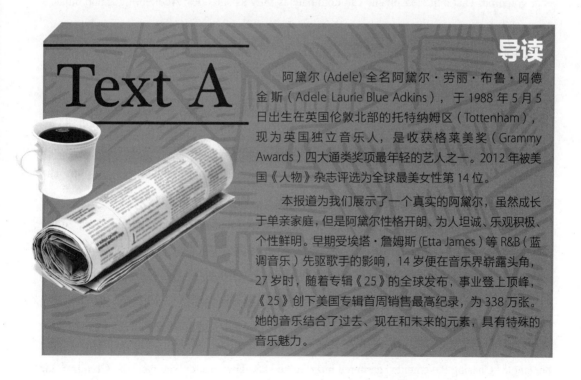

Text A

导读

阿黛尔 (Adele) 全名阿黛尔·劳丽·布鲁·阿德金斯（Adele Laurie Blue Adkins），于 1988 年 5 月 5 日出生在英国伦敦北部的托特纳姆区（Tottenham），现为英国独立音乐人，是收获格莱美奖（Grammy Awards）四大通类奖项最年轻的艺人之一。2012 年被美国《人物》杂志评选为全球最美女性第 14 位。

本报道为我们展示了一个真实的阿黛尔，虽然成长于单亲家庭，但是阿黛尔性格开朗、为人坦诚、乐观积极、个性鲜明。早期受埃塔·詹姆斯（Etta James）等 R&B（蓝调音乐）先驱歌手的影响，14 岁便在音乐界崭露头角，27 岁时，随着专辑《25》的全球发布，事业登上顶峰，《25》创下美国专辑首周销售最高纪录，为 338 万张。她的音乐结合了过去、现在和未来的元素，具有特殊的音乐魅力。

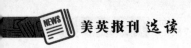

Adele is music's past, present and future

By Sam Lansky

When you talk to people about Adele, pretty much everyone uses the word authentic sooner or later. But over the course of a week with her, it's not one she uses to describe herself or her music. Nor is she into other industry jargon. At one point, she volunteers that she hates the word brand, for example. "They all use that word," she says. "It makes me sound like a fabric softener, or a packet of crisps."

Unlike nearly all her peers, Adele has no product-endorsement[1] deals. She seems uninterested in the contemporary practice of working to maintain a specific image. She just doesn't want to be perceived as a jerk. "Some artists, the bigger they get, the more horrible they get, and the more unlikable," she says. "I don't care if you make an amazing album—if I don't like you, I ain't getting your record. I don't want you being played in my house if I think you're a bastard."

Adele will be played in a lot of houses in 2016. Her voice has the impact of a thousand tons of bricks. The zeitgeist can't seem to get enough—the memes spawned by "Hello" alone were numerous enough to clog social media for weeks. Yet she's the only pop star you can listen to with your grandma. That's the reason she can dominate as fully as she does: Adele bridges pop music's past and its future.

IN PERSON, Adele is frank and funny, peppering her speech with profanity and self-deprecating asides. Perhaps that's why it's startling to register how young she still is. 25, like the two albums before, is named for the age she was when she recorded it. Born Adele Laurie Blue Adkins and raised in the working-class London neighborhood of Tottenham[2] by a single mom, she recalls her childhood through the lens of being a new mother. Her son Angelo is 3. "The environment in which my kid is growing up couldn't be further away from the way I grew up," she says. "But there was never any embarrassment about showing love in my family."

Early on, she was inspired by R&B artists such as Lauryn Hill[3] and Alicia Keys, along with legends like Etta James[4]. At 14, she earned a spot at the BRIT School[5], an elite performing-arts school that also counts Amy Winehouse and Leona Lewis as alumnae. She was scouted on MySpace and signed with indie label XL at age 18. When she began recording her debut album, 19, her expectations were low. "I was a brand-new artist," she says. "No one cared." But a warm reception in the U.K. and a high-proile performance on Saturday Night Live in 2008 showcasing her single "Chasing Pavements" garnered buzz in the U.S. That winter, she won the Grammy[6] for Best New Artist.

Superstardom came the following year when she released another single, "Rolling in the Deep," a stomping anthem that set the tone for the record that followed and topped charts around the world. Released in 2011, 21 was largely about the end of a relationship that hit on classic themes of heartache and empowerment. Her songs often sounded simpler than they were. The easy melody and spare production of a track like "Someone Like You," for instance, makes it seem universal. Yet it's also an emotionally complex piece of writing.

By the time Adele was a household name, she was ready for some time off. After giving birth, she did the most radical thing an artist at her level could do: she went mostly dark to spend time with her boyfriend, charity executive Simon Konecki, and their son Angelo. "I was very conscious to make sure that our bond was strong and unbreakable," she says. "I had to get to that point before I'd come back."

This left her with little in the way of material for a new album, however. First she tried writing songs about motherhood, most of which she tossed. "I loved it," she says "For me, it was great. Better than 25. But he's the light of my life—not anyone else's." She didn't want to write about the issues in her partnership with Konecki. "We're in a grownup, adult, mature relationship," she says. "I didn't want to write about us, because I didn't want to make us feel uncomfortable." Nor did she want to resort to shallow material. "Can you imagine if I was singing about texting?" She cackles. "You would never get me singing about having a drink in the club."

It wasn't until Adele turned the lens back on herself that she was able to make progress. "That's when I decided to write about myself and how I make myself feel, rather than how other people make me feel," she says. She also decided not to rush it. "It doesn't matter how long it takes," she says. "You're only as good as your next record."

（From *TIME*, Dec. 28, 2015–Jan. 4, 2016）

▐ NOTES

1. product-endorsement 产品代言

2. Tottenham 托特纳姆，位于英格兰大伦敦北部哈林盖伦自治市的一个区域。是阿黛尔的故乡，也是热刺足球俱乐部（Hotspur Football Club）的所在地。该俱乐部成立于 1882 年，传统主场球衣为白色，所以热刺球迷有"白百合"之称。阿黛尔是热刺的忠实球迷。

3. Lauryn Hill 劳伦·希尔，美国说唱歌手、唱片制作人、演员。1975 年 5 月出生于美国新泽西州东奥兰治，曾为 Fugees 乐队的女主唱。1993 年出演《修女也疯狂 2》中 Rita Louise Watson 一角。1998 年首张个人专辑 *The Miseducation Of Lauryn Hill* 不但出现在所有杂志的年度最佳

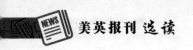

专辑推荐名单上，并且与专辑中的首支单曲"(Doo Wop)That Thing"双双登上 Billboard 冠军王座。

4. Etta James (1938-2012) 埃塔·詹姆斯，一代灵歌天后，R&B 歌手的先驱，乐坛传奇女歌手。原名 Jamesetta Hawkins（洁米塞塔·霍金斯），12 岁正式改名为 Etta James。 因经常以 "Etta James & the Peaches" 之名发行唱片，所以又被人称为 Miss Peaches（桃子小姐）。代表作品有 *Mystery Lady: The Songs of Billie Holiday*。2003 年被美国录音艺术与科学学院（National Academy of Recording Arts and Sciences, NARAS）授予终身成就奖。

5. BRIT School 伦敦表演艺术与技术学校，位于伦敦克罗伊登区，1991 年由英国政府及英国唱片业基金会出资合办，以音乐、表演、戏剧、传媒、制作等科目为重点。毕业生有 Adele、Kate Nash 等知名歌手，被誉为培养明星的摇篮。

6. Grammy 格莱美奖，英文 Gramophone（留声机）的变异谐音。由国家录音艺术与科学学院（NARAS）每年 2 月份颁发。作为世界比较有影响力的音乐大奖，格莱美奖有"音乐界的奥斯卡"之美誉。格莱美四大通类（General Field categories）指的是综合领域内的四个奖，由于这个领域不分音乐类别竞争，所以叫四大通类，是格莱美含金量最高的奖，包括最佳新人（Best New Artist），年度制作（Record of the Year），年度歌曲（Song of the Year）和年度专辑（Album of the Year）。

USEFUL WORDS

alumna	[ə'lʌmnə]	*n.*	[C] a female graduate of a school, college, etc. 女校友
anthem	['ænθəm]	*n.*	[C] a song that is used to represent a particular nation, society, or group and that is sung on special occasions 国歌；会歌
authentic	[ɔː'θentɪk]	*adj.*	genuine 真实的
bastard	['bæstərd]	*n.*	[C] an insulting word which some people use about a person, especially a man, who has behaved very badly 杂种
cackle	['kækl]	*v.*	to laugh in a loud unpleasant way 咯咯地笑，高声谈笑
clog	[klɑːg]	*v.*	to block or become blocked with an accumulation of thick, wet matter. (Here) fill up or crowd (something) so as to obstruct passage 堵塞
conscious	['kɑːnʃəs]	*adj.*	intentional 自觉的；有意的
contemporary	[kən'tempəreri]	*adj.*	modern; of the present 当代的
crisp	[krɪsp]	*n.*	[C] very thin slices of fried potato that are eaten cold as a snack 炸薯片
dominate	['dɑːmɪneɪt]	*v.*	to have the most important place or position (in) 处在支配地位；处在最重要的地位
garner	['gɑːrnər]	*v.*	to gain or collect 获得；收集
household	['haʊshoʊld]	*adj.*	well-known 家喻户晓的
inspire	[ɪn'spaɪər]	*v.*	to encourage in (someone) the ability to act, esp. with a good result 鼓励；启发

meme	[miːm] *n.*	[C] an idea or element of social behavior passed on through generations in a culture, esp. by imitation 文化基因
perceive	[pəˈsiːv] *v.*	to have or come to have knowledge of (something) through one of the senses (esp. sight) or through the mind; see 察觉；看出；领悟
scout	[skaʊt] *v.*	to go through an area searching for sth. 搜寻
self-deprecating	[ˈsɛlfˈdɛprɪˌketɪŋ] *adj.*	criticizing oneself or represent oneself as foolish in a light-hearted way. 自我嘲笑的
stomp	[stɑːmp] *v.*	to walk with very heavy steps. (Here) a dance involving a rhythmical stamping step 顿足爵士舞
superstardom	[ˈsuːpəstɑːdəm] *n.*	[U] the identity or status of being an unusually famous performer, esp. a popular musician or a film actor 超级明星的身份（或地位）
zeitgeist	[ˈzaɪtɡaɪst] *n.*	[U] the defining spirit or mood of a particular period of history as shown by the ideas and beliefs of the time 时代精神；时代潮流

EXERCISES

I. Vocabulary

Choose among the four alternatives one word or phrase that is closest in meaning to the underlined part in each statement.

1. She seems uninterested in the <u>contemporary</u> practice of working to maintain a specific image.

    A. future   B. previous   C. present   D. contemptuous

2. She just doesn't want to be <u>perceived</u> as a jerk.

    A. detected   B. absorbed   C. felt   D. seen

3. Her voice has the impact <u>of a thousand tons of bricks</u>.

    A. very thickly   B. very strongly

    C. very solidly   D. very confidentially

4. But there was never any <u>embarrassment</u> about showing love in my family.

    A. decency   B. politeness   C. kindness   D. awkwardness

5. She was <u>scouted</u> on Myspace and signed with indie label XL at age 18.

    A. assaulted   B. searched   C. mocked   D. listed

6. The easy melody and <u>spare</u> production of a track like "Someone Like You," for instance, makes it seem universal.

    A. extra   B. simple

    C. prepared   D. unnecessary

7. By the time Adele was a <u>household</u> name, she was ready for some time off.

    A. domestic   B. daily   C. routine   D. famous

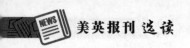

8. "I was very <u>conscious</u> to make sure that our bond was strong and unbreakable," she says, "I had to get to that point before I'd come back".

   A. intended   B. confident   C. conscience   D. ambitious

9. That's the reason she can <u>dominate</u> as fully as she does: Adele bridges pop music's past and its future.

   A. control   B. understand   C. donate   D. change

10. Yet it's also an emotionally <u>complex</u> piece of writing.

   A. complementary   B. amplified   C. complicated   D. wonderful

II. Comprehension

Decide whether the following statements are true or false according to the information given in the press clipping. Mark T or F to each statement.

1. Adele likes to be treated as a product with brand, which is easy for people to recognize.

2. Like all the other pop stars, Adele also advertizes many products.

3. If Adele dislikes some singer, she would not listen to his/her music.

4. Adele's music is so attractive that both the young and the old like to listen to it.

5. Born in a rich family, Adele lived a happy life during the childhood.

6. Adele was eager to be successful when she began recording her first album, 19.

7. "Rolling in the Deep" is an important song because it sets the tone for the following record and topped charts around the world.

8. After giving birth, Adele gave up her career and decided to stay with her husband Simon Konecki.

9. As to the material for a new album, Adele prefers motherhood to her partnership with Knoecki.

10. Adele is ambitious to issue the next record as soon as possible.

III. Questions for discussion

1. Zhang Ailing, a legendary Chinese writer, once stated, "Fame is to be achieved in the early age." When Adele won the Grammy for Best New Artist, she was only in her twenties. How do you comment on her success at such a young age?

2. Do you like Adele's music? Do you think it has the magic to bridge pop music's past and its future?

3. Please describe what kind of person Adele is, according to the article. Do you like her? And why?

4. Which one do you think is much more important, personal honor or family loyalty? If you were Adele, would you make the same decision to stay with your family?

5. Some people think it is rather embarrassing and unnecessary to say the word "love" to family members. Please make some comments on this viewpoint.

美英国家的艺术博物馆

美国

西方博物馆一般划分为艺术博物馆、历史博物馆、科学博物馆和特殊博物馆四类。艺术博物馆展示绘画、雕刻、装饰艺术、实用工艺和工业艺术，也有的展示古物、民俗和原始艺术。世界著名的艺术博物馆有法国卢浮宫（Louvre）、美国大都会艺术博物馆（Metropolitan Museum of Art）和伦敦的大英博物馆（British Museum）。艺术博物馆是永久性地展示城市繁荣的场所。

艺术博物馆在美国的政治意义重大，它不仅是美国国家财富的象征，更是美国民主信念的表达。因为美国艺术博物馆的建设受到法国卢浮宫和英国南肯辛顿博物馆的影响，一开始就坚持向大众开放，它所收藏的珍宝是为了全体国民的利益。伴随民主教育理念的发展，博物馆也成为教育机构的一部分，是普通民众汲取知识的重要场所。

美国艺术博物馆的兴起主要依靠 19 世纪富有的工业家，他们是艺术赞助和博物馆建设的主力军。1857 年经济危机的出现，使富商们意识到货币资产价值可能严重萎缩，而艺术品的精神价值不可估量，所以艺术收藏不失为一种理想的投资途径，并且这不仅是自身社会地位的彰显，同时也是新美国成功、财富及力量的象征。1917 年，美国国会实施联邦税法，规定个人或企业向艺术博物馆等非盈利组织捐赠时，可以扣除艺术品当时的市场价值，免除任何税费。此法规使得艺术品投资者们将艺术品捐赠给公共艺术博物馆时，实现了利益最大化。与此同时，捐赠行为也极大程度地提高了美国资产阶级的社会声誉，可谓经济利益和精神世界得到双重满足。(李晓敏，2012) 在此时期，美国各个公共艺术博物馆的藏品迅速丰富。美国政府通过建立艺术博物馆，不仅将美国打造成经济之都，更使之成为文化和艺术之都。

美国拥有很多规模较大的艺术博物馆，较受欢迎的有以下一些：

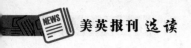

美国著名艺术博物馆一览

序号	名称（英文）	名称（中文）	建立时间	所在地
1	Metropolitan Museum of Art	大都会艺术博物馆	1871	纽约
2	The Art Institute of Chicago	芝加哥艺术博物馆	1891	芝加哥
3	National Gallery of Art	美国国家艺术馆	1937	华盛顿特区
4	The Museum of Modern Art	现代艺术博物馆	1929	纽约
5	Boston Museum of Fine Arts	波士顿美术博物馆	1876	波士顿
6	Detroit Institute of Arts	底特律艺术博物馆	1885	底特律
7	Nelson-Atkins Museum of Art	纳尔逊 - 阿特金斯艺术博物馆	1933	堪萨斯
8	Philadelphia Museum of Art	费城艺术博物馆	1876	费城
9	The Dallas Museum of Art	达拉斯艺术博物馆	1903	达拉斯
10	Whitney Museum of American Art	惠特尼美国艺术博物馆	1931	纽约
11	San Francisco Museum of Modern Art	旧金山现代艺术博物馆	1935	旧金山
12	The Getty Center	盖蒂中心	1997	洛杉矶

英国

博物馆的最初萌芽可以追溯到公元前四世纪。亚历山大大帝在建立亚欧非大帝国时，将搜集来的珍贵艺术品交给亚里士多德，以供其进行教学研究。亚历山大去世后，他的部下托勒密·索托继续南征北战，收集到更多的艺术品。公元前三世纪，为了收藏这些艺术品，托勒密·索托在埃及的亚历山大城创建了缪斯神庙，这被认为是人类历史上最早的"博物馆"。Museum 即由 "缪斯"（希腊文 Μουσαι，拉丁文 muses) 一词演变而来。

英国艺术博物馆的初衷是发展商业。早期的艺术博物藏品主要来自私人收藏的捐赠，主要用于研究，参观者也大多是特权阶层。17、18 世纪，英国萌发的启蒙运动，掀起了批判专制主义和宗教愚昧，宣传自由、平等和民主的社会思潮。新的公共博物馆由此产生，并将对公众开放作为对当时思潮的积极响应。随着博物馆开放程度的日益扩大，博物馆逐渐成为普通大众集会的社会场所。1753 年，英国政府决定建立大英博物馆，这也是世界上第一个对普通公众开放的大型博物馆。1824 年，国家画廊设立，以便让所有公众都能欣赏到伟大的绘画，普遍提高民众们的欣赏水平和艺术素养。

英国的艺术博物馆大多位于交通极为便利的市中心，均设有停车场、咖啡店和纪念品商店。英国约有 2000-2500 所博物馆，近一半的英国居民每年至少会参观一次博物馆。英国艺术博物馆通过展览，发挥着巨大的潜移默化的导向作用，提高了公众的审美水平，净化和愉悦了公众的心灵，真正起到了文化传播的桥梁作用。

英国著名艺术博物馆一览

序号	名称（英文）	名称（中文）	建立时间	所在地
1	Ashmolean Museum	阿什莫尔博物馆	1683	牛津
2	British Museum	英国国家博物馆（大英博物馆）	1753	伦敦
3	The National Gallery	英国国家美术馆（国家画廊）	1824	伦敦
4	Tate Modern	泰特现代美术馆	2000	伦敦
5	Victoria and Albert Museum	维多利亚和艾伯特博物馆	1852	伦敦
6	National Portrait Gallery	国家肖像馆	1856	伦敦
7	Kelvingrove Art Gallery and Museum	凯文葛罗夫艺术博物馆	1901	格拉斯哥
8	Hunt Museum	汉特博物馆	1974	利默里克
9	Elgin Museum	埃尔金博物馆	1856	埃尔金
10	Montrose Museum & Arts Gallery	蒙特罗斯博物馆与画廊	1842	安格斯
11	National Museum of Scotland	苏格兰国家博物馆	1931	爱丁堡

Text B

导读

2016 年诺贝尔文学奖授予了 75 岁的美国摇滚乐传奇人物——鲍勃·迪伦（Bob Dylan），颁奖理由是"在伟大的美国歌曲传统内创造了新的诗歌表达。"（for having created new poetic expressions within the great American song tradition）鲍勃·迪伦也成为自黑人小说家托妮·莫里森（Toni Morrison）1993 年获奖后的首位美籍诺贝尔文学奖得主。时任美国总统奥巴马立刻送上祝福，并称鲍勃·迪伦是他最喜欢的诗人之一，获此殊荣是实至名归。

鲍勃·迪伦的获奖引发了摇滚歌词是否属于文学的持久争议。支持者将其比作美国的"莎士比亚"、游吟诗人传统的杰出继承者，他的歌词被视作经典广为引用。此次诺贝尔文学奖的授予是肯定了文学的口头形式，承认了文学与诗歌以多种形态存在于文化之中；鲍勃·迪伦的歌词其实是音乐形式之下的文本创作，是被传唱的诗歌。而反对者则认为诺贝尔文学奖评委会的这个决定，其实是在反对书，反对阅读。

其实，鲍勃·迪伦早在 1996 年、2006 年就曾获诺贝尔文学奖提名，也是唯一获得普利策奖（特别荣誉奖）的摇滚明星。1991 年获国家录音艺术与科学学院颁发的终身成就奖，2001 年获得奥斯卡最佳原创歌曲奖，2012 年奥巴马为其颁发总统自由勋章。

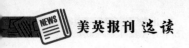

Bob Dylan wins Nobel Prize in literature

By Tribune news services

Bob Dylan, Nobel laureate. In the book world's equivalent of a Supreme Court ruling, the Nobel judges declared Thursday that Dylan is not just a rock star but a poet of the very highest order.

Dylan, 75, becomes the first musician in the 115-year history of the Nobel to win the prize in literature. He was honored for "having created new poetic expressions within the great American song tradition."

It is the ultimate ascension for the man who set off a lasting debate over whether lyrics, especially rock lyrics, can be regarded as art. Dylan, who gave the world "Like a Rolling Stone," "Blowin' in the Wind" and dozens of other standards, now finds himself on a list that includes Samuel Beckett[1], Toni Morrison[2] and T.S. Eliot[3], whom Dylan referred to in his epic song "Desolation Row."

"Congratulations to one of my favorite poets, Bob Dylan, on a well-deserved Nobel," tweeted President Barack Obama, who in 2012 presented the singer-songwriter with a Presidential Medal of Freedom.

Dylan rarely gives interviews, and a representative said the star had no immediate comment. He is on tour and was scheduled to play in Las Vegas on Thursday night.

The startling announcement out of Stockholm[4] was met with both euphoria and dismay.

Many fans already quote Dylan as if he were Shakespeare, there are entire college courses and scholarly volumes devoted to his songs, and judges work Dylan quotations into their legal opinions all the time, such as "The times they are a-changing" and "You don't need a weatherman to know which way the wind blows."

With this year's Nobel announcement, many people, especially Americans, weren't scratching their heads and asking "Who?!" the way they did after hearing the names of such winners as Patrick Modiano[5] and J.M.G. Le Clézio.

Others, though, lamented a lost moment for books.

"An ill-conceived nostalgia award wrenched from the rancid prostates of senile, gibbering hippies," wrote "Trainspotting"[6] novelist Irvine Welsh. "I totally get the Nobel committee," tweeted author Gary Shteyngart. "Reading books is hard." The Vatican newspaper *L'Osservatore Romano* said some "real writers" probably aren't pleased.

But several leading authors praised the news.

Nobel laureate Toni Morrison said in a statement that she was pleased and that Dylan was "an impressive choice." Salman Rushdie, who has written songs with U2's Bono, tweeted that Dylan is "the brilliant inheritor of the bardic tradition. Great choice." Perennial Nobel candidate Joyce Carol Oates tweeted that "his haunting music & lyrics have always seemed, in the deepest sense, literary."

Dylan's award also was welcomed by a venerable literary organization, the Academy of American Poets[7].

"Bob Dylan receiving the Nobel Prize in literature acknowledges the importance of literature's oral tradition, and the fact that literature and poetry exists in culture in multiple modes," executive director Jennifer Benka said in a statement.

Critics can argue whether "Visions of Johanna" is as literary as "Waiting for Godot," but Dylan's stature among musicians is unchallenged. He is the most influential songwriter of his time, who brought a new depth, range and complexity to rock lyrics and freed Bruce Springsteen, Joni Mitchell and countless other artists to break out from the once-narrow boundaries of love and dance songs.

Dylan already was the only rock star to receive a Pulitzer Prize (an honorary one), and is, in fact, an author, too: He was nominated for a National Book Critics Circle[8] prize for his memoir, "Chronicles: Volume One."

He is the first American to win the Nobel literature prize since Morrison in 1993, and his award probably hurts the chances of such older American writers as Philip Roth and Don DeLillo, since the Nobel judges try to spread the honors around.

"Rather doubt Philip Roth and Don DeLillo wish they'd written "Mr. Tambourine Man" vs. AMERICAN PASTORAL and UNDERWORLD," tweeted Roth biographer Blake Bailey, referring to acclaimed novels by Roth and DeLillo. "But sure, OK."

Dylan's life has been a hybrid of popular and literary influences. A native of Duluth, Minnesota, he worshipped Elvis Presley and James Dean as a boy, but also read voraciously and seemed to absorb virtually every style of American music.

His lyrics have referred to (and sometimes lifted from) the Bible, Civil War poetry and Herman Melville[9]. He has contended that his classic "Blood on the Tracks" album was inspired by the stories of Anton Chekhov.

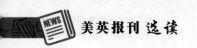
His songs can be snarling and accusatory ("Idiot Wind," "Positively 4th Street"); apocalyptic ("A Hard Rain's A-Gonna Fall"); dense and hallucinatory ("Desolation Row"); tender and wistful ("Visions of Johanna"); bracingly topical ("Hurricane" and "Only a Pawn in Their Game"); and enigmatic and absurdist ("Stuck Inside of Mobile with the Memphis Blues Again").

"Blowin' in the Wind" was an instant protest anthem for the 1960s, yet sounded as if it had been handed down through the oral tradition from another century, with such lines as "How many times must the cannon balls fly before they're forever banned?"

"Like a Rolling Stone," his takedown of a rich and pampered young woman forced to fend for herself, was pronounced the greatest song of all time by Rolling Stone magazine. The six-minute recording from 1965 is regarded as a landmark that shattered the notion a hit song had to be three minutes.

His career has been such a complicated pastiche of elusive, ever-changing styles that it took six actors—including Cate Blanchett—to portray him in the 2007 movie based on his life, "I'm Not There." He won an Oscar in 2001 for the song "Things Have Changed" and received a lifetime achievement award from the Academy of Recording Arts and Sciences[10] in 1991.

Dylan is the most unorthodox Nobel literature prize winner since 1997, when the award went to Italian playwright Dario Fo, whose works some say also need to be performed to be fully appreciated. By a sad coincidence, Fo died Thursday at 90.

The literature award was the last of this year's Nobel Prizes to be announced. The six awards will be handed out on Dec. 10, the anniversary of prize founder Alfred Nobel's death in 1896.

(From *Chicago Tribune*, Oct. 13, 2016)

📖 NOTES

1. Samuel Beckett 塞缪尔·贝克特，爱尔兰前卫小说家、剧作家、诗人。荒诞派戏剧的重要代表人物，20 世纪最有影响力的作家之一。1969 年荣获诺贝尔文学奖。代表作品有《等待戈多》（*Waiting for Godot*）（1952）。

2. Toni Morrison 托妮·莫里森，美国黑人女作家，编辑，普林斯顿大学（Princeton University）荣誉退休教授。1931 年 2 月 18 日出生于俄亥俄州洛雷恩（Lorain, Ohio）的一个普通工人阶级家庭，四个孩子中排行第二。她的小说以史诗般的主题、生动的对话和对人物细致的刻画见长，代表作品有《最蓝的眼睛》（*The Bluest Eye*）（1970），《苏拉》（*Sula*）（1973），《所罗门之歌》（*Song of Solomon*）（1977），和《宠儿》（*Beloved*）（1987）。她所主编的《黑人之书》（*The Black Book*），被誉为"美国黑人史的百科全书"。1993 年获诺贝尔文学奖。

3. T.S. Eliot 托马斯·斯特尔那斯·艾略特（Thomas Stearns Eliot），英国诗人、散文家、剧作家和文学社会批评家。生于美国密苏里州的圣路易斯，25 岁时移居英国，39 岁时放弃美国国籍，正式加入英国国籍。1915 年发表诗歌《阿尔弗雷德·普鲁弗洛克的情歌》（*The Love Song of J. Alfred Prufrock*），被视为现代派运动的经典之作。1948 年因"对现代诗歌杰出、开拓性的贡献"获得诺贝尔文学奖。代表作品有《荒原》（*The Waste Land*）（1922）、《四个四重奏》（*Four Quartets*）（1945）等。

4. Stockholm 斯德哥尔摩，瑞典首都，享有"北方威尼斯"的美誉。斯德哥尔摩是阿尔弗雷德·诺贝尔（Alfred Nobel）的故乡，也是诺贝尔奖颁奖仪式举行地。

5. Patrick Modiano 帕特里克·莫迪亚诺，法国小说家。与 2008 年诺贝尔文学奖得主勒·克莱齐奥（Jean Marie Gustave Le Clézio）、乔治·佩雷克（Georges Perec）并称为"法国当代作家三杰"。2014 年诺贝尔文学奖获得者，因为他的作品"唤起了对最不可捉摸的人类命运的记忆"。其代表作有《暗店街》（*Rue des boutiques obscures*）（1978）、《八月的星期天》（*Dimanches d'août*）（1986）等。

6. *Trainspotting*《猜火车》，苏格兰著名作家欧文·威尔士所写的一部小说，真实地描绘了苏格兰地区下层人民的生活。

7. Academy of American Poets 美国诗人学会，于 1934 年在纽约成立，会员制的非盈利组织，宗旨是推动诗歌艺术的发展。为推动诗歌阅读，每年四月都会举办全国诗歌月（National Poetry Month）。此外，学会每年主办各种评奖活动，包括华莱士·斯蒂文斯终生成就奖（Wallance Stevens Award）、沃尔特·惠特曼奖（Walt Whitman Award）以及哈罗德·莫顿·兰登翻译奖（Harold Morton Landon Translation Award）等。

8. National Book Critics Circle 美国全国书评家协会，成立于 1974 年。非营利性组织，有近 600 名会员，是美国书评编辑和评论家的专业联盟。每年三月举办一次美国全国书评家协会奖。

9. Herman Melville 赫尔曼·梅尔维尔（1819-1891），美国小说家、诗人。象征主义文学大师，与纳撒尼尔·霍桑（Nathaniel Hawthorne）齐名。生前最后三十年作品几乎被人遗忘，直到 20 世纪 20 年代，作品价值才被美国文学界发现。代表作品有《泰比》（*Typee*）（1846）、《大白鲸》（*Moby-Dick*）（1851）等。

10. Academy of Recording Arts and Sciences 美国国家录音艺术与科学学院，是音乐家、制片人、录音师和录音专业人士的组织，格莱美奖的举办方。成立于 1957 年，总部位于圣莫尼卡。

USEFUL WORDS

accusatory   [əˈkjuːzətəri]   *adj.* containing or expressing accusation 非难的；责问的

acknowledge   [əkˈnɒlɪdʒ]   *v.*   to accept or recognize (as); recognize the fact or existence (of) 认可；承认

ascension   [əˈsenʃn]   *n.*   a movement upward 上升，升高

contend   [kənˈtend]   *v.*   to claim; say with strength 主张；断定

enigmatic   [ˌenɪgˈmætɪk]   *adj.* mysterious and difficult to understand 神秘难解的

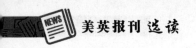

euphoria	[juːˈfɔːriə] *n.*	[U] a feeling of intense happiness and excitement 狂喜
fend	[fend] *v.*	~*for*, to look after oneself without relying on help from anyone else 照料（自己）
lament	[ləˈment] *v.*	to express sadness, regret, or disappointment about sth 感到悲痛；感到遗憾；感到失望
laureate	[ˈlɔːriət] *n.*	winners of the Nobel Prize 诺贝尔奖获奖者
lyrics	[ˈlɪrɪk] *n.*	[C] words of a song 歌词
nominate	[ˈnɒmɪneɪt] *v.*	to suggest or name (someone) officially for election to a position, office, honor, etc. 提名
perennial	[pəˈreniəl] *adj.*	recurring again and again 反复发生的；一再的
present	[ˈpreznt] *v.*	to give (something) away, esp. at a ceremonial occasion 赠送；给予；呈现
prostate	[ˈprɒsteɪt] *n.*	an organ in the body of male mammals situated at the neck of the bladder that produces a liquid which forms part of semen 前列腺
ruling	[ˈruːlɪŋ] *n.*	[C] an official decision made by a judge or court 裁决
shatter	[ˈʃætər] *v.*	to break into a lot of small pieces 粉碎
stature	[ˈstætʃər] *n.*	the importance and reputation that a person have 名望
tweet	[twiːt] *v.*	(a small bird) to make a short, high-pitched sound（小鸟）啾鸣，吱吱地叫
voraciously	[vəˈreɪʃəsli] *adv.*	in an eagerly voracious manner 非常渴望地；贪婪地
wrench	[rentʃ] *v.*	to pull hard with a twisting or turning movement 猛扭，猛拧，猛扳

EXERCISES

I. Vocabulary

Choose among the four alternatives one word or phrase that is closest in meaning to the underlined part in each statement.

1. "Congratulations to one of my favorite poets, Bob Dylan, on a well-deserved Nobel," tweeted President Barack Obama, who in 2012 <u>presented</u> the singer-songwriter with a Presidential Medal of Freedom.

   A. demonstrated   B. represented   C. submitted   D. awarded

2. He is on tour and was <u>scheduled</u> to play in Las Vegas on Thursday night.

   A. forced   B. required   C. arranged   D. docketed

3. "An ill-conceived nostalgia award <u>wrenched from</u> the rancid prostates of senile, gibbering hippies," wrote "Trainspotting" novelist Irvine Welsh.

   A. hurled away   B. twisted off   C. did away with   D. got away from

4. Salman Rushdie, who has written songs with U2's Bono, tweeted that Dylan is "the brilliant <u>inheritor</u> of the bardic tradition."

   A. heir   B. hare   C. inhabitor   D. inherence

5. "Bob Dylan receiving the Nobel Prize in literature <u>acknowledges</u> the importance of literature's oral tradition, and the fact that literature and poetry exists in culture in multiple modes," executive director Jennifer Benka said in a statement.

    A. admits   B. recognizes   C. notices   D. realizes

6. He was <u>nominated</u> for a National Book Critics Circle prize for his memoir, "Chronicles: Volume One."

    A. constituted   B. put forward   C. assigned   D. appointed

7. "Rather doubt Philip Roth and Don DeLillo wish they'd written "Mr. Tambourine Man" vs. AMERICAN PASTORAL and UNDERWORLD,"tweeted Roth biographer Blake Bailey, referring to <u>acclaimed</u> novels by Roth and DeLillo.

    A. derogatory   B. praised   C. laudatory   D. accelerant

8. He has <u>contended</u> that his classic "Blood on the Tracks" album was inspired by the stories of Anton Chekhov.

    A. competed   B. struggled   C. asserted   D. argued

9. The six-minute recording from 1965 is regarded as a landmark that shattered the notion a <u>hit</u> song had to be three minutes.

    A. successive   B. popular   C. well-written   D. elaborate

10. The six awards will be <u>handed out</u> on Dec. 10, the anniversary of prize founder Alfred Nobel's death in 1896.

    A. bestowed   B. distributed   C. allocated   D. portioned

II. Comprehension

Decide whether the following statements are true or false according to the information given in the press clipping. Mark T or F to each statement.

1. The Nobel Prize in Literature has become the world's most prestigious literature prize.

2. Dylan is the first American poet in the 115-year history of the Nobel to win the prize in literature.

3. There is a consensus that rock lyrics can be regarded as art. Therefore, the announcement of Nobel laureate is met with euphoria.

4. Bob Dylan is one of the favorite poets of President Barack Obama's.

5. Dylan was ecstatic when he got the news that he won the Nobel Prize in Literature, so he gave interview immediately.

6. Many people, especially Americans weren't shocked with this year's Nobel announcement because they often quote Dylan as if he were Shakespeare.

7. Bob Dylan is the most influential songwriter of his time, because he brought a new depth, range and complexity to rock lyrics.

8. Being the first American to win the Nobel literature prize, Bob Dylan is an epoch-making musician in the history of the United States of America.

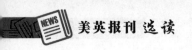

9. Dylan's life has been a hybrid of popular and literary influences. He reads avidly and absorbs every style of American music.

10. "Like a Rolling Stone" is the only poem written by Dylan, depicting a rich and pampered woman forced to look after herself.

III. Questions for discussion

1. Nobel Prize was established by Alfred Nobel for the greatest benefit to mankind. How much do you know about Alfred Nobel and the Nobel Prize? Can you name some Nobel laureates?

2. The link between music and great poetry goes back at least as far as ancient Greece. Yet song lyrics are not generally considered serious literature today. Do you agree that music is an important oral form of literature?

3. For almost a week after Bob Dylan was named the winner of the Nobel Prize in literature, no one knew how he felt about the prestigious award—not even the Nobel judges. They couldn't establish direct contact with Bob Dylan. Comment on Dylan's muted reaction.

4. Some people say, "nobody would expect a singer to win a Nobel." The Japanese writer Haruki Murakami has been rumored to better deserve a Nobel Prize. Do you think so? Why or why not?

5. Chen Xiaoming, a Peking University professor specializing in literary criticism, comments on the win that Dylan just elicits a sense of nostalgia. How do you think about it?

《新闻周刊》简介

《新闻周刊》（*Newsweek*）与《时代周刊》（*Time*）和《美国新闻和世界报道》（*U.S News & World Report*）并称为美国三大周刊，主要报道最新时政新闻，并辟有多个专栏对国际时事、前沿科技、商业、文化和政治进行深度分析，配有大量照片和图表。

《新闻周刊》最初的英语名字是 *News-Week*，创刊于 1933 年 2 月 17 日，创始人为托马斯·马丁（Thomas J.C. Martyn）。1937 年，马尔柯姆·米尔（Malcolm Muir）出任主编及总裁，将 *News-Week* 改成 *Newsweek*，并引入新的署名专栏和国际版面。1961 年，华盛顿邮报公司将其收归旗下。在归属华盛顿邮报公司逾半个世纪之后，《新闻周刊》于 2010 年 8 月 2 日以 1 美元价格出售给 91 岁美国大亨、慈善家西德尼·哈曼（Sidney Harman），期待实现平面媒体向全媒体的华丽转型。受网络发展的冲击，该期刊广告量严重下滑，发行量大幅下跌，读者大量流失。2013 年 12 月 24 日《新闻周刊》发布了创刊 80 年的最后一本纸质杂志后，退出纸媒市场。一年多后，《新闻周刊》再次付梓，回归传统纸媒市场，开始在美国和欧洲发行，首期发行 7 万册。

《新闻周刊》报道犀利、大胆、自由。自由派游说组织"美国民主行动（Americans for Democratic Action）"曾对美国媒体的倾向进行打分——100 分表示立场最倾向自由派；《新闻周刊》高达 72 分，超过《时代周刊》、《纽约时报》等。《新闻周刊》曾在克林顿性丑闻等负面报道中一马当先。

登录《新闻周刊》的官方网站，可以阅读该报刊的电子版。

Unit Eight
Education

报刊英语中的文体风格

　　所谓文体是指文本构成的模式，反映了文本从内容到形式的整体特点，是内容和形式的高度统一。文本内容决定了使用什么样的文体，而文体一旦形成，又反作用于表达内容。英语报刊由于受到大众性、简洁性、趣味性、时效性和客观性的制约，内容要求既要客观报道最新发生的新闻事实，又要文字精炼、通俗易懂、生动有趣。这种文本内容决定了报刊英语独特的文体风格，而报刊英语独特的文体风格又对文本内容起到了一定的制约作用。了解英美报刊的各种文体风格及文字特色，有助于更好地理解英语新闻报道中所要传递的信息，提高美英报刊阅读能力。

　　依照美英报刊的行文结构，报刊英语的文体风格主要体现在以下两个方面：

1 标题精练浓缩

　　报刊标题是新闻内容的精华提炼和高度概括，是新闻报道的点睛之笔。读者通常通过扫视标题来选择自己感兴趣的新闻报道，因此标题是新闻报道给读者的第一直觉。新闻界有"1/3 时间写标题、1/3 时间写导语、1/3 时间写主题"的说法，可见标题的重要性。

　　报刊标题有其独特的排版、文字、语法和修辞等方面的文体特色。常见的英语报刊标题排版有三种：垂直式标题、单行式标题和缩进式标题；垂直式标题重要性不以标题长度来显示，主要通过标题的厚度（多层）来呈现。这方便读者看到大部分标题，能够突出强势新闻，层次分明。《时代周刊》常采用这种排版。单行式标题能简洁地反映消息的主要事实。缩进式标题一般为两到三行，每行向右逐步缩进。这种标题形式新颖，易于激发读者兴趣。英语报刊标题在文字上多使用缩写词、简缩词、小词、短词等；在语法上常使用省略手法、多使用一般现在时态、动词不定式、现在分词和过去分词；常见的修辞有押韵、比喻、典故、习语、对照、夸张等。报刊文章标题在第三单元已详细介绍，在此不再赘述。

2 内容丰富多样

美英报刊的文章内容丰富、涵盖范围广，涉及政治、经济、科技、文化、体育、军事、社会、娱乐、天气等领域。按照报道形式，主要可以分为四类：消息报道、专栏、社论和广告。

（一）消息报道类文体风格

美英报刊消息报道类文章文体最大特点是简洁。简洁的标准是精确、清晰和简练。为了达到这个标准，消息报道通常采用以下两种基本写法：

1. 倒金字塔体（the inverted pyramid style）

倒金字塔体，也称之为倒卷帘体或倒叙法，是英语新闻写作的标准文体或规范形式。当今报纸约有 90% 的消息都是用倒金字塔体写成的。倒金字塔体先写消息中最重要的事实，随之是次要事实，以最次要的事实结尾。倒金字塔体起源于美国南北战争时期，记者稿件通过电报的传送时常中断，为了及时传送消息，记者就把战况写在最前面，然后按照事实的重要性依次写下去。后来这种写法被《纽约时报》的编辑采用，一直使用至今。

倒金字塔体中最重要的是导语，它是整条消息的核心部分，以最有限的版面表达了尽可能多的内容，消息的主体是对导语的扩展。导语中涵盖了新闻六要素：什么人（who），什么事（what），什么时间（when），什么地点（where），为什么（why）和怎么样（how）。比如：

Japan police probe 48 suspicious deaths
after poisoning of two elderly patients

Two men died in a Yokohama hospital after being fed a chemical through IV drips, prompting an investigation into other cases.

Police in Japan are investigating the suspicious deaths of 48 elderly patients at the same hospital after autopsies on two of them revealed they had been poisoned by intravenous drips laced with a chemical found in disinfectant.

The murder investigation initially focused on two men who died within days of each other in the middle of last month. Both had been poisoned, and a tiny hole was found in an IV drip administered to one of them.

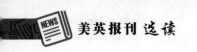

The investigation has widened to include 46 other people who have died since the beginning of July, all of whom were being treated on the same floor of Oguchi hospital in Yokohama as the two murdered men, according to Kyodo.

...

(The Guardian, Oct. 3, 2016)

通过本篇消息报道的导语，读者了解到两名患者在横滨市大口医院（where）注射毒点滴（why）死亡后（when），引发日本警察（who）调查（how）另外 46 人的死因（what）。

2. 编年史体（the chronological style）

编年史体又称为顺序法或者香肠式，按照新闻事实发生的时间顺序来写，这种文体层层推进消息内容，事件高潮多出现在最后，能起到引人入胜的效果。编年史体多用于体育比赛、商业发展或新闻人物讣告类的报道。

（二）专栏类文体风格

专栏是报刊定期出现的一种栏目形式，从消息报道发展而来。它对于活跃报纸版面、丰富报纸内容起着举足轻重的作用。按照刊载时间长短和频率，专栏可以分为长期专栏和短期专栏、定期专栏和不定期专栏；按照谈论话题，又可以分为时政专栏、经济专栏、社会问题专栏、科学专栏、人物专栏、教育专栏等；按照文章体裁分，可分为文学专栏、新闻集纳和通讯专栏、杂文专栏和专栏评论（林克勤，2005）。专栏通常是叙事兼说理，作者个人思想在说理中得到充分表达。在行文风格上，专栏可以采取第一人称，将"我"置身于评论当中，以个人的身份发表见解，这有利于作者与读者之间平等交谈与沟通，避免了生硬之感。

（三）社论类文体风格

社论作为代表媒体观点的评论性文章，堪称报刊的灵魂。一般来说，美英报刊的社论在政治性和社会舆论导向工具性方面有着较大自由度。新闻界的最高奖项普利策奖自 1917 年设立以来，就有社论写作奖（the Pulitzer Editorial Prize）。迄今为止，社论版仍是美国报刊生命力最强的部分。当代美国大中型报纸一般设有每天刊登的社论版，如《纽约时报》几乎每天都会发三四篇社论；《华盛顿邮报》每天也会维持两到三篇。

社论是报刊英语中最严肃的一种文体。黑白灰三色的运用使社论版显得更加理性和庄严。社论版的版头通常与要闻版头版在同一水平线，用词正式、严谨，句式上多用长句和复杂句，在篇章上通常采用提出论点—正 / 反论证—得出结论的结构。美英报刊社论的选题不局限于社会要闻，有些是读者日常生活中会碰到的问题，这不仅不会破坏这一文体的权威性,反而会提高读者对社论的关注度。比如: Make the District a place to die with dignity (*The Washington Post*, Oct. 1, 2016), 探讨的就是重症晚期的病人选择安乐死的自主权问题。即使是严肃的话题,社论作者也会运用幽默等修辞手法使写作风格更加个性化。

（四）广告类文体风格

美英报刊上的广告多使用大幅照片或图画,配以简洁生动的文字。这种图文搭配很好地起到了吸引读者注意力、帮助读者了解广告宣传事物并接受该事物的作用。

报刊英语广告中会频繁使用 make, get, give, have, see, buy, come, go, know, keep 等特定动词和 new, crisp, good, fine, free, big, fresh, great, delicious, real 等形容词。代词如 you 和 we 的使用也要高于一般文体,拉近商家和客户之间的距离。在句法上,广告多使用简单句、分离句、非主谓句、省略句和主动结构,并频繁使用疑问句和祈使句加强广告的说服力。广告的说服性要求广告英语有较强的艺术感染力,所以广告英语是最具修辞色彩的应用文体,像拟人、夸张、比喻、双关等修辞手法常常出现在广告文体中。

比如:

Marry me sounds so much better than just merry christmas. (*Time*, Nov. 30, 2015)

这是永恒印记（Forevermark）钻戒刊登在《时代周刊》的广告。广告语中巧妙地使用了 marry 和 merry 一对音近词,并构成对比。对于恋人来讲,还有什么是比钻戒更好的圣诞节礼物呢? 这则广告成功地激发了读者对永恒印记钻戒的购买欲。

此外,值得一提的是,伴随着网络的飞速发展和传统媒介的数字化,各媒介出现融合的发展趋势,催生了如手机报、电子杂志等新媒介。媒介融合下报刊英语的文体风格也在悄悄发生着变化,新闻的原创性和独家性要求大大提高,文体界限弱化,一篇新闻报道可能兼具两种或以上基本文体的表达特征。"手机文体"、"网络文体"等新型新闻报道文体相继产生。并且图文并重不再是上述报刊广告文体的专属特点,视觉新闻也逐渐成为新闻报道的重要组成部分。正如前文所提到的电报的使用产生了倒金字塔体,科技的每一次突破都会影响到新闻写作,进而影响到报刊英语的文体风格。

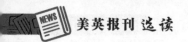

导读 众所周知，每年填写高考志愿都会耗费学生和家长无数的脑细胞，到底该选择什么样的高校？这同样也是困扰美国学生的问题。高校排名在某种意义上代表着学校教学质量的好坏，成为学生选择学校的重要参考依据。

美国高等教育质量评估由认证机构组织实施。认证评估小组由高等教育专家和关心高等教育的公众代表组成。认证机构为非盈利组织，经费来自接受认证的院校，所以文中指出，这好比"狐狸守鸡舍"。随着毕业率和就业前景的低迷，当前的认证系统受到越来越多的质疑。一些大公司，如 JetBlue, Starbucks, Anthem Inc. 等开始与高校合作，注资帮助自己的员工修完学位，他们在高校质量评价中起着越来越重要的作用。

Will employers gain influence in rating the quality of a college degree?

By Jeffrey J. Selingo

It's an anxiety-ridden decision for millions of students each year: how to compare the quality of the colleges they're considering so they can ensure a pay off from what will likely turn out to be the largest investment of their lifetime.

While a plethora of college rankings serve as a crude proxy for quality among thousands of colleges in the U.S., most students don't attend the brand-name institutions that tend to top the rankings. In reality, students are often limited by finances, academics, or family and job obligations and have just a few choices about where to go. According to a recent study by the American Council on Education[1], the average freshman at a public university attends a campus that is within 100 miles of home.

Quality control of higher education is governed by a national network of regional accreditors approved by the U.S. Department of Education[2]. Without accreditation, a college can't access federal financial aid for its students. But accreditors are run and financed by the colleges themselves. It's kind of like the fox guarding the hen house[3]. Colleges determine quality measures they need to ultimately meet.

In recent years, such self-regulation has come under increased scrutiny as questions have been raised about colleges that continue to operate with low graduation rates or that produce graduates deep in debt and without any job prospects. Last month, an advisory board within the Education

Department voted to strip one of the largest accreditors in the country of federal recognition because of its lax oversight.

While there is widespread agreement among college officials and policymakers that the current accreditation system is broken, this is less consensus on what should replace it. While that debate rages on, a group that is the largest consumer of college graduates is increasingly taking on a greater role in quality control: employers.

Employers are beginning to define quality in higher education through their tuition-assistance programs. Some 71 percent of employers offer tuition benefits to their workers, according to Deloitte, and spend nearly $22 billion on the benefit annually. Most employers offer a flat-rate benefit each year and have long controlled *how* that money is used—for classes related to a person's job or other positions in the organization. Now, employers want more oversight in *where* their dollars are used.

"Busy workers don't have time to distinguish between colleges and universities," Bonny Simi, president at JetBlue[4] Technology Ventures, said during a panel discussion I moderated at a U.S. Education Department summit last week. "They probably haven't heard about the problems at some institutions and don't pay attention to graduation rates or accreditation. We're doing that work for them and eliminating some of the complexity."

Simi leads JetBlue Scholars, a new program started by the airline that takes the place of the traditional tuition benefit (JetBlue never offered tuition assistance before starting the program earlier this year). About 6,000 of JetBlue's 18,000 employees have a bachelor's degree, Simi said. Many more have some college credit but no degree.

JetBlue Scholars is designed to get employees with at least 15 credits to complete their degree. The airline works with just seven pre-approved providers, including Straighterline and Saylor.org. They evaluate credits that can be awarded for workers' previous work experience or military service and offer one course at a time to employees.

All the costs are covered by JetBlue. The course work is completed virtually at Thomas Edison State University[5] in New Jersey, which awards the degrees. Some 400 employees are enrolled in the program. Their average age is 42.

JetBlue is far from alone. Other large employers are taking similar approaches in picking one or just a small group of colleges where employees can use their educational benefit.

Starbucks[6], for example, has partnered with Arizona State University[7] to allow employees in the U.S. who have earned at least two years' worth of credits to complete their degree for free

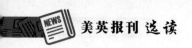

(like JetBlue, just a quarter of Starbucks employees had a bachelor's degree). And Anthem Inc., one of the nation's largest health benefits companies, has joined up with Southern New Hampshire University[8] to offer free self-paced associate and bachelor's degree programs for their employees.

In making these exclusive deals, the companies are often not only negotiating lower tuition prices than they would pay if the employees enrolled on their own, but they are also making judgments about quality. Like students worried about wasting their money at a sub-par college, employers are also trying to reduce their risks.

Given how much money employers spend on tuition benefits, where companies decide to spend their dollars has ripple effects[9]. Already, for-profit colleges have seen their enrollments plummet, in part because fewer adults are using tuition benefits at their institutions.

Employers have long played a part in determining quality in higher education by simply deciding where to recruit traditional undergraduates into full-time jobs. Now as colleges and policymakers debate how to measure outcomes and regulate institutions that receive $150 billion in federal aid each year, employers are making their own assessments that just might put some colleges with poor outcomes out of business.

（From *The Washington Post*, July 8, 2016 ）

NOTES

1. American Council on Education（ACE）美国教育委员会，是美国较有影响力的高等教育组织，于1918 年在华盛顿哥伦比亚特区创立。目前该委员会拥有 1800 所成员机构，包括被认可的学位授予高校和与高等教育相关的协会、组织或企业。ACE 就与高等教育相关的重大问题进行公共政策倡议、调研等，对美国高等教育发展起到了重要的领导作用。

2. U.S. Department of Education（ED）美国教育部，1980 年和其他联邦机构合并成立，截至 2016 年，有大约 4400 名雇员，其宗旨是发展优质教育，并确保人人都有平等受教育的机会。不同于其他国家的教育部，ED 不参与课程标准的设置，主要负责编列联邦补助方案以及执行联邦关于民权及隐私的教育法案。

3. The meaning is to entrust the safety of the chickens to a predator that eats chickens. 此处比喻美国的高等教育质量监管体制存在的问题。大学自己制定自己最终要达到的教学质量标准。

4. JetBlue 捷蓝航空公司。成立于 1999 年 2 月，总部坐落在长岛市，最大枢纽设于约翰肯尼迪国际机场。捷蓝航空公司是一家廉价航空公司也是美国第五大航空公司。"911 事件"后，美国航空业比较低迷，但捷蓝航空仍是几家能盈利的航空公司之一。

5. Thomas Edison State University 托马斯爱迪生州立大学（原 Thomas Edison State College）。创办于 1972 年 7 月 1 日，位于新泽西州特伦顿 (Trenton)，是新泽西州 11 所公立大学之一。提供专科、本科和硕士学位，涵盖 100 多个研究领域。该校于 2015 年由"学院(college)"升格为"大学(university)"。

6. Starbucks 星巴克。全球最大的咖啡连锁公司，成立于 1971 年，总部坐落在美国华盛顿州西雅图市。1998 年进入中国台湾，1999 年 1 月，坐落在北京中国国际贸易中心的星巴克成为中国大陆第一家门店。其商标是一幅 16 世纪斯堪的纳维亚的双尾美人鱼木雕图案。

7. Arizona State University (ASU) 亚利桑那州立大学。创办于 1885 年 2 月 26 日，位于亚利桑那州的州府和最大城市菲尼克斯，是一所研究型公立大学，其学术研究在世界上享有盛名。学校在航天、光学、计算机及商业管理方面均处于美国乃至世界领先地位。

8. Southern New Hampshire University 新罕布什尔南方大学。原名 New Hampshire College，简称 SNHU。创校于 1932 年，位于曼彻斯特市的市郊，离美国商业重镇波士顿仅一个小时的车程。该校被列为是北新英格兰地区最好的商业教育机构，其中 MBA 专业和在线教育项目曾赢得最佳商业教育的荣誉。

9. ripple effects 涟漪效应，连锁反应。

📖 USEFUL WORDS

access	['ækses]	*v.*	to obtain 获取
accreditation	[ə,kredɪ'teɪʃn]	*n.*	the act of granting credit or recognition (especially with respect to educational institution that maintains suitable standards) 委托；委派
consensus	[kən'sensəs]	*n.*	general agreement among a group of people 共识
distinguish	[dɪ'stɪŋgwɪʃ]	*v.*	to mark as different ~ *between/from* 辨别；区分
eliminate	[ɪ'lɪmɪneɪt]	*v.*	to remove completely 根除
evaluate	[ɪ'væljueɪt]	*v.*	to calculate the value or degree of 评定……的价值；评价
exclusive	[ɪk'skluːsɪv]	*adj.*	not divided or shared with other 独有的
flat	[flæt]	*adj.*	(of taxes) not increasing as the amount taxed increases（费率等）固定的
lax	[læks]	*adj.*	not careful or strict about maintaining high standards 松懈的；不严格的
moderate	['mɒdərət]	*v.*	to preside over 主持（会议）
obligation	[,ɑːblɪ'geɪʃn]	*n.*	a duty; necessity 义务；责任；必要
panel	['pænl]	*n.*	a group of speakers who answer questions to inform or amuse the public, usu. on a radio or television show（广播或电视中）答问小组，座谈小组 ~ *discussion*（在听众面前进行的有组织的、预先选定的）专题讨论会；座谈会
plethora	['pleθərə]	*n.*	an amount is greater than you need, want, or can cope with 过剩
plummet	['plʌmɪt]	*v.*	to fall steeply or suddenly 垂直落下，骤然跌落

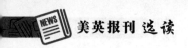
proxy	['prɑːksi] *n.*	[C] a person or thing that is acting or being used in the place of someone or something else 代理人；代替者；替代物
rage	[reɪdʒ] *v.*	to be full of violent force 狂暴；凶猛；剧烈
recruit	[rɪ'kruːt] *v.*	to register formally as a participant or member 招收；招募
scrutiny	['skruːtəni] *n.*	[U] the act of examining something closely (as for mistakes) 仔细研究；仔细观察
strip	[strɪp] *v.*	to take away possessions from someone ~ *of* 剥夺
sub-par	[sʌb'pɑr] *adj.*	under the average standard 平均标准以下的，低于一般水准的

EXERCISES

I. Vocabulary

Choose among the four alternatives one word or phrase that is closest in meaning to the underlined part in each statement.

1. In reality, students are often limited by finances, academics, or family and job <u>obligations</u> and have just a few choices about where to go.

   A. requirements   B. responsibilities   C. categories   D. obscure

2. Colleges determine quality measures they need to <u>ultimately</u> meet.

   A. finally   B. intimately   C. basically   D. ulteriorly

3. Without accreditation, a college can't <u>access</u> federal financial aid for its students..

   A. spend   B. apply   C. approach   D. obtain

4. Last month, an advisory board within the Education Department voted to strip one of the largest accreditors in the country of federal recognition because of its lax <u>oversight</u>.

   A. rule   B. organization   C. supervision   D. procedure

5. Busy workers don't have time to <u>distinguish</u> between colleges and universities.

   A. differentiate   B. discuss   C. distinct   D. disguise

6. They <u>evaluate</u> credits that can be awarded for workers' previous work experience or military service and offer one course at a time to employees.

   A. withdraw   B. assess   C. admit   D. evolve

7. Some 400 employees are <u>enrolled</u> in the program.

   A. passed   B. awarded   C. registered   D. empowered

8. Other large employers are taking similar <u>approaches</u> in picking one or just a small group of colleges where employees can use their educational benefit.

   A. approvals   B. measures   C. adornments   D. methods

9. Already, for-profit colleges have seen their enrollments <u>plummet</u>, in part because fewer adults are using tuition benefits at their institutions.

   A. summit   B. comet   C. drop   D. increase

10. Employers have long played a part in determining quality in higher education by simply deciding where to <u>recruit</u> traditional undergraduates into full-time jobs.

A. employ   B. find   C. persuade   D. introduce

II. Comprehension

Decide whether the following statements are true or false according to the information given in the press clipping. Mark T or F to each statement.

1. It is difficult for millions of students each year to decide which university they should go to.

2. With the financial support from the government, students in the United States can choose brand-name universities as they like.

3. Colleges should determine quality measures they need to ultimately meet, because they know students as well as the requirements of the employers very well.

4. With current accreditation system, even a high-quality college may operate with low graduation rates or produce graduates deep in debt and without any job prospects.

5. Both college officials and policymakers agree that the broken accreditation system should be replaced by a new system.

6. Employers begin to offer money to help their employees to complete their degree.

7. JetBlue is the only one to offer free degree programs for the employees so far.

8. Starbucks has partnered with Southern New Hampshire University to allow employees in the U.S. who have earned at least two years' worth of credits to complete their degree for free.

9. Employers are also making judgments about quality, because they do not want to waste their money.

10. Where companies decide to spend their dollars has a great effect on some colleges or universities.

III. Questions for discussion

1. Choosing colleges is an anxiety-hidden decision to make. Do you still remember the moment you made such a decision?

2. Most students would like to attend the brand-name universities that top the rankings. How about you?

3. It is necessary to rank the universities, because it will help students as a reference. Do you agree? What do you think about the ranking of universities?

4. Some experts suggest the quality of a college/university should be judged by its graduate employment rate. Please comment on this viewpoint.

5. Some big companies, such as JetBlue, Starbucks, and Anthem Inc., cooperate with universities to offer free courses for their employees to complete their degrees. How do you understand this statement?

美英国家的教育体制

美国

美国现行的教育体制有两个理想的前提：一是保证所有人接受小学和初中阶段的基础教育；二是保证所有人都有进一步接受更高教育的机会和权力（理查德、张民强，2004）。这两个前提体现了美国社会对平等观念的追求，也切实体现了美国宪法中人人平等的精神。按照法律规定，任何年龄阶段的美国公民，无论信仰什么宗教，来自什么民族或属于什么阶级，都可以平等地接受教育。这是美国教育制度一个显著的特点，也被称为单轨制。这种单轨制从十九世纪中期就开始实行，保障了美国公民平等受教育的权利。经过一个多世纪的发展，美国教育随着社会变迁和政治、经济等因素的影响，体制逐步趋于完善。

美国的教育以各州为主体负责。联邦政府虽然也设有教育部，但其主要是教育政策研究和咨询机构，负责制定教育政策，并不参与政策的执行，也不监管地方学校。美国学校分为公立、私立两类。公立学校由联邦政府和州政府拨款，须遵守各州议会制定的有关教育法律，接受各州州政府的监督。私立学校根据国家有关规定自行筹集资金，基本不受任何政府监管。

美国教育体制大体可以分为四个阶段：学前教育（pre-school education）、初等教育(elementary education)、中等教育 (secondary education) 和高等教育 (higher education)。学前教育包括保育园（nursery school）和幼儿园（kindergarten）。保育园和幼儿园阶段旨在辅助家庭，帮助儿童养成良好习惯，为儿童进入小学做好身心准备；初等教育通常指五年制的小学，部分州也有六年制。小学教育旨在发展儿童的社会认知，促进儿童心智健康发展，培养儿童的创造力。中等教育包括三年的初中（middle school）和四年的高中（high school）。顺利完成高中学业，就可以拿到高中文凭，未获得高中文凭的学生可以参加 GED（General Educational Development）测试，取得同等学历证书。中小学教育都属于国家义务教育。美国高等教育比较发达，高校数量多、类型多，并且有公立和私立之分。哈佛、耶鲁、麻省理工、斯坦福大学都是比较知名的私立大学。美国高中生毕业后可进入两年制学院（two-year college）的初级学院（junior college），学习相当于四年制大学一、二年级课程，完成高等教育的初级阶段，毕业后拿到副学士学位（Associate Degree）。社区学院（community college）也属于两年制学院，为学生提供职业教育，所开课程为学生毕业后就业作准备。两年制学院目标是推广普及高等教育，招生要求不高，学费低廉，这也是美国高中生能有半数以上进入高等院校的原因之一。美国高等教育还包括四年制学院（four-year college）和综合性大学（comprehensive university）。四年制学院又称之为文理学院，规模较综合性大学小，注重本科教育，没有研究院。但教授对学生关注度高，旨在培养文理兼长、平衡博学的人。学生毕业时可获得学士学位（Bachelor Degree）。综合性大学集本科教育、研究生教育和学术研究为一体，除了提供学士学位以外，还提供硕士研究生学位（Master Degree）和博士研究生学位（Doctor of Philosophy，即 Ph.D）。

美国的教育投资位居世界之首，高投入带来高产出，文化教育的高水平也决定了美国在世界科技方面的领先地位。自 1901 年诺贝尔奖设立至今，约四成诺贝尔奖获得者来自美国，这与健全完善的教育体制密不可分。

英国

大约 6 世纪时，基督教传入英国，学校教育在英国拉开帷幕，并深深烙上宗教的印记。此后随着资本主义的发展和工业革命的出现，教育从宗教化走向世俗化，国家通过出台各种政策为各阶层民众创造接受学校教育的机会。漫长的历史沉淀和一系列的变革使英国的教育体制呈现出传统和创新的双重特点。

按照课程设置和学历划分，英国存在英格兰、威尔士、北爱尔兰教育体制和苏格兰教育体制，本部分主要介绍前者。英国教育体制大体可以分为三个阶段：义务教育（compulsory education）、延续教育（further education）和高等教育（higher education）。英国是世界上最早实施义务教育的国家之一，1870 年便颁布了《初等教育法》，保障儿童和青少年受教育的机会。1973 年《教育法》规定英国义务教育年限为 12 年，5 到 16 岁青少年必须接受义务教育，适龄儿童强制入学，享受全免费的国家福利。16 岁后英国学生可根据自己的情况选择继续学习或工作。继续学习就进入延续教育阶段，这是英国教育体制中比较有特色的部分，它分两个方向：学术方向和职业方向。学术方向重点培养学术研究人才，学生要继续学习两年，并参加高级普通教育证书（General Certificate of Education Advanced Level, 简称 A-level）考试。职业方向重点培养在各行各业中具有专门知识和技能的人才，开设职业课程和部分本科课程，学生修完可以获得 HND (Higher National Diploma)，毕业后可选择就业或继续接受高等教育。英国的高等教育在世界上负有盛名，除白金汉大学是唯一一所私立大学外，其余为公立大学。英国大学由古典大学、近代大学、新大学和开放大学构成。古典大学主要指牛津大学和剑桥大学。19 世纪末以来，牛津和剑桥一直是培养英国统治阶层和科学家的场所。截至 2016 年，从牛津走出 27 名英国首相；从剑桥走出 96 名诺贝尔奖获

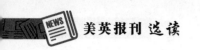

得者。近代大学建立于19世纪上半叶，包括伦敦大学和达勒姆大学。新大学指20世纪60年代由国家创办的大学，包括约克大学等。开放大学是20世纪70年代出现的以广播、电视、函授与暑期学校相结合的成人高等教育机构。英国大学既是教学中心，也是科研中心，提供学士、硕士、博士学位。

正如中国驻英国使馆前教育参赞王百哲所说："英国是一个有悠久教育传统的国家。它的教育体系经过几百年的沿革，相当的完善和复杂，且具有非常大的灵活性。英国的教育是鼓励式教育，不断地鼓励学生独立解决问题，以各种方法激励学生越来越好地学习。"（晓晓，2012）

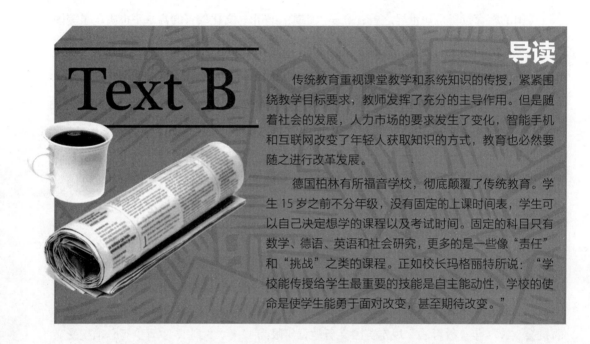

导读

传统教育重视课堂教学和系统知识的传授，紧紧围绕教学目标要求，教师发挥了充分的主导作用。但是随着社会的发展，人力市场的要求发生了变化，智能手机和互联网改变了年轻人获取知识的方式，教育也必然要随之进行改革发展。

德国柏林有所福音学校，彻底颠覆了传统教育。学生15岁之前不分年级，没有固定的上课时间表，学生可以自己决定想学的课程以及考试时间。固定的科目只有数学、德语、英语和社会研究，更多的是一些像"责任"和"挑战"之类的课程。正如校长玛格丽特所说："学校能传授给学生最重要的技能是自主能动性，学校的使命是使学生能勇于面对改变，甚至期待改变。"

No grades, no timetable: Berlin school turns teaching upside down

By Philip Oltermann

A teacher with a pupil at the Evangelical School Berlin Centre. Photograph: Handout

Anton Oberländer is a persuasive speaker. Last year, when he and a group of friends were short of cash for a camping trip to Cornwall, he managed to talk Germany's national rail operator into handing them some free tickets. So impressed was the management with his chutzpah that they invited him back to give a motivational speech to 200 of their employees.

Anton, it should be pointed out, is 14 years old.

The Berlin teenager's self-confidence is largely the product of a unique educational institution that has turned the conventions of traditional teaching radically upside down. At Oberländer's school, there are no grades until students turn 15, no timetables and no lecture-style instructions. The pupils decide which subjects they want to study for each lesson and when they want to take an exam.

The school's syllabus reads like any helicopter parent's[1] nightmare. Set subjects are limited to maths, German, English and social studies, supplemented by more abstract courses such as "responsibility" and "challenge". For challenge, students aged 12 to 14 are given €150 (£115) and sent on an adventure that they have to plan entirely by themselves. Some go kayaking; others work on a farm. Anton went trekking along England's south coast.

The philosophy behind these innovations is simple: as the requirements of the labour market are changing, and smartphones and the internet are transforming the ways in which young people process information, the school's headteacher, Margret Rasfeld, argues, the most important skill a school can pass down to its students is the ability to motivate themselves.

"Look at three or four year olds—they are all full of self-confidence," Rasfeld says. "Often, children can't wait to start school. But frustratingly, most schools then somehow manage to untrain that confidence."

The Evangelical School Berlin Centre (ESBC) is trying to do nothing less than "reinvent what a school is", she says. "The mission of a progressive school should be to prepare young people to cope with change, or better still, to make them look forward to change. In the 21st century, schools should see it as their job to develop strong personalities."

Making students listen to a teacher for 45 minutes and punishing them for collaborating on an exercise, Rasfeld says, was not only out of sync with the requirements of the modern world of work, but counterproductive. "Nothing motivates students more than when they discover the meaning behind a subject of their own accord."

Students at her school are encouraged to think up other ways to prove their acquired skills, such as coding a computer game instead of sitting a maths exam. Oberländer, who had never been away from home for three weeks until he embarked on his challenge in Cornwall[2], said he learned more English on his trip than he had in several years of learning the language at school.

Germany's federalised education structure, in which each of the 16 states plans its own education system, has traditionally allowed "free learning" models to flourish. Yet unlike Sudbury[3], Montessori[4] or Steiner[5] schools, Rasfeld's institution tries to embed student self-determination within a relatively strict system of rules. Students who dawdle during lessons have to come into

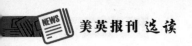

school on Saturday morning to catch up, a punishment known as "silentium". "The more freedom you have, the more structure you need," says Rasfeld.

The main reason why the ESBC is gaining a reputation as Germany's most exciting school is that its experimental philosophy has managed to deliver impressive results. Year after year, Rasfeld's institution ends up with the best grades among Berlin's *gesamtschulen*, or comprehensive schools, which combine all three school forms of Germany's tertiary system[6]. Last year's school leavers achieved an average grade of 2.0, the equivalent of a straight B—even though 40% of the year had been advised not to continue to *abitur*[7], the German equivalent of A-levels[8], before they joined the school. Having opened in 2007 with just 16 students, the school now operates at full capacity, with 500 pupils and long waiting lists for new applicants.

Given its word-of-mouth success, it is little wonder that there have been calls for Rasfeld's approach to go nationwide. Yet some educational experts question whether the school's methods can easily be exported: in Berlin, they say, the school can draw the most promising applicants from well-off and progressive families. Rasfeld rejects such criticisms, insisting that the school aims for a heterogenous mix of students from different backgrounds. While a cross adorns the assembly hall and each school day starts with worship, only one-third of current pupils are baptised. Thirty per cent of students have a migrant background and 7% are from households where no German is spoken.

Even though the ESBC is one of Germany's 5,000 private schools, fees are means tested and relatively low compared with those common in Britain, at between €720 and €6,636 a year. About 5% of students are exempt from fees.

However, even Rasfeld admits that finding teachers able to adjust to the school's learning methods can be harder than getting students to do the same.

Aged 65 and due to retire in July, Rasfeld still has ambitious plans. A four-person "education innovation lab" based at the school has been developing teaching materials for schools that want to follow the ESBC's lead. About 40 schools in Germany are in the process of adopting some or all of Rasfeld's methods. One in Berlin's Weissensee district recently let a student trek across the Alps[9] for a challenge project. "Things are only getting started," says Rasfeld.

"In education, you can only create change from the bottom—if the orders come from the top, schools will resist. Ministries are like giant oil tankers: it takes a long time to turn them around. What we need is lots of little speedboats to show you can do things differently."

(From *The Guardian*, July 1, 2016)

NOTES

1. helicopter parent 直升机父母，指那些像直升机一样整天盘旋在孩子的身边，时刻等待孩子召唤的父母。凡事代劳、过分操控只能使子女的自理能力低下。

2. Cornwall 康沃尔，位于英格兰西南部。西北毗邻凯尔特海，南部靠近英吉利海峡，东部是塔玛河流经的德文郡。康沃尔拥有 536000 人口，占地 3563 平方公里。特鲁罗是康沃尔的唯一城市。

3. Sudbury (University of Sudbury) 萨德伯里大学，创立于 1913 年，位于加拿大安大略省萨德伯里，是一所罗马天主教大学。英语和法语双语授课，开设课程有宗教研究、哲学、土著研究和民俗学（法语），是劳伦森大学联合会的创始成员。

4. Montessori 蒙台梭利，生于 1870 年 8 月 31 日，意大利第一位女医学博士、杰出的幼儿教育家，创立了蒙台梭利教育法。代表作品有《发现孩子》、《童年的秘密》、《教育人类学》等。蒙台梭利认为要为儿童准备可以最大限度进行自由活动的环境，不能盲目限制儿童的自由行动，要鼓励孩子自由探索与发展，滋养孩子的好奇心。

5. Steiner 斯坦纳，生于 1861 年 2 月 27 日，奥地利社会哲学家。创立了人智学（anthroposophy），主张用人的本性、心灵感觉和独立于感官的纯思维与理论解释生活。他提出要教师管理学校，开设需要学生动脑的课程，培养学生的想象力，追求真理和责任感。

6. Germany's tertiary system 第三级高等教育。德国教育共分为五个部分，第一级基础教育，第二级初阶，第二级进阶，第三级高等教育，以及衍生教育。在第三级高等教育中，大约有 400 所高等院校，包括综合大学，神学院和教育学院，69% 的学生在这些学校里接受教育。共有 215 所应用技术大学，约有 29% 的学生在此学习。其余为艺术院校，约有 2% 的学生在艺术类院校就读。

7. *abitur* 德国中学生的毕业高考，其重要性不亚于中国高考。Abitur 成绩不是一次考试的成绩，而是综合高中阶段最后两年内不同学科的成绩和最后的毕业考试成绩加权计算累计后得出来的一个复合成绩。1 分是最高分，4.0 分以上为不及格。

8. A-levels，A-level 相关课程（详见 P181），A-level 成绩是英国大学入学考试课程以及大学招收新生的入学标准。A-levels 被全球 110 多个国家和地区认可，因此有人将其戏称为"世界高考"。

9. Alps，阿尔卑斯山，欧洲最高、最长的山脉，呈弧形，长约 1200 千米，最高峰为勃朗峰（Mount Blanc），海拔约 4810 米。跨越八个国家：奥地利、法国、德国、意大利、列支敦士登、摩纳哥、斯洛文尼亚和瑞士。被世人称为"大自然的宫殿"和"真正的地貌陈列馆"。

USEFUL WORDS

adorn	[əˈdɔːn]	*v.*	to make sth look more beautiful 装饰
chutzpah	[ˈxʊtspə]	*n.*	[U] the quality of being not afraid or embarrassed to do or say things that shock, surprise, or annoy other people 胆识
collaborate	[kəˈlæbəreɪt]	*v.*	to work together, especially on a book or on some research（尤指著书或进行研究时的）合作

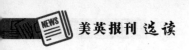

convention	[kən'venʃn] *n.*	(an example of) generally accepted social behaviour 惯例；习俗
counterproductive	[ˌkaʊntərprə'dʌktɪv] *adj.* tending to hinder the achievement of a goal 产生相反结果的
dawdle	['dɔːdl] *v.*	to waste tie; be slow 混日子；磨蹭
embark	[ɪm'baːk] *v.*	to set out on (an enterprise or subject of study) ~ *on* 开始从事
embed	[ɪm'bed] *v.*	to fix firmly and deeply 嵌入
exempt	[ɪg'zempt] *v.*	to state officially that someone is not affected by a particular rule, duty, or obligation ~*from* 免除
heterogenous	[ˌhetə'rɒdʒənəs] *adj.* not originating within the body; of foreign origin 异种的；异源的
kayak	['kaɪæk] *v.*	to travel in a small canoe 划独木舟
motivate	['moʊtɪveɪt] *v.*	to give an incentive for action 激发…的积极性
persuasive	[pər'sweɪsɪv] *adj.* likely to persuade a person to believe or do a particular thing 有说服力的
radically	['rædɪkli] *adv.*	thoroughly, completely 彻底；完全
speedboat	['spiːdboʊt] *n.*	a small power-driven boat built for high speed 快速汽艇
supplement	['sʌplɪmənt] *v.*	to make additions to 补足，增补
syllabus	['sɪləbəs] *n.*	(*pl. -buses or -bi*) an arrangement of subjects for study, esp. A course of studies leading to an examination 教学大纲；课程提纲
tertiary	['tɜːʃəri] *adj.*	third in order, third in importance, or at a third stage of development. 第三的
transform	[træns'fɔːrm] *v.*	to change completely in form, appearance, or nature 改变；转变
trek	[trek] *v.*	to journey on foot, especially in the mountains 徒步旅行

EXERCISES

I. Vocabulary

Choose among the four alternatives one word or phrase that is closest in meaning to the underlined part in each statement.

1. The Berlin teenager's self-confidence is largely the product of a unique educational institution that has turned the <u>conventions</u> of traditional teaching radically upside down.

   A. assemblies　　　B. patterns　　　C. agreements　　　D. custom

2. The school's <u>syllabus</u> reads like any helicopter parent's nightmare.

   A. curriculum　　　B. name　　　C. summary　　　D. sketch

3. Set subjects are limited to maths, German, English and social studies, <u>supplemented</u> by more abstract courses such as "responsibility" and "challenge".

   A. subscribed　　　B. supplied　　　C. complemented　　　D. accelerated

4. But <u>frustratingly</u>, most schools then somehow manage to untrain that confidence.

   A. dishearteningly　　　　　　B. disappointingly

   C. unexpectedly　　　　　　D. excitingly

5. Making students listen to a teacher for 45 minutes and punishing them for <u>collaborating</u> on an exercise, Rasfeld says, was not only out of sync with the requirements of the modern world of work, but counterproductive.

   A. laboring   B. cooperating   C. confirming   D. surpassing

6. Germany's federalised education structure, in which each of the 16 states plans its own education system, has traditionally allowed "free learning" models to <u>flourish</u>.

   A. glamour   B. foster   C. flush   D. thrive

7. Students who <u>dawdle</u> during lessons have to come into school on Saturday morning to catch up, a punishment known as "silentium".

   A. dismiss   B. absent   C. linger   D. dwell

8. The main reason why the ESBC is gaining a reputation as Germany's most exciting school is that its experimental philosophy has managed to <u>deliver</u> impressive results.

   A. present   B. impress   C. restrict   D. disclose

9. Even though the ESBC is one of Germany's 5,000 private schools, fees are <u>means</u> tested and relatively low compared with those common in Britain, at between €720 and €6,636 a year.

   A. methods   B. income   C. classifications   D. varieties

10. About 40 schools in Germany are in the process of <u>adopting</u> some or all of Rasfeld's methods.

   A. adapting   B. adjusting   C. accepting   D. absorbing

II. Comprehension

Decide whether the following statements are true or false according to the information given in the press clipping. Mark T or F to each statement.

1. Anton succeeded in getting some free tickets from Germany's national rail operator to continue his camping trip to Cornwall.

2. ESBC's curriculum is welcomed by helicopter parents.

3. The mission of a traditional school should be to prepare young people to cope with change, or better still, to make them look forward to change.

4. According to Rasfeld, the most important responsibility of school is to motivate students.

5. The best way of motivating students is to let them discover the meaning behind a subject voluntarily.

6. Students in ESBC enjoy absolute freedom because the school advocates students' self-determination.

7. ESBC is so innovative that few students would like to go there.

8. Educational experts assert that ESBC's methods can easily be exported.

9. According to the news, it is very expensive to study in ESBC.

10. It is difficult to find teachers who are able to adjust to the school's learning methods.

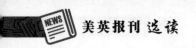
III. Questions for discussion

1. Before entering universities, we had received elementary and secondary education. Say something about your educational experience.

2. Can you briefly introduce to the Western people the education system in China?

3. In China, attitudes towards National Matriculation Test (NMT) vary from person to person. Some people believe that NMT should be abolished because it is too stressful. Some others say it is the only fair way for students and hence, it should be maintained. What's your opinion?

4. If you are short of cash for a camping trip, a situation that Anton Oberländer and his friends have encountered, what would you do?

5. Do you think it is necessary to advocate innovation in Chinese education? Why or why not?

《时代周刊》简介

　　《时代周刊》（Time），简称为"时代"，创刊于 1923 年 3 月 3 日，是美国三大时事性周刊之一，在美国乃至全世界都颇有影响力。其报道内容广泛，立足美国、关注全球。对国际问题发表主张，并跟踪国际重大事件，有世界"史库"之称。

　　《时代周刊》最初的名字是《事实》（Facts），创始人为布里顿·哈登（Briton Haddon）和亨利·卢斯（Henry Luce）。《时代周刊》强调简洁性，忙人一个小时内也可以读完，使用口号"简约《时代》，方以遣暇"（"Take Time—It's Brief"）。写给"忙人"看的宗旨是使读者能迅速地找到自己最需要了解和关注的报道，在最短的时间获得最多的信息量。《时代》满足了读者的要求，自 20 世纪 30 年代后迅速流行起来。

　　《时代周刊》最初的写作文体极为独特，常用倒装句。标志性的红色边框从 1927 年使用至今，期间只变过四次：第一次是 9-11 恐怖袭击发生之后，使用黑色边框以示哀悼；第二次是为 2008 年 4 月 28 日的地球日使用绿色边框；第三次是 2011 年 9 月 19 日，使用金属银色纪念 9.11 十周年；第四次是 2012 年 12 月 31 日，奥巴马当选《时代》年度人物，同样使用了银色边框。《时代周刊》对新闻的关注极其敏锐，记者的身影和笔端触及到世界的每一个角落。除了美国主版、国际版，《时代》还有出版于伦敦的欧洲版（Time Europe，旧称 Time Atlantic），出版于香港的亚洲版（Time Asia）和出版于悉尼的南太平洋版。涉及外国国家时，《时代周刊》会拿美国国内版图和它们的版图比较，援引它们的政治情况，追溯报道事件的来龙去脉，并借助图表等，帮助读者理解复杂的国际问题。

《时代》拥有全球最大的新闻周刊发行量，至 2016 年，已发行三百多万册，读者达到两千六百万。特色专刊有 20 世纪最有影响力的 100 人（ *Time 100* ）、年度风云人物（ *Person of the Year* ）和红叉封面(*Red X covers*)。也曾为迈克尔·杰克逊(Michael Jackson)和史蒂夫·乔布斯（ Steve Jobs ）创办过纪念特刊。

登录《时代》的官方网站，可以阅读该报刊的电子版。

Unit Nine Travel

报刊英语中的修辞

修辞就是在语言使用过程中，根据交际的内容、语言环境，运用多种语言手段和表达方式以达到更好语言效果的一种语言活动，使语言具有美感。报刊英语中经常会灵活运用一些修辞手段，增加文章的生动性和有趣性，并达到用经济的语言表达丰富内容的文体效果。本部分将就报刊英语中常用的几种修辞进行分析，探讨修辞效果。

1 比喻

比喻是报刊英语中常见的一种修辞，能使语言更加精炼和生动。报刊英语的显著特点就是"大量使用比喻性同义词，大量使用各种比喻手段，以借助于某些有比喻意义的文体来满足表意、修辞以及文体风格的需要。"（从莱庭，1999）下面将分别以明喻、暗喻、借喻和提喻几种常见的修辞手段逐一举例说明。

（一）明喻（simile）

两个不同的事物具有某种相似的特征，从而加以比较，本体和喻体具有某种共同特征，并且同时出现。报刊英语中常用的明喻词有 as, like 等。明喻的使用可以让表达更生动形象。比如：

X Factor mogul Simon Cowell has also joined the remain camp, pointing to the idea of being isolated <u>as an island</u>. (*The Mirror*, June 24, 2016)

此例句指的是英国著名音乐人西蒙·考威尔对英国是留在欧盟还是脱离欧盟的态度。他指出如果脱欧，那么英国就会被孤立得像"一座岛屿"，表明其留欧的态度。

Heidelberg curls up against the Neckar River in a narrow pass between a pair of mountains, <u>like a flower</u> preserved between two books. (*The New York Times*, Aug. 16, 2016)

这个例句中，把"海德尔堡"比喻为"藏于两书之间的一朵花"，明喻词为 like，形象地描绘出了 Heidelberg 周围和谐美丽的景致。

（二）隐喻（metaphor）

隐喻是报刊英语中比较常见，并且涵盖范围很广的一种比喻，又被称为"简缩了的明喻"，指的是两个不同的事物也具有某种相似之处，但是由于该相似性是隐含的，所以不用像 as、like 这样的比喻词，而是直接把本体说成喻体，直接把复杂、抽象的本体喻化为人们熟悉的喻体，变抽象为具体，使呆板的本体变得更有可感性，进而增强语言的表现力。比如：

To millions of adventurers and campers, America's national forests are a boundless backyard for hiking trips, rafting, hunting and mountain biking. (*The New York Times*, Aug. 21, 2016)

此句中，相对于"徒步旅行者、漂流者、打猎者和山地自行车者"而言，"美国的国家森林"就是"无垠的后院"。

Trump's bad week is a nightmare for the GOP (*The Washington Post*, Sept. 30, 2016)

此句中，因为总统候选人唐纳德·特朗普的"漏税事件"被曝光，对于美国共和党而言，"特朗普糟糕的一周"就像"一个噩梦"。

"Republicans are a bunch of frightened rabbits," Giuliani said. "Unfortunately, we have a party made up of a bunch of people who get frightened very easily, and their hands start to shake whenever something happens that they don't like." (*The Washington Post*, Sept. 30, 2016)

此句把美国的"共和党人"比喻成"一群惊恐的兔子"。

（三）借喻（metonymy）

借喻是通过相近的联想，不直接说出人和事物的名称，而是"借一事物的名称指代另一事物"（周学艺，2010）。"是新闻写作中常用的修辞手段，它可以节省篇幅，避免重复，增加语言的形象性和表达效果"（端木义万，2013）。如用地名代指机构，Whitehall 指代"英国政府首相办公室所在地"。Pentagon 指代"美国国防部"，Big Apple 指代"纽约城"。

"They support their schools, they support their infrastructure, they support the military, but the billionaires, no, they don't have to do that because they have their friends on Capitol Hill. They pay zero in taxes, " Sanders told ABC on Sunday. (*The Guardian*, Oct. 2, 2016)

此例句中，"Capitol Hill"是"国会山"，在新闻报道中，通常代指"美国国会"。

Big Data Shows How Wall Street Profited From the Financial Crash (*Newsweek*, Oct. 2, 2016)

在这个例句中，借用 "Wall Street"（华尔街）指"美国的金融市场"，这也是新闻中

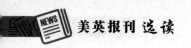

常用的借喻方式。

（四）提喻 (synecdoche)

又称为举隅法，借助于两事物的部分相似，用一事物 A 代指另一事物 B，但不直接说事物 B 的名称。通常是以局部代表全部或以全部指代部分，用具体代替抽象，单个代指类别，或者反之。

Trump went into the first presidential debate Monday night in Hempstead, N.Y., with swagger, ahead or tied in some national and battleground-state polls and, momentarily at least, relatively disciplined on the stump. But his performance was widely panned and revealed his thin skin. (*The Washington Post*, Sept. 30, 2016)

此例句中，用 "thin skin" 代表特朗普的"薄弱点"。在美国总统竞选过程中，和 Hillary Clinton 的第一轮总统辩论时，特朗普因表现欠佳，饱受抨击，再次暴露了他演讲中的跑题、重复等薄弱点。

More than three years after the Boston Marathon bombing, the story of the 2013 deadly attack on the race and its aftermath is making its way to both the big and small screens. (*Reuters*, Sept. 30, 2016)

此报道中，用 "big and small screens" 来代指"各种大大小小的媒体"都对 2013 年波士顿马拉松爆炸事件进行报道。

②委婉语 (euphemism)

委婉语修辞，指使用较含蓄的词来表达不便直言或不文雅的事情，从而避免粗俗和不雅，即"原本用来谈论生理疾病、死、卖淫、同性恋等令人尴尬、不快或禁忌的话题。有的较文雅礼貌，有的含糊其辞，以使听者顺耳，读者舒服"（周学艺，2010）。这是报刊英语中委婉语修辞正面的、积极的意义，通常社会领域中的委婉语属于这类，如"残疾人"一般不会称为 the disabled, the retarded 等，而是称为 the physically challenged 或 the physically inconvenient。准确理解这些委婉语的意义有助于对新闻内容的正确把握。

Children are often charged hundreds of dollars to join soccer clubs in the United Kingdom. In some of the more disadvantaged neighborhoods, it can be nearly impossible to find parks or public spaces that are suited to play in, members of the soccer club said. (*The Washington Post*, Oct.1, 2016)

例句中，"the more disadvantaged neighborhoods" 实际上指的是"贫民区"。原文"更不利的社区"委婉地表达了"该社区比较贫穷"之义，因此"经济上不足以提供场所供孩子练习足球"。

在政治领域内,委婉语通常是政客们为其政治服务的一种手段。有人也会故意歪曲事实,将丑陋隐匿于看似美好的大话、空话之中。这是委婉语修辞在新闻报道中负面消极的意义。

🔲3 排比 (parallelism)

排比的修辞手法是指一组三个或三个以上的短语或句子并列使用,通常结构相同或相似,内容相关,语气一致,字数大体相等。排比通常结构工整对仗,节奏鲜明,气势较强,能起到很好的强调效果。该修辞格多用于报刊文章、政治演讲、广告等文体中。

"We are going to make America wealthy again," Trump said as he wrapped up. "We are going to make America strong again. We are going to make America powerful again. We are going to make America safe again. And we are going to make America great again." (*The Washington Post*, Oct. 2, 2016)

特朗普用一系列的 "We are going to make America" 来表达将使美国变得更好的决心,以求赢得更多的选票。

"Maybe we'll have a good relationship. Maybe we'll have a horrible relationship. Maybe we'll have a relationship right in the middle." (*The Christian Science Monitor*, Oct. 5, 2016)

这也是美国共和党总统候选人特朗普在谈及美国与俄罗斯关系时用的一系列排比,意指在他看来,美国同俄罗斯未来关系具有不确定性及多种可能性。

🔲4 夸张 (hyperbole)

夸张是有意夸大或缩小所叙述之事,以达到突出事物的本质特征,强化表达效果的目的。报刊英语中夸张修辞使用极为频繁,一定程度上是报刊英语追求新奇的手段之一。夸张通常运用充满想象力、言过其实的语言来突出强调效果。

Philippine President Rodrigo Duterte raised the rhetoric over his bloody anti-crime war to a new level Friday, comparing it to Hitler and the Holocaust and saying he would be "happy to slaughter" 3 million addicts. (*Los Angeles Times*, Sept. 30, 2016)

此句谈到菲律宾总统杜特尔特对于毒品犯罪的坚决态度,表示要像希特勒和犹太人大屠杀那样,不惜杀害 300 万人,夸张的手法表现出其要打赢这场战争的决心。

除上面列举的几种外,报刊英语中的修辞还包括音韵修辞、拟人、典故、矛盾修辞法等多种修辞手法。新闻报道中,需要根据具体的语境选择合适的修辞。修辞手法的运用确实不仅能帮助作者用更生动形象的语言来表达主题,而且能使读者有效提高阅读的兴趣并充分领会文章的内涵。

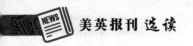
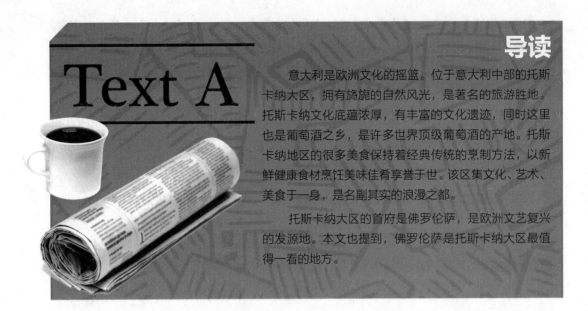

Text A

导读

意大利是欧洲文化的摇篮。位于意大利中部的托斯卡纳大区，拥有旖旎的自然风光，是著名的旅游胜地。托斯卡纳文化底蕴浓厚，有丰富的文化遗迹，同时这里也是葡萄酒之乡，是许多世界顶级葡萄酒的产地。托斯卡纳地区的很多美食保持着经典传统的烹制方法，以新鲜健康食材烹饪美味佳肴享誉于世。该区集文化、艺术、美食于一身，是名副其实的浪漫之都。

托斯卡纳大区的首府是佛罗伦萨，是欧洲文艺复兴的发源地。本文也提到，佛罗伦萨是托斯卡纳大区最值得一看的地方。

Plan the ultimate Tuscany[1] trip, from private cooking lessons to hot spring dips

By Alex Palmer

There's no shortage of highlights that make Tuscany an ideal place to visit—the cypress-accented landscape, friendly locals, and a wealth of history, to name a few. But a top draw for anyone visiting this region of central Italy is the food.

Tuscan food isn't fussy. Most dishes are just a few ingredients, prepared quick without elaborate presentation. But those ingredients are fresh and local—often sourced from farms a few miles away—and that preparation follows customs that have developed over centuries. It's about as far as you can get from the revolving door of trends and hot new restaurants that define New York's foodie scene.

While Italy's efficient train system makes it easy to get from one major city to another, to experience the Tuscan countryside, rent a car. This allows you to visit hole-in-the-wall restaurants and wineries, trace the rolling hills and expansive valleys, and spot local wildlife. (Yes, the roads are narrow and windy, but it's worth it.)

Book a few nights at the Renaissance Tuscany[2] (renaissancetuscany.com) for a taste of the Tuscan countryside. Set atop a hillside on the Il Ciocco estate, the hotel showcases the local landscape, with stunning views of the Apuan Alps[3] and the Tuscan-Emilian Apennines mountain range. And the property's menu includes dishes created from local ingredients, like gnocchi made from chestnut flour or a plate of cured meats including hare and wild boar, caught on the Il Ciocco property.

For a deeper dive into Tuscan cuisine, the Renaissance Tuscany offers a menu of indigenous culinary experiences. Those who sign up accompany chef Alessandro Manfredini on a trip to the farmers market in the nearby medieval city of Barga, selecting ingredients based on your own preferences. Then join him in the kitchen to whip up a multi-course Italian feast (we made fresh tagliatelle and veal scallopini with local porcini mushrooms) that can be enjoyed for lunch or dinner.

This private cooking experience with the chef for dinner only (includes everything except the visit to the market with the chefs) costs about $166 per person at current exchange rates. The full experience, with a market visit, ranges from $200 to $266 per person, depending on the day of the week.

Of course, no Italian meal is complete without wine, so pay a visit to Podere Cóncori (podereconcori.com), a family-owned biodynamic[4] winery just a few minutes from the Renaissance Tuscany. While the Garfagnana region, where Podere Cóncori is located, is not known for its wines as much as other parts of Tuscany, this winery has created a thriving operation, with its aromatic Melograno ("pomegranate" in Italian) well worth trying.

About 30 miles south of Barga lies the provincial capital of Lucca[5], a rampart-enclosed city of cobblestone streets and clock towers that offers local crafts and high-end shopping that could compete with Fifth Ave. For lunch, stop by Buca di Sant'Antonio (bucadisantantonio.com), which has been serving terrific Tuscan food since 1782. Copper pots and brass musical instruments decorate the walls and ceiling, and local specialties such as prosciutto toscano and mushroom risotto grace the menu.

As charming as Lucca is, the must-see city in Tuscany remains Florence[6], birthplace of the Renaissance and home to Michelangelo's[7] "David" statue, the famed Ponte Vecchio bridge, and the astonishing Duomo. It also houses no shortage of excellent restaurants, from the friendly and delicious Taverna del Bronzino (built in the former studio of a Renaissance artist; tavernadelbronzino.com), to the high-end Il Santo Graal (ristorantesantograal.com) in the city's trendy Oltrano neighborhood, on the south side of the Arno River.

There is so much to explore in Florence that visitors would be wise to stay here for at least two or three days—or better yet, stay just outside the city, at the Il Salviatino (salviatino.com). This luxury hotel built in a refurbished 15th century palazzo sits less than three miles from Florence,

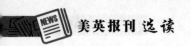
providing terrific views of the city from the serenity of an expansive Italian garden—and a free shuttle to and from Florence every hour.

Visitors can enjoy terrific Tuscan food without leaving the property. Il Salviatino's La Cucina restaurant, set in the stunning library of the hotel, serves a rotating menu of classic dishes, such as gnudi with ricotta and spinach, as well as pici (a thick noodle pasta you're likely only to find in the area) with porcini mushrooms and wild fennel. But any meat-eater will want to order the bistecca alla Florentina—a Tuscan T-bone steak, prepared rare, sliced tableside and drizzled with olive oil. It's a substantial meal, even for two people, but for fans of steak, it will be a culinary highlight.

One of Tuscany's most popular natural resources is its hot springs. Going back centuries, locals have enjoyed the comfort and healing properties of the mineral-rich water. The Lunigiana territory in the north and the Val d'Orcia region in the south boast dozens of public springs where visitors can drop in for the day.

But for those interested in experiencing Tuscan hot springs on a more involved level, consider checking in at Fonteverde Tuscan Resort & Spa (fonteverdespa.com). It offers eight pools infused with mineral water from hot springs, including an expansive infinity pool, spiral-shaped "bioacquam" pool, and even a small wading pool just for dogs.

Wellness is on the menu as well, with health-oriented spreads for breakfast and lunch, including fresh juice, salads, and fish. And don't miss aperitivo hour. It's a much classier version of American happy hour, where instead of discounted drinks, you sip on cocktails like Negronis and snack on small appetizers—olives, potato chips, or finger sandwiches. It's hard to beat the aperitivo hour at Fonteverde's Il Falconiere Bar.

The property is about a 45-minute drive from a few of Italy's best wine regions, such as Montalcino and Montepulciano. The latter is a medieval city dotted with restaurants, shops, and wine stores, most of which offer free tastings of the area's famed Vino Nobile wine, as well as pairings with cheese or local cured meats.

Consider going out of the city to visit one of the many wineries in the area, such as Bindella (bindella.it). Opened about three decades ago, it has established a reputation for itself as a local favorite. In a region with so much history and tradition, there's still room for new arrivals.

(From *New York Daily News*, July 14, 2016)

NOTES

1. Tuscany 托斯卡纳，意大利中部的一个大区，其首府是佛罗伦萨，意大利文艺复兴时期的发源地。以风光秀丽，物产丰富及其悠久的历史而闻名，盛产红酒。

2. Renaissance Tuscany 指的是 Renaissance Tuscany II Ciocco Resort & Spa 托斯卡纳西科度假酒店。位于托斯卡纳大区的中世纪小镇——巴尔加（Barga）的山坡上，是一家豪华型酒店，有现代化的配置，酒店周围环绕着占地 600 公顷的庄园。

3. Apuan Alps 阿普安阿尔卑斯山（意大利语：Alpi Apuane），意大利托斯卡纳大区（Tuscany）北部的一个山脉，是亚平宁山脉（Apennine Mountains）的一部分。

4. biodynamics 生物动力学，针对农业发展方向问题，奥地利社会哲学家鲁道夫·施泰纳博士（Dr. Rudolf Steiner）在 1924 年所作的一系列讲座中，首次提出用传统的肥料代替化学肥料和杀虫剂，从而建立可持续发展的生态农业，也就是生物动力农业。此外，它还强调农业是一个完整有机的系统，包括土壤、月亮，行星等都是有机联系的整体，动植物的生长要与这些因素相配合，建立良好的、相互促进的平衡关系。本文提到的 Biodynamic winery（生物动力葡萄酒），是生物动力农业的一种。近年来，生物动力农业很流行，但关于此种方法是否值得推崇，一直存有争议。

5. Lucca 卢卡，意大利中部城市，位于托斯卡纳大区，是比萨和佛罗伦萨之间的一座平原小城，也是卢卡省的省会城市，建于公元前 180 年，古迹保存比较完善，著名的景点有卢卡城墙。

6. Florence（意大利语为 Firenze）佛罗伦萨（旧译"翡冷翠"），不仅是托斯卡纳区的首府，也是文艺复兴的发源地和中心，是意大利最美丽的城市之一。存有大量的艺术作品、精美建筑、以及历史遗迹，号称是"中世纪的雅典"。

7. Michelangelo 米开朗基罗（1475-1654），意大利文艺复兴时期著名的雕塑家、画家、建筑师和诗人，对于西方艺术的发展起着无可比拟的影响。代表性的雕塑作品有两个，一个是《圣殇》（Pieta），另外一个就是本文提到的《大卫》（David）。

USEFUL WORDS

accent	['æksent]	*v.*	to emphasize a part of sth; emphasize a word, sound, or feature 强调；突出 accented 强调的；突出的
aromatic	[ˌærə'mætɪk]	*adj.*	fragrant, spicy 芳香的，有香味的
cobble	['kɒbl]	*n.*	(also 亦作 cobblestone) stone worn round and smooth by water and used for paving 由水冲磨成圆而光滑的石头（用以铺路），鹅卵石
dip	[dɪp]	*n.*	act of bathing, putting in or into a liquid for a moment 浸泡，浸，蘸
elaborate	[ɪ'læbərət]	*adj.*	very detailed and complicated; carefully prepared and finished 复杂的；精心制作的
expansive	[ɪk'spænsɪv]	*adj.*	able or tending to expand or characterized by expansion; spacious 易膨胀的；广阔的

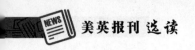
fennel	['fenl] *n.*	yellow-flowered herb, used as a flavouring 茴香（用来调味）
foodie	['fuːdi] *n.*	a person devoted to refined sensuous enjoyment (especially good food and drink) 美食家
fussy	['fʌsi] *adj.*	(of dress, style, etc) over-ornamented; having too many unimportant details, etc. (指衣服、文体等) 装饰过分的；有太多不重要细节的
gnocchi	['njɒki] *n.*	(Italian) a small dumpling made of potato or flour or semolina that is boiled or baked and is usually served with a sauce or with grated cheese （面粉或马铃薯做的）汤团；团子
healing	['hiːlɪŋ] *adj.*	tending to cure or restore to health 有治疗功能的，能治愈的
highlight	['haɪlaɪt] *n.*	luminous area on a photograph, picture, etc which shows reflected light; reflection of light on a shiny object; (fig) most conspicuous or prominent part （通常用复数）像片、图画等光亮的部分；闪光灯上光的反射；（喻）最显著的部分；最精彩的部分
hole-in-the-wall		*adj.* small, unpretentious, out-of-the-way 狭小的，简陋的
indigenous	[ɪn'dɪdʒənəs] *adj.*	(~ to) native, belonging naturally 土生的，天生的
infuse	[ɪn'fjuːz] *v.*	to fill, as with a certain quality 注入，倾注
refurbish	[ˌriː'fɜːrbɪʃ] *v.*	to make clean or bright again; make or polish (as if new) 使清洁；翻新，革新
revolve	[rɪ'vaːlv] *v.*	(cause to) go round in a circle （使）旋转
serene	[sə'riːn] *adj.*	clear and calm; tranquil 晴朗的；宁静的
serenity	[sə'renəti] *n.*	宁静，沉着
substantial	[səb'stænʃl] *adj.*	solidly or strongly built or made; large, considerable; possessing considerable property; well-to-do; essential; virtual 构造牢固的，坚实的；大的，相当可观的；拥有相当财富的，富有的；实际上的，大体上的，实质的
whip	[wɪp] *v.*	(~ up) to prepare or cook quickly or hastily 快速地准备或做饭

EXERCISES

I. Vocabulary

Choose among the four alternatives one word or phrase that is closest in meaning to the underlined part in each statement.

1. Plan the ultimate Tuscany trip, from private cooking lessons to hot spring dips.

   A. erosion   B. bathing   C. scouring   D. rinsing

2. There's no shortage of highlights that make Tuscany an ideal place to visit—the cypress-accented landscape, friendly locals, and a wealth of history, to name a few.

   A. intensified   B. italicized

   C. emphasized   D. peculiar

3. Tuscan food isn't fussy. Most dishes are just a few ingredients, prepared quick without <u>elaborate</u> presentation.

   A. tedious   B. devious   C. complicated   D. forthright

4. Set atop a hillside on the Il Ciocco estate, the hotel <u>showcases</u> the local landscape, with stunning views of the Apuan Alps and the Tuscan-Emilian Apennines mountain range.

   A. embodies   B. displays   C. reflects   D. obstructs

5. This allows you to visit hole-in-the-wall restaurants and wineries, trace the rolling hills and <u>expansive</u> valleys, and spot local wildlife.

   A. horizontal   B. profound   C. confined   D. spacious

6. Then join him in the kitchen to <u>whip up</u> a multi-course Italian feast (we made fresh tagliatelle and veal scallopini with local porcini mushrooms) that can be enjoyed for lunch or dinner.

   A. prepare for   B. tidy up   C. lash   D. gulp

7. This winery has created a <u>thriving</u> operation, with its aromatic Melograno ("pomegranate" in Italian) well worth trying.

   A. boisterous   B. distressing   C. prosperous   D. blooming

8. This luxury hotel built in a <u>refurbished</u> 15th century palazzo sits less than three miles from Florence.

   A. spruced   B. redesigned   C. excavated   D. repolished

9. Going back centuries, locals have enjoyed the comfort and <u>healing</u> properties of the mineral-rich water.

   A. restoring   B. specializing   C. trimming   D. preventing

10. It offers eight pools <u>infused</u> with mineral water from hot springs, including an expansive infinity pool, spiral-shaped "bioacquam" pool, and even a small wading pool just for dogs.

   A. imparted   B. filled   C. implanted   D. covered

II. Comprehension

Decide whether the following statements are true or false according to the information given in the press clipping. Mark T or F to each statement.

1. Tuscany boasts distinctive landscape, friendly locals, and a wealth of history. But the food there is the biggest attraction for visitors.

2. Most dishes in Tuscany are easy to cook, and the ingredients are fresh and local. The preparation of foods in this area still follows the customs.

3. In Tuscany, if you want to have a private cooking experience with the chef for dinner, it will only cost about $166 per person at current exchange rates.

4. The provincial capital of Lucca is located in the south of Barga, and is a place which could compete with Fifth Ave for the similarity they share in food.

5. Florence, as the birthplace of the Renaissance, offers both some famous arts and excellent

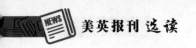

restaurants. Compared with Lucca, Florence is more charming.

6. Il Salviatino, a luxury hotel, is located outside Florence. And from this hotel, there is a free shuttle to and from Florence every hour.

7. Tuscany's most popular natural resource is its hot springs. Both the locals and the visitors could dip in for the day.

8. If you are interested in experiencing hot springs on a more involved level, you may refer to the Lunigiana territory in the north where you can enjoy eight pools infused with mineral water from hot springs.

9. Tuscany has the best wine regions in Italy, such as Montalcino and Montepulciano. They offer both free tastings of the area's famed Vino Nobile wine and pairings with cheese or local cured meats.

10. From the news, we may infer the author might be from America. What the author enjoys most in Tuscany is its hot springs.

III. Questions for discussion

1. To travel on the spur of the moment has been popular recently. Do you agree to this fashion? While we are visiting scenic spots, apart from merely taking pictures, what are the other ways to appreciate the beauty and the local culture?

2. "It's about as far as you can get from the revolving door of trends and hot new restaurants that define New York's foodie scene". Why does the author mention New York while being in Tuscany? Please explain the sentence, based on the context.

3. Visitors come to Tuscany for many reasons. Some come for beautiful landscapes, some explore its rich culture, while others like to enjoy its cuisine. If you were the visitor, what would you come for? And why?

4. What does the last sentence "In a region with so much history and tradition, there's still room for new arrivals" possibly imply? Please discuss with your partner.

5. Supposing you have just finished your trip in Tuscany and come back, what are the most impressive experiences you would like to share with your friends?

美英国家的著名景点掠影

美国

（一）科罗拉多大峡谷（The Grand Canyon）

又称为"美国大峡谷"，是世界上最为壮观的自然奇迹之一。位于亚利桑那州的西北部，大峡谷以小科罗拉多河为起点，是全长 2190 千米的科罗拉多河在科罗拉多高原上侵蚀切割形成的 19 个主要峡谷中最长、最宽、最深、最著名的一个。大峡谷山石多为红色。主要特色有：1）被称为"活着的地质教科书"，从大峡谷底部到顶部分布着从寒武纪到新生代各个不同地质年代的代表性生物化石，并且从下到上有不同的气候，鲜明的植物群和动物生物化石群。2）马蹄形的玻璃走廊（Skywalk），从大峡谷的崖边向外伸延出 21 米，使在峡谷崖边空中漫步成为可能。该走廊也被称为"二十一世纪的世界奇观"。1919 年，托马斯·威尔逊（Thomas Wilson）总统将大峡谷地区辟为"大峡谷国家公园"（Grand Canyon National Park）。

（二）黄石国家公园（Yellowstone National Park）

主要位于怀俄明州（Wyoming），靠近加拿大的边界。1872 年美国总统尤利西斯·格兰特（Ulysses Grant）许可建立，是美国最古老的国家公园，总面积达 8985 平方公里。景区以喷泉和温泉而闻名，其中最著名的是"不老泉"(Old Faithful)，每隔几小时就会喷出巨大的水柱直冲天空，每次时间持续长达 4 分钟。景区内有超过 3000 个温泉。黄石国家公园拥有美丽的瀑布、起伏的丘陵和丰茂的山谷，是很多珍惜野生动物的家园，以拥有良好的生态环境而著名。

（三）自由女神像（Statue of Liberty）

是法国 1886 年为纪念美国独立战争期间的美法联盟而送的礼物，位于纽约市纽约港口的自由岛上，游客乘坐游轮前往岛上参观。雕像金属铸造，是非常巨大的新古典主义艺术品，由法国雕塑家 Frédéric Auguste Bartholdi 设计，历时 10 年完成。雕塑是身着希腊风格服饰的女神形象，头戴象征着世界七大洲的冠冕，手持火炬，高高举起，象征着自由精神。整个雕像高 46 米，加上基座共为 93 米，重达 225 吨，非常雄伟，是美国最著名的旅游景点之一。

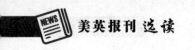

（四）尼亚加拉瀑布（Niagara Falls）

位于加拿大的安大略省和美国纽约州边界的尼亚加拉河上，是三个瀑布的总称，分别是马蹄型瀑布（Horseshoe Falls）（位于加拿大境内）、美利坚瀑布（American Falls）和新娘面纱瀑布（Veil of the Bride Falls）（这两个都位于美国境内）。由于河流落差大，瀑布喷射出的水从几英里外就可以看到，水势澎湃，发出雷鸣般的响声，景象非常壮观震撼。

英国

（一）伦敦（London）

伦敦是英国乃至欧洲最大的城市，英格兰的首府，同时是英国的首都，是政治、经济和文化中心，拥有悠久浓厚的历史底蕴和极其众多的风景名胜，是世界著名的旅游胜地。

1. 泰晤士河（River Tames）：全长 346 公里，贯穿整个伦敦城。被丘吉尔（Winston Churchill）称为"穿过英国历史的河流"，见证了英格兰的历史变迁。伦敦城的主要建筑物大多分布在泰晤士河的两岸。

2. 伦敦塔（Tower of London）：位于泰晤士河的北岸，是一座拥有悠久历史的城堡。1066 年征服者威廉 (William the Conqueror) 征服英格兰后开始建立。从 1100 至 1952 年被用为监狱。伦敦塔是一组塔群，包括珍宝馆、白塔和格林塔等。

3. 大本钟（Big Ben）：于 1859 年建成。2012 年，为庆祝英国女王 (Queen Elizabeth II) 登基 60 周年改名为 Elizabeth Tower。大本钟同时朝向四个方向，钟楼高 95 米，直径 7 米，重 13.5 吨，是英国的地标性建筑。

4. 白金汉宫（Buckingham Palace）：位于威斯敏斯特城内，是一座四层楼的正方形围院建筑，是英国君主居住和办公的地方，也是一些重要的国家庆典活动场所。

5. 唐宁街 10 号（No. 10 Downing Street）：唐宁街 10 号，位于伦敦威斯敏斯特的白厅街旁，是英国首相的官邸，因其黑色木门上的白色数字"10"十分醒目，故名为"唐宁街 10 号"。

与之相近的白厅街（Whitehall），连接着议会大厦和唐宁街，是重要而知名的大街，因为在这条街上设置着国防部、财政部、外交部、内政部、海军部等英国中央政府机构，所以白厅常作为英国行政部门的代名词。

6. 大英博物馆（British Museum）：是世界上历史最悠久的博物馆，始建于 1753 年，1759 年正式开放。该馆也是规模最大的综合性博物馆，是历史、艺术和文化的收藏中心，藏品来自于世界各地，馆内藏品超过 800 万件。就藏品的数量和丰富程度上，在全球首屈一指。

（二）英国巨石阵（Stonehenge）

位于英格兰的威尔特郡，又叫"圆柱石林"，是著名的史前建筑遗迹，世界上最壮观的巨石文物之一。由许多整块的兰砂岩组成，巨石阵的主体，是几十根巍峨的石柱，它们排成几个完整的同心圆。考古学家推测巨石阵大约建于公元前 3000 年至公元前 2000 年。关于巨石阵到底是如何建成的，至今仍然是人类未解之谜。

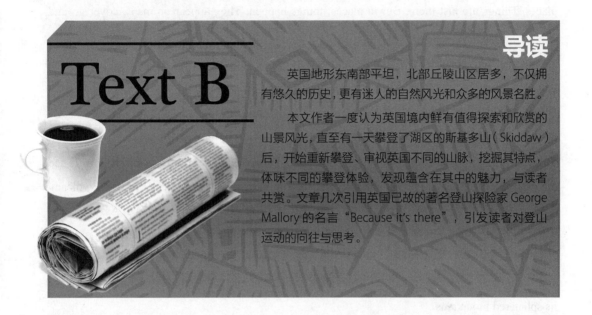

Text B

导读

英国地形东南部平坦，北部丘陵山区居多，不仅拥有悠久的历史，更有迷人的自然风光和众多的风景名胜。

本文作者一度认为英国境内鲜有值得探索和欣赏的山景风光，直至有一天攀登了湖区的斯基多山（Skiddaw）后，开始重新攀登、审视英国不同的山脉，挖掘其特点，体味不同的攀登体验，发现蕴含在其中的魅力，与读者共赏。文章几次引用英国已故的著名登山探险家 George Mallory 的名言"Because it's there"，引发读者对登山运动的向往与思考。

'The spaciousness is breathtaking …' In praise of Britain's mountains

By Simon Ingram

The beauty of the UK's uplands, from the Highlands to the Lakes, is that you don't have to travel far to find adventure, spectacle or solitude, says Simon Ingram.

Why climbing a mountain? Don't say "Because it's there."[1] It's said that when the great, doomed mountaineer George Mallory[2] used the phrase in 1923 it was uttered dismissively, without the gravitas it later gained. Just because climbing a mountain may serve no obvious practical purpose, there are plenty of better reasons to get to its summit than its mere existence. Far better.

I didn't walk to the top of anything high until I was 20, when I was dragged. Until then—as with many people who look overseas rather than exploring their own backyard—I was considering emigrating, to Canada. I believed the nonsense about Britain being a claustrophobic place where you could never find the crystalline magnificence you visualise when you think of escape, wilderness and all that stuff.

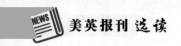

Then that day I climbed Skiddaw, in the Lake District[3], I saw layers of blue mountains spilling from my feet, only 1½ hours from where I'd lived all of my life, and realised I'd been missing something. In 2004, I took a job on *Trail* magazine (which I now edit), and learned two things quickly: the more you see of Britain, the bigger Britain gets; and you haven't seen it at all until you've seen it from a mountain.

So first, get it out of your head that a mountain is a thing. A bollard is a thing. Mountains are places. Things are just there. But in places, things happen. They appear on maps, cover ground, create weather and bear life.

Our ancient peoples saw them as the homes of gods and monsters. Our greatest poets found muses in them. They've harboured scientists, smugglers, occultists and ghost hunters. They were, and are, uninhabited, inhospitable islands of wild. Agriculturally barren and obstinate to passage, mountains are the last landscapes to become useful, and so are left to the fringes.

And being the wonderful geological hotchpotch Britain is, you don't have to travel far to feel a complete shift in the way the mountains cut their dash. There is true variety here: the volcanic summits of the Cuillin ridge on the Isle of Skye[4]; the strange, free-standing peaks of Assynt, north-west Scotland, eulogised by poet Norman MacCaig; the exquisite tapestry of mountains, lakes and slate villages of the Lake District that were such an inspiration for Turner, Wordsworth, Ruskin and Coleridge[5]; Snowdonia, with its Tolkeinian mines, climbs and folk tales—all underpinned by its splintered mountains …

The most wonderful attribute of all of these is their scale. They can all be explored on foot, mostly in a weekend. Leave London—or other cities en route—by sleeper train on a Friday night and you'll wake up in the Highlands on Saturday morning. A flight covers the distance between London and Inverness quicker than you can cross London by tube.

Once in the uplands, you can have a real adventure with few of the collateral hazards of other mountain areas. You can camp safe in the knowledge that no animals will pull you shrieking from your tent into the night. You won't get altitude sickness. You're never more than 10 miles from a road. There are no crevasses to fall into, no deserts to get lost in or hostile tribes to be wary of. And there's so much freedom here: in many countries, you keep out unless told otherwise. Thanks to the right to roam, in most parts of Britain it's the other way around.

That said, our mountains do have teeth. That old joke about Everest being good training for the Highlands of Scotland is only funny if you've never experienced the Cairngorms in winter, or looked up at Snowdon's sharp summit when it's white. It's alarming how extreme Britain can be:

the first taste of this engenders a mixture of sudden, shocked respect. Chuck it in the deep freeze and suddenly, electrifyingly, Britain stops playing nice.

But you'll come to crave the feelings. The chill, the silence and the space. The darkest night you've ever seen from the window of a stove-lit bothy. The tired-happy exhilaration of being a mile high having walked there. The thrill of holding on for your life, and living. Of swinging a bag on to your back that contains all you need to sustain yourself, then doing it. The act of boiling life down to the basics—get up, move, eat, sleep, get down—is the ultimate in perspective realignment. And the few who make the effort to get into Britain's wild rafters share the biggest secret of all: up above the millions in this crowded … this apparently suffocatingly crowded nation, the spaciousness and enormity is breathtaking.

"Because it's there" is the last reason to climb a mountain. Perhaps another of George Mallory's comments carries more truth: "What we get from this adventure is sheer joy. And joy is, after all, the end of life." Everest, Helvellyn, Snowdon, Ben Nevis[6]. To those who know, that joy inhabits the same lofty step—where the mountains of Britain stand as tall as any in the world. One of Mallory's gifts to Everest was to name its great valley the Western Cwm, a Welsh word, because it reminded the mountaineer of Snowdon.

Mallory's mentor was another mountaineer-philosopher, Geoffrey Winthrop Young. A line from his poem, *A Hill*, about the implacability of the British mountains' lure, gave me a title for my book about the same:

Only a hill, but all of life to me, Up there between the sunset and the sea

So, why climb a mountain? Stop asking. Just climb one.

• *Simon Ingram is the author of Between the Sunset and the Sea*

(From *The Guardian*, June 14, 2016)

NOTES

1. Because it's there. 1923 年，英国著名登山家 George Mallory 打算挑战世界最高峰—珠穆朗玛峰，记者采访他时，他说的一句话。这句话后来成为登山界的名言。

2. George Mallory (1886-1924) 英国著名的登山探险家。在 20 世纪 20 年代早期，三次参加英国组织的征服地球最高峰—珠穆朗玛峰的探险。1924 年，和队友 Andrew Irvine 第三次攀登珠峰，在接近珠峰顶端的东北部时，与地面失去联系。直到 1979 年，Eric Simson 带领探险队，找到了 George Mallory 的尸体。但他和队友在遇难前是否已经到达了珠峰的峰顶，仍然是个谜。

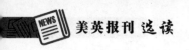

3. Lake District 著名的湖区国家公园 (Lake Districts National Park)，位于英国的西北部，方圆大约 2300 平方公里。因拥有湖泊（主要的有 14 个）、山峰和树林而闻名。文中的斯基多山（Skiddaw），就是位于湖区的一座山。湖区的最高山是斯可斐峰（Scafell Pike）。另外，湖区也因 19 世纪英国文学史上著名的"湖畔派"诗人居住于此而闻名，尤其是 William Wordsworth 常年生活在湖区内，并在此写下了很多著名的诗篇，如 *The Daffodils* 等。著名儿童文学家碧雅翠丝·波特（Helen Beatrix Potter）也是这个湖区的常客，备受全世界儿童喜欢的《彼得兔的故事》(*The World of Peter Rabbit and His Friends*)(1902)，也是从湖边的美景引发而来。

4. Cuillin ridge on the Isle of Skye Isle of Skype 是位于苏格兰西北部的一个岛屿，因风景秀丽而闻名。库林山（Cuillin）是位于这个岛屿上的山，又名 Black Cuillin，最高海拔为 992 米。

5. Turner, Wordsworth, Ruskin and Coleridge

   Joseph Mallord William Turner（1775-1851），英国绘画史上最著名的艺术家之一，擅长风景画，代表作品有 *The Painter of Light* 等。

   William Wordsworth（1770-1850），英国浪漫主义诗人，1843 年获得英国 "桂冠诗人"的称号，和 Samuel Taylor Coleridge（1772-1834）、Robert Southey（1774-1843）同被称为"湖畔派"诗人（Lake Poets），他们都为英国文学史上浪漫主义时期的早期代表。

   John Ruskin（1819-1900），英国维多利亚时代的艺术评论家，多才多艺，同时也是作家，艺术家，哲学家。代表作品为著作 *Modern Painters*。

6. Everest, Helvellyn, Snowdon, Ben Nevis

   Everest，即 Mt. Everest（又称为 Mt. Qomolangma），珠穆朗玛峰，是喜马拉雅山（the Himalayas）的最高峰，海拔为 8848.13 米，终年被雪覆盖。因其高度和险峻而闻名世界，许多登山爱好者以征服此山作为人生梦想，本文中提到的 George Mallory 就是其中之一。

   Helvellyn，赫尔维林山，是 Lake District 里的一座山，为英格兰的第三高峰。

   Snowdon，雪墩山，威尔士最高山峰，海拔为 1085 米，位于雪墩国家公园（Snowdonia National Park）（仅次于 Lake Districts National Park 的第二大国家公园）。

   Ben Nevis，本尼维斯山，位于苏格兰，是英国最高峰，海拔 1343 米。南坡缓，东北坡陡，山顶终年积雪。

USEFUL WORDS

barren	['bærən]	*adj.*	unproductive; completely wanting or lacking 贫瘠的；无效的
claustrophobic	[ˌklɔːstrə'foʊbɪk]	*adj.*	suffering from claustrophobia(a morbid fear of being closed in a confined space); abnormally afraid of closed-in places （患）幽闭恐怖症的；引起幽闭恐怖的
collateral	[kə'lætərəl]	*adj.*	serving to support or corroborate; accompany, concomitant 并行的；附属的
crevasse	[krə'væs]	*n.*	deep, open crack, esp. in ice on a glacier （冰河等的）裂缝，破口

crystalline	['krɪstəlaɪn]	*adj.*	transmitting light; able to be seen through with clarity 水晶（般）的，水晶做的；透明的
dismissive	[dɪs'mɪsɪv]	*adj.*	showing indifference or disregard 表示轻视的、默然的
doomed	[du:m]	*adj.*	marked by or promising bad fortune 命中注定的
eulogise	['ju:lədʒaɪz]	*v.*	to praise formally and eloquently 表扬，赞扬
exhilaration	[ɪg,zɪlə'reɪʃn]	*n.*	the feeling of lively and cheerful joy 高兴，兴奋
gravitas	['grævɪtɑ:s]	*n.*	formality in bearing and appearance 庄严的举止，庄严
hotchpotch	['hɑːtʃpɑːtʃ]	*n.*	a motley assortment of things 杂烩，混杂
implacable	[ɪm'plækəbl]	*adj.*	(formal) that can not be appeased; relentless（正式用语）不能平息的；无情的
implacability	[ɪmplækə'bɪlɪtɪ]		*n.* 难以安抚的性质或状态
lofty	['lɔːfti]	*adj.*	of high moral or intellectual value; elevated in nature or style 崇高的，高尚的
muse	[mju:z]	*n.*	the Muses, (GK myth) the nine goddesses, daughters of Zeus, who protected and encouraged poetry, music, dancing, history and other branches of art and learning.（希神）缪斯女神（宙斯的第九个女儿，保护并鼓励诗歌、音乐、舞蹈、历史和其他艺术与学术的女神）
obstinate	['ɑːbstɪnət]	*adj.*	tenaciously unwilling or marked by tenacious unwillingness to yield 固执的，倔强的，不易屈服的
solitude	['sɑːlətuːd]	*n.*	the state or situation of being alone 孤独，独居，荒僻的地方
splinter	['splɪntər]	*v.*	to break up into splinters or slivers 破裂，组成小派别
suffocate	['sʌfəkeɪt]	*v.*	to cause or have difficulty in breathing（使）窒息，（使）呼吸困难
suffocatingly		*adv.*	令人窒息地
tapestry	['tæpəstri]	*n.*	a heavy textile with a woven design; used for curtains and upholstery 挂毯
underpin	[ˌʌndər'pɪn]	*v.*	to support from beneath 从下端支持，支撑

✍EXERCISES

I.   Vocabulary

Choose among the four alternatives one word or phrase that is closest in meaning to the underlined part in each statement.

1. The beauty of the UK's uplands, from the Highlands to the Lakes, is that you don't have to travel far to find adventure, <u>spectacle</u> or solitude, says Simon Ingram.

   A. peculiar scene   B. remarkable scene   C. desolate scene   D. horrible scene

2. It's said that when the great, doomed mountaineer George Mallory used the phrase in 1923 it was uttered <u>dismissively</u>, without the gravitas it later gained.

   A. solemnly   B. gravely   C. indifferently   D. joyously

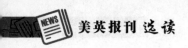

3. Agriculturally barren and obstinate to passage, mountains are the last landscapes to become useful, and so are left to the fringes.

A. shallow   B. fertile   C. arid   D. unproductive

4. There is true variety here: the volcanic summits of the Cuillin ridge on the Isle of Skye; the strange, free-standing peaks of Assynt, north-west Scotland, eulogised by poet Norman MacCaig.

A. praised   B. mentioned   C. repudiated   D. confounded

5. Once in the uplands, you can have a real adventure with few of the collateral hazards of other mountain areas.

A. horizontal   B. vertical   C. diagonal   D. accompanying

6. You can camp safe in the knowledge that no animals will pull you shrieking from your tent into the night.

A. screaming   B. weeping   C. roaring   D. grieving

7. It's alarming how extreme Britain can be: the first taste of this engenders a mixture of sudden, shocked respect.

A. presumes   B. causes   C. endangers   D. accumulates

8. The tired-happy exhilaration of being a mile high having walked there.

A. exclamation   B. excitement   C. howl   D. reminiscence

9. To those who know, that joy inhabits the same lofty step—where the mountains of Britain stand as tall as any in the world.

A. humble   B. course   C. high   D. intrigue

10. A line from his poem, *A Hill*, about the implacability of the British mountains' lure, gave me a title for my book about the same.

A. repression   B. exclusion   C. resistance   D. attraction

II. Comprehension

Decide whether the following statements are true or false according to the information given in the press clipping. Mark T or F to each statement.

1. Before starting for Mount Everest in 1923, when interviewed by the reporter, George Mallory was very passionate and confident to conquer the highest point on the earth.

2. The author used to think Britain did not have any mountains which could arouse his interest to explore. It was not until the day he climbed Skiddaw that he realized he had missed something about British mountains.

3. According to the news, mountains tend to be areas unsuitable for cultivation, for it is agriculturally barren and obstinate to passage.

4. The Lake District occupies exquisite tapestry of mountains, lakes and slate villages, which is an inspiration for literature figures, such as Wordsworth and MacCaig.

5. "The most wonderful attribute of all of these is their scale" means that in Britain the mountains are low enough for most of people to conquer within a short time.

6. Climbing British mountains seems to be very safe, and no animals will attack you because wild animals are preserved in certain areas.

7. To climb a mountain in Britain might be an amazing experience, which involves a mixture of sudden, shocked respect.

8. Britain is a crowded nation for the large population, but the mountains in this country are very spacious, for the comparatively larger area they occupy.

9. In Mount Everest there is a valley Western Cwm named by George Mallory, for it reminded him of Snowdon in Britain.

10. The attitude towards mountains in Britain held by the author has changed from being negative to positive, and the author gradually began to extoll British mountains.

III. Questions for discussion

1. "Because it's there" is the famous quote from George Mallory in 1923 before he took the third attempt to conquer Mount Everest. Based on the news, please describe what kind of person George Mallory was, and share with your partner your understanding of his remarks.

2. Have you ever been to the U.K.? How much do you know about mountains in this country? Please refer to the Internet and find more information.

3. "Mountains are places. Things are just there. But in places, things happen". These sentences seem a little confusing, while rich in meaning. Could you explain what "mountains" and "things" respectively refer to?

4. Climbing a mountain, especially a steep, intimidating one, is very challenging, but some mountaineers deliberately challenge those treacherous mountains which are seemingly impossible to be conquered. What are the motives driving them to face these challenges?

5. At the end of the news, the author quotes a line from Geoffrey Winthrop Young, who was George Mallory's mentor. What does the author intend to convey by quoting this?

《卫报》简介

　　《卫报》（The Guardian）是一份英国的全国性日报，著名的综合性报刊。《卫报》属于卫报传媒集团（Guardian Media Group，GMG）的一部分，与同在卫报传媒集团下的《观察者报》(*The Observer*) 是"姐妹报",与《泰晤士报》、《每日电讯报》被合称为英国三大报。《卫报》是定位于高端市场的主流大报,一定程度上是严肃、可信、独立新闻的代名词,其读者主要为政界人士、白领和知识分子。2013 年 8 月《卫报》的平均日发行量为 189,000 份,在英国排名第三。

《卫报》原名为《曼彻斯特卫报》(*The Manchester Guardian*),1821 年由 John Edward Taylor 创刊于曼彻斯特,当时是一份地方周报,周六出版。1872 年 Charles Prestwich Scott 成为该报的总编,并在 1907 年从 Taylor 儿子手中买下这份报纸,在他当总编的 57 年间,报纸逐渐被整个英国所认可,奠定了其成为英国著名报纸的基础。1936 年其子 J.R.Scott 放弃继承权,并把报纸的所有权全部转给 Scott Trust(斯格特信托基金),这一举措保证了报纸的独立性,不依赖于任何政党,坚守自由、民主立场的办报传统,报纸的品质得到了保证,同时赢得了世界的瞩目。1955 年,改为日报。1959 年去掉 "Manchester" 这一地方色彩的字眼,改为现名,总部 1964 年迁往伦敦,但曼彻斯特和伦敦都有其印刷厂。因《卫报》早期的印刷错误,误把 Guardian 误拼为 Gaurdian,以讽刺、揭发各种丑闻的杂志 Private Eye 曾给《卫报》起绰号为 Grauniad(缩写为 Graun),该报至今仍偶尔被称为 Grauniad。

2005 年 9 月开始,《卫报》宣布从对开面改为使用柏林报纸板式,是英国第一家使用这种板式的报纸。这种板式通常的尺寸为 470 mm × 315 mm,其优点在于比小报略宽,比大报的板式又略小,非常便于折叠、携带和阅读。改版后,《卫报》的发行量一度迅速上涨。

登录《卫报》的官方网站,可以阅读该报刊的电子版。

Unit Ten
Global Spotlight

报刊英语中的话语权力

报刊是大众传媒的重要方式之一。报刊英语中新闻报道的生命是其真实性，即反映客观事实，是根据事实进行公正真实的报道。因此以客观、中立的态度为公众报道新闻事件是新闻媒体应该恪守的原则。

但是，由于新闻报道代表的权益主体不同，在报道时带着不同的主观意识，因此平时我们看到的新闻报道，总是呈现出某种倾向性观点，虽然不一定会支配我们的想法，但在一定程度上会影响人们的观点。换言之，新闻报道并不总是像其宣称的那样公正、客观。受新闻媒体的政治立场以及新闻写作者的观点态度等多种因素的影响，新闻媒体对所报道的新闻事件都暗含了自己的观点、立场和态度，其意识形态隐藏在新闻报道的字面意思之后，而隐含的主观意识形态会对读者的认知判断造成潜移默化的影响，这种影响一定程度上构成报刊英语的话语权力。可见，报刊英语中的语言、意识形态以及话语权力之间存在着复杂的关系。

为了客观、理性地理解新闻报道，读者需要对报道话语进行批评性分析。批评性话语分析（Critical Discourse Analysis）是由 20 世纪 70 年代末开创的批判语言学发展而来。英国语言学家 R.Fowler 等人在 1979 年的《语言与控制》（*Language and Control*）一书中，率先提出了批判语言学的概念，开启了批判语篇分析方法。后来 N.Fairclough 指出"意识形态普遍存在于语言之后，因此语言同时也是社会控制和权力关系得以实现的一种重要手段，并直接参与社会现实和社会关系的构成。"（戴炜华、陈宇昀，2004）批判性话语分析为分析新闻语篇提供了重要的理论和方法支持，我们可以借此对报刊英语中新闻语篇的语言进行分析，剖析语言的特点和规律，揭示出隐含在字里行间的新闻媒体的意识形态，探讨语言、权力和意识形态三者之间的关系。

下面几个片段选自《华盛顿邮报》（*The Washington Post*）2016 年 9 月 26 日报道的一

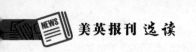

篇题为 "Defense secretary: US will sharpen 'military edge' in Asia" 的新闻。主要讲了美国国防部长 Ashton Carter 在 San Diego 发表的关于要重振在亚洲力量的言论，主要涉及南海争端问题，政治倾向性十分明显。

下面将从词语选择、引语两个方面，分析《华盛顿邮报》是如何通过大众媒体的语言渗透，表明对华态度，从而影响受众意识形态倾向性的。

1 词语选择

With a broad <u>complaint</u> that China is "sometimes behaving <u>aggressively</u>," Carter alluded to Beijing's building of artificial islands in disputed areas of the South China Sea.

"Beijing sometimes appears to want to <u>pick and choose</u> which principles it wants to benefit from and which it prefers to try to undercut," he said. "for example, the universal right to freedom of navigation that allows China's ships and aircraft to transit safely and peacefully is the same right that Beijing criticizes other countries for other countries for exercising in the region, but principles are not like that. They apply to everyone, to every nation, equally." (from *Defense secretary: US will sharpen 'military edge' in Asia*, *The Washington Post*, Sept. 29, 2016)

这部分故意选用 "complaint"，"aggressively"，"pick and choose" 等词语，揭示了近年来，随着中国经济迅速发展，中国的崛起对世界格局影响的日益凸显，美国个别媒体开始营造舆论导向，污蔑中国片面追求自身利益，并谋求霸权地位。

2 引语

"The United States will continue to sharpen our military edge so we remain the most powerful military in the region and the security partner of choice," he said.

He said his visit had inaugurated "a major new era in a longstanding alliance."

"I am proud to say this alliance is as close as it's been in years."

引语，尤其是直接引语，通常是新闻记者借助于当事人的话来表述自己的立场观点，进而影响受众观点。上面几段引文，分别是 Ashton Carter 谈论的关于美国对于亚洲问题的态度，那就是要坚持并加强其一贯的强硬霸权地位，以及在谈及与菲律宾关系时，突出要结盟支持菲律宾，进而插手区域性问题的鲜明观点。本篇新闻的作者直接引用了他的话，隐含着较多的意识形态意蕴，影响受众观点的目的显而易见。

这篇新闻的立场和报道倾向，其实是美国近年来对中国态度在媒体中的迁移反应，没有跳出美国涉华报道的思维框架，那就是在美国民众中传播 "中国威胁论" 的导向。

其实，英文报刊不仅在关于他国的新闻报道中会有意识形态的倾向性表现，而且在针对本国的新闻报道中，也存在着导向的差别。例如 2016 年美国大选中，美国著名的《纽约时报》（*The New York Times*）政治倾向明显，很早就明确表态支持民主党候选人希拉里·克林顿（Hillary Clinton）。在各种报道中，不遗余力地抬高希拉里，说其是美国现代史上"无论广度还是深度上都最具资格"的总统竞选人之一，与此同时，贬低其竞争对手唐纳德·特朗普（Donald Trump）。2016 年 10 月，《纽约时报》声称已获取相关文件，显示特朗普可能从 1995 年开始就以某种方式避税，并刊登一系列报道深度挖掘和曝光所谓的"特朗普偷税"行为，其中 10 月 2 日的一篇题为"Donald Trump and His Allies Struggle to Move Past Tax Revelation"的新闻，用意更是明显，指出特朗普及其同盟对是否偷税问题欲盖弥彰的做法。《纽约时报》的这些做法，无非就是想用媒体所掌握的话语权，影响美国选民的投票倾向，提高希拉里在最终的总统大选中获胜的机率。

因此，在阅读报刊英语中的新闻报道时，要运用批判性话语分析，提高语言鉴赏及评论能力。要透过现象看本质，分析报刊英语中新闻报道所隐含的意识形态倾向和话语权力的指向，看清新闻报道本来该有的事实原貌，做出自己正确的评价。

Text A

导读

现代奥林匹克运动会（简称"奥运会"），1896 年第 1 届在雅典开始举行，每 4 年一届。奥运会是世界上规模最大的，最受瞩目的综合性运动会，宗旨是促进人类向真善美发展，口号是"更高，更快，更强"。2016 年 8 月 5 日至 8 月 21 日的里约奥运会是第 31 届奥运会，从筹备到开幕之前，因为其不断缩减的财政预支，安保、环境等诸多问题，一直备受质疑。

本文呈现了里约奥运会开幕式的盛况，既有独具特色的南美风情，又有绚丽的艺术表演，打造了一场简约却不简单的狂欢盛宴。同时，巴西国内民众对于在本国举办奥运会持不同态度，也分别给予了报道。

Rio[1] brings its samba[2] style to the opening ceremony of the Summer Olympics[3]

By Joshua Partlow and Chico Harlan

RIO DE JANEIRO—The Summer Olympic Games kicked off Friday night in an opening ceremony with a gutted budget but a soaring feel, as a stadium nestled here below a hillside pulsed

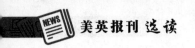

with lights, fireworks, circus-like acrobats and a samba singalong typical of this nation's partying style.

Brazil, the first South American country to host the Olympics, used the start of the Games to tell a version of the country's history—from slavery to mega-cities—that comes as hard economic times are testing its fun-loving style.

The celebration featured a 12-year-old rapper, a supermodel, and beams of light used to dazzling effect—part of what Daniela Thomas, one of the event's co-directors, called "MacGyver" ingenuity, in reference to the stripped-down budget[4].

Projections of light and imagery cast the stadium floor in ethereal greens and blues, and in a matter of minutes Brazil provided eons of choreographed history—with performers sometimes taking a back seat to the visual effects. Images on the turf first showed a creation-of-Earth story— molecules, smoke, creatures crawling from the sea. Soon, a new splash of light gave the stadium the feel of a rain forest, with the sounds of animals chirping to make the point.

The performers came in. A line of indigenous tribes carving out homes in the rain forest. Portuguese arrived on ships in the colonial era. Africans towed to shore, shackled, moving through the stadium with feet secured in blocks. Then, the music quickened, and projections showed what appeared to be blocks rising from the ground. As those blocks turned into skyscrapers—an homage to Rio's development—a team of dancers leapt from rooftop to rooftop, in what resembled an action movie chase scene.

Earlier, the Brazilian singer Regina Casé, who warmed up the crowd at Maracanã stadium[5], told the thousands of cheering spectators what they wanted to hear: "Here in Brazil, we like to party."

A video on four jumbo screens showed a montage of Brazil's sweeping vistas—rumbling waves, above-the-Amazon hang gliders, and aerial views of the famous Christ statue in Rio de Janeiro[6].

Over 400 years before it became the last country in the Western Hemisphere to abolish slavery in 1888, Brazil imported about 5 million African slaves, 10 times more than the United States. The opening ceremony at the 1996 Summer Games, which were held in Atlanta, did not include any reference to slavery, angering some groups.

Before the 206 competing nations, plus one refugee team, paraded into the stadium, Brazil showed off some of its musical riches, with a much-loved samba singer, Zeca Pagodinho[7]. The audience sang along. This was followed by a dance routine featuring dancers spinning on the floor, which was based on capoeira[8], a Brazilian martial art, and was accompanied by Brazilian female rapper Karol Conka.

After the hour-long show, athletes paraded into the stadium—led first, per tradition, by Greece, which hosted the initial Games. The order then proceeded alphabetically; athletes from Cameroon wore traditional flowing robes, those from communist-led Cuba had outfits designed by a French luxury footwear designer. The team from the United States—Estados Unidos, in Portuguese—paraded in earlier than it usually does, this time wearing blue blazers and being led by legendary swimmer Michael Phelps[9].

TheU.S. team received a warm reception as Secretary of State John F. Kerry looked on from the stands.

The athletes included the decorated and the obscure, representing nations with rich and thin sporting histories. Afghanistan, with three athletes, was led by Kamia Yousufi, 20, competing in the 100-meter dash. Meantime, tennis star Andy Murray fronted the team for Great Britain; his rival on the pro tour, Rafael Nadal, carried the flag for Spain.

Rio's preparations for the Games were marked by a catalogue of bad news: sluggish venue construction, rising crime and coastal waters so polluted that Olympic swimmers were advised to avoid swallowing even a few spoonfuls.

But, for one night at least, Rio de Janeiro was basking in what it does best. This is a country expert in revelry, which every year fills its streets with dancing, stranger-kissing, inebriated glee at Carnival. The drumming and samba, the feathers and sequins, the models and athletes: Brazilians have been preparing for the opening ceremony for years.

Hundreds of millions of people around the world tuned in to Maracanã stadium—the 74,000-seat venue hosting the ceremony, which was co-created by the filmmaker Fernando Meirelles and Thomas to honor Brazil's sports, multi-ethnic history, world-famous music and raw natural beauty, from the Amazon rainforest to the white-sand beaches of Rio.

The program featured the choreographed show at the start, followed by the parade of athletes, including the appearance of the refugee Olympic team[10]—a first—and ending with the arrival of the team from the host country, Brazil.

Many people had expected the Olympic flame to be lit by 75-year-old soccer legend Pelé, but he said that he would not participate in the ceremony because of his health.

Coming two years after the most expensive Olympics ever—the $50 billion Winter Games in Sochi, Russia—Rio's welcome to the world was jubilant but restrained. This has become the

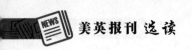

austerity Olympics, with the country's economic fortunes plunging since it won the bid for the Games in 2009. Brazil is now locked in one of its worse recessions in history, dragged down by slumping oil prices and allegations of staggering corruption.

For the opening ceremony, the budget available for Meirelles, who directed the Oscar-nominated film "City of God," was one-tenth of what British director Danny Boyle had for the 2012 Summer Olympics ceremony in London. In an interview on the 2016 Rio Olympics website, Meirelles talked about how his ambitions were forced to shrink along with the vanishing budget. What began as more than $100 million was cut in half, a show of 3,000 people sliced to 700.

"At first I was very upset. You start thinking something very big and then you have to cut, cut, cut," he added. "On the other hand, it is good in some way because we are in a moment in the world where we need to be reasonable with the way we spend money."

That scaled down ambitions fit well with the frustrated mood across many parts of Rio.

The run-up to the games has been punctuated by demonstrations, an anti-Olympic backlash driven by people who felt the time was not right for lavish spending. Protesters blocked the torch's progress as it made its way around the country and attempted to douse it with fire extinguishers and buckets of water; in a few cases they were met by police firing tear gas and rubber bullets.

Just hours before the opening ceremony, security forces fired tear gas and a percussion grenade after youths set fire to a Brazilian flag and a Rio 2016 volunteer's T-shirt and tried to get close to the Maracanã stadium. One man was arrested.

The trouble came after a march targeting what demonstrators called "the Exclusion Games" had come to a peaceful end in at the leafy Afonso Pena square near the stadium. Beatriz Nunes, 34, a teacher at the march, said that when some protesters tried to cross a police line, officers responded with tear gas and the percussion grenade.

Earlier in the day, a few thousand protestors marched along the Copacabana seafront in a sea of red shirts. They took aim at two targets—Brazil's interim President Michel Temer[11], who took over in May when President Dilma Rousseff was suspended and ordered to face a controversial impeachment trial, and the Olympic Games themselves.

"We don't have the conditions to receive the Games," said Leonardo Ladeira, a 22-year-old protestor. "At this moment it is a chaotic activity."

Yet it's not all recriminations and rancor in Rio and beyond.

Many Brazilians have embraced their opportunity to host the Games, and are excited for them to begin. Residents have lined the streets and cheered the passing torch as it has made its way into Rio.

"I think they are a wonderful thing for Rio in terms of the spirit," said Aline Campos, 45, who works in a financing company in the city's center. "It is a very beautiful coming-together of people, and people are happy they are here."

Harlan reported from Washington. Dom Phillips, Adam Kilgore and Rick Maese in Rio de Janeiro contributed to this report.

（From *The Washington Post*, Aug. 5, 2016）

NOTES

1. Rio 里约热内卢，Rio de Janeiro 的简写，简称为"里约"，位于巴西的东南部，濒临大西洋，曾经是巴西的首都，全国人口第二大城市，也是南半球著名的旅游胜地。大部分为热带草原气候，部分地区是热带雨林气候，常年高温。2016 年夏季奥林匹克运动会在该市举办，里约也因此成为奥运史上首个主办奥运会的南美洲城市。

2. samba 桑巴，最早由黑人奴隶带到巴西，经与当地其他文化相融合，成为公认的巴西及里约狂欢节的象征，是这个国家最有代表性的音乐形式。

3. the Summer Olympics 夏季奥林匹克运动会，此处指 2016 年在里约热内卢举行的第 31 届夏季奥林匹克运动会。古代奥运会始于公元前 776 年。1896 年在雅典召开首届夏季奥林匹克运动会，这也是首届现代奥运会，自此，基本上每四年举行一次（有两届奥运会因战火停办）。夏季奥运会是全世界规模最大的综合性运动会。

4. stripped-down budget 指奥运会举办国巴西由于长期严重的经济衰退，国内经济不景气。里约奥组委将预算一再削减，因此饱受质疑。据媒体报道，里约奥运开幕式的预算从最初的 1.139 亿美元最终被削减至 5590 万美元。

5. Maracanã stadium 里约热内卢的马拉卡纳体育场，是世界上最大的足球场，能容纳 20 万名观众，里约奥运会开幕式和闭幕式的举办场地。

6. Christ statue in Rio de Janeiro 里约热内卢基督像，建成于 1931 年，位于科科瓦多山（Corcovado Mountain）（又名驼背山，耶稣山，基督山）的山顶。高 30 米（不包括 8 米基座），宽 28 米，重量超过 1 千吨。面向大西洋，伸开双臂，远观像一个巨大的十字架，非常壮观，是里约的地标性建筑。

7. Zeca Pagodinho 巴西歌手，桑巴唱作人，在里约奥运会上唱了歌曲 *Deixa A Vida Me Levar*（中文名称：生活引领我）。另外，本段中提到的 Karol Conka，是巴西最有名的说唱歌手（rapper）之一。

8. capoeira 卡波耶拉，又叫巴西战舞，是一项源于非洲的巴西舞蹈，结合了民间舞蹈、健身、音乐、自我防卫和体操等元素，是巴西本土文化的象征。2014 年被联合国教科文组织列为非物质文化遗产加以保护。

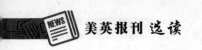

9. Michael Phelps 美国著名游泳运动员，有"飞鱼"（Flying Fish）之称。2016 年里约奥运会上收获了自己奥运会史上第 23 枚金牌，赛后宣布正式退役。

10. refugee Olympic team 指由 5 名南苏丹难民、2 名叙利亚难民、2 名刚果难民和 1 名埃塞俄比亚难民，共 10 名来自不同国家的难民组成的代表队，他们不代表自己的国家，而是聚集在奥林匹克五环旗下为梦想而战。开幕式上，当这支代表队入场时，受到了全场热烈欢迎。国际奥委会主席巴赫（Thomas Bach）提到难民代表团时曾说，这支队伍代表了全世界难民对美好生活的期待和向往。

11. interim President Michel Temer 时任巴西代总统米歇尔·特梅尔。2016 年 4 月，巴西总统 Dilma Rousseff 被弹劾，暂时停职，75 岁的副总统 Michel Terner 担任代总统。2016 年 8 月 31 日由代总统转为总统。

USEFUL WORDS

austerity	[ɔː'sterəti]	*n.*	quality of being simple and plain (in way of living, of places, styles) 朴素，质朴
backlash	['bæklæʃ]	*n.*	an adverse reaction to some political or social occurrence 强烈反对
choreograph	['kɔːriəgræf]	*v.*	to plan and oversee the development and details of 精心编制
dazzle	['dæzl]	*v.*	to make sb unable to see clearly or act normally because of too much light, brilliance, splendor, etc. 使某人因强光、绚烂、壮丽等而看不清楚或行动失常，使眼花，使目眩
dazzling		*adj.*	令人眼花缭乱的，耀眼的
eon	['iːən] (=aeon)	*n.*	period of time too long to be measured 永世，亿万年（极长而无法计算的时期）
ethereal	[i'θɪriəl]	*adj.*	characterized by lightness and insubstantiality; as impalpable or intangible as air 飘逸的；精致的，飘渺的
glee	[gliː]	*n.*	great merriment 欢乐，欣喜
grenade	[grə'neɪd]	*n.*	a small explosive bomb thrown by hand or fired from a missile 手榴弹
inebriate	[ɪn'iːbrɪeɪt]	*v.*	to make a drunk; intoxicate 使醉；使大醉
ingenuity	[ˌɪndʒə'nuːəti]	*n.*	skill at solving problems; cleverness; the property of being ingenious 足智多谋；心灵手巧；独创性
jubilant	['dʒuːbɪlənt]	*adj.*	(formal) triumphant; showing joy（正式用语）欢欣的；喜悦的；喜气洋洋的
jumbo	['dʒʌmbou]	*adj.*	of great mass; huge and bulky 庞大的；巨大的
montage	[ˌmaːn'taːʒ]	*n.*	selection, cutting and arrangement of photographic film, etc to make a consecutive whole; process of using many pictures, designs, etc sometimes superimposed, to make a composite picture. 蒙太奇（把已经拍好的许多镜头等加以选择，剪接以及编排成连贯的影片）
nestle	['nesl]	*v.*	to lie in a sheltered position（舒适地）安顿

percussion	[pər'kʌʃn] *n.*	the striking together of two (usually hard) objects; sound or shock produced by this 撞击，碰撞；撞击声
revelry	['revlri] *n.*	noisy, joyous festivity and merrymaking 吵闹作乐的饮宴，狂欢作乐
rumble	['rʌmbl] *v.*	to make a deep, heavy, continuous sound 发出隆隆声或辘辘声
rumbling	*adj.*	隆隆响的
sluggish	['slʌgɪʃ] *adj.*	inactive; slow-moving 不活泼的；行动缓慢的
soaring	[sɔːrɪŋ] *adj.*	ascending to a level markedly higher than the usual 猛增的，剧增的
vista	['vɪstə] *n.*	the visual percept of a region 街景，远景

📝 EXERCISES

I. Vocabulary

Choose among the four alternatives one word or phrase that is closest in meaning to the underlined part in each statement.

1. The Summer Olympic Games kicked off Friday night in an opening ceremony with a gutted budget but a soaring feel, as a stadium nestled here below a hillside <u>pulsed</u> with lights, fireworks, circus-like acrobats and a samba singalong typical of this nation's partying style.

   A. reflected   B. dashed   C. impelled   D. throbbed

2. The celebration featured a 12-year-old rapper, a supermodel, and beams of light used to dazzling effect—part of what Daniela Thomas, one of the event's co-directors, called "MacGyver" <u>ingenuity</u>, in reference to the stripped-down budget.

   A. localization   B. coincidence   C. cleverness   D. obligation

3. Africans <u>towed</u> to shore, shackled, moving through the stadium with feet secured in blocks.

   A. dragged   B. impelled   C. emitted   D. courted

4. Projections of light and imagery cast the stadium floor in ethereal greens and blues, and in a matter of minutes Brazil provided <u>eons</u> of choreographed history.

   A. posterity   B. eternity   C. ancestor   D. descendant

5. A video on four <u>jumbo</u> screens showed a montage of Brazil's sweeping vistas.

   A. magical   B. gigantic   C. monstrous   D. cracked

6. This is a country expert in revelry, which every year fills its streets with dancing, stranger-kissing, inebriated <u>glee</u> at Carnival.

   A. merriment   B. hospitality   C. chaos   D. tranquility

7. Brazil is now locked in one of its worse recessions in history, dragged down by <u>slumping</u> oil prices and allegations of staggering corruption.

   A. slumbering   B. descending   C. ascending   D. slurring

8. The run-up to the games has been <u>punctuated</u> by demonstrations, an anti-Olympic backlash driven by people who felt the time was not right for lavish spending.

    A. boosted   B. acclaimed   C. inspected   D. interrupted

9. Protesters blocked the torch's progress as it made its way around the country and attempted to <u>douse</u> it with fire extinguishers and buckets of water.

    A. reinforce   B. drench   C. irrigate   D. extinguish

10. Yet it's not all recriminations and <u>rancor</u> in Rio and beyond.

    A. sympathy   B. yearning   C. indifference   D. enmity

II. Comprehension

Decide whether the following statements are true or false according to the information given in the press clipping. Mark T or F to each statement.

1. As the first South American country to host the Olympics, Brazil held a grand and lavish opening ceremony.

2. Although Rio tells a version of the country's story—from slavery to mega-cities in the opening ceremony, samba style is still the main feature of the event.

3. From performance, we can tell Brazil used to be a colony of Portugal, imported a lot of African slaves, and slavery in this country lasted more than 400 years.

4. Brazil is the last country in Western Hemisphere to abolish slavery in 1888. And the opening ceremony involved a lot of reference to slavery, which was different from 1996 Summer Games in Atlanta.

5. The 206 competing nations, plus one refugee team, parade into the stadium alphabetically, but Greece who hosted the initial Games always led first as the tradition, and the host country Brazil is the last one.

6. Refugee Olympic team did not represent any country in Rio Olympics, and it is composed of 12 athletes from different countries.

7. After Brazil won the bid for the Games in 2009, it has suffered recession, which caused the budget cut heavily.

8. At Rio opening ceremony, Andy Murray fronted the team for Great Britain, while Rafael Nada carried the flag for Spain, and they are rivals on the pro tour.

9. Many Brazilians protested against Rio Olympics, for they think this country could not afford such a lavish party. They marched and demonstrated their opposition, but encountered some tear gas and a percussion grenade.

10. Some Brazilians embraced their opportunity to host the Games, just because Rio Olympics could bring great profit to them.

III. Questions for discussion

1. Olympic opening ceremony has been considered a grand event, and the host countries tend to lavish on it. But it was reported that the budget available for Rio opening ceremony was only one-tenth of that for the 2012 Summer Olympics ceremony in London. Can we say the more money we spend on the Olympic opening ceremony, the better it is? What are the right ways to hold a successful Olympic opening ceremony?

2. Since Rio won the bid for the Games, it has encountered severe and continuous economic recession. Please analyze the possible advantages brought about by the Rio Olympics, which might infuse a new life to Brazil.

3. To win a gold medal seems to be the ultimate goal for an athlete, for it means a lot both for the athlete and the country the athlete represents. Do you agree to the idea that a gold medal in Olympics is the most important thing for an athlete?

4. During the parade of athletes, the appearance of refugee Olympic team caused a great sensation, and received warm applause from the whole audience. Why did the audience react in such a way? Please analyze the possible reasons.

5. Rio Olympics ended with a spectacular carnival-inspired closing ceremony on 21 August, 2016. During the Games, there must have been some impressive moments for you. List at least two examples and share with your partner.

宗教对西方文化的影响——以基督教为例

宗教属于社会意识形态，是人类发展到一定阶段出现的特定思想信仰。一种特定民族文化的形成和演化，都是跟宗教的发展密切相关的。"西方文化是指源自希伯来的宗教文化和古希腊理性主义的人本文化相结合而发展起来的欧洲文化，它后来又传到美国和加拿大以及澳洲。就基督教的产生来说，其本身就是'两希文明'的结晶"（王志捷，2009）。基督教作为世界三大宗教之一，始于公元1世纪，有2000多年的发展历史，在西方文化中占有核心地位，影响了整个西方思想文化的发展。可以说，基督教的思想已经深深地融入了西方文化，维系着西方人的精神世界。

一、基督教对西方政治文化的影响

虽然早期的基督教与政治分离并受到罗马统治者的迫害，但是在上千年的欧洲中世纪

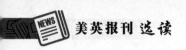

历史中,基督教会借助掌握的政治力量对欧洲社会实行了全面操控,垄断了所有的思想文化。近现代西方社会虽然实行了政教分离,但是其价值观对于现代西方的政治理念有着深刻的影响。很多西方国家都将"天赋人权","法律面前人人平等"这些思想写在宪法的开头。

二、基督教对西方道德生活的影响

社会生活中,法律来规范人们的外部行为。要人们自觉遵守社会准则,保持正常的社会秩序,则需要道德的约束。基督教与道德的关系历来密切。基督教的原则要求是:要爱人如己,并宣称这是神的旨意和命令。用宗教的语言对其成员提出强制性的行为规范,并启发和要求人们自己遵守,这实际上就是道德的要求。在历史上,基督教是西方人的价值观依据。在现代社会,维系社会的道德也是其主要的社会功能。

三、基督教对西方文学的影响

宗教在文学发展过程中,起到不可忽视的积极作用,西方的文学与基督教会的思想和活动密不可分。作为基督教最高神学经典的《圣经》,本身就是全世界公认的人文科学的重要文献和文学作品。它为西方文学作品提供了最基本的素材宝库,西方文学作品中深深地打着《圣经》的烙印。中世纪的宗教文学,基本上是以基督教为题材。之后的文艺复兴时期仍旧如此,如但丁(Dante Alighieri)的《神曲》(Divine Comedy),被视为世界上伟大的作品之一,有着深厚的宗教哲理。在英国文学史上占有重要地位的著名诗人弥尔顿(John Milton)的《失乐园》(Paradise Lost)、《复乐园》(Paradise Regained),也是以基督教的题材为核心。也有作家通过隐喻来表达自己的宗教思想,如美国作家霍桑(Nathaniel Hawthorne)的《红字》(The Scarlet Letter)。海明威(Ernest Miller Hemingway)的《老人与海》(The Old Man and the Sea)则是根据耶稣受难的细节,将老人构想成是耶稣的化身。

四、基督教对西方教育的影响

要研究西方的教育史,必然追溯到基督教。在欧洲,许多古老的大学由教会创办,如巴黎大学,就是在大教堂学校的基础上发展而来。教会办的神学院为西方近、现代高等教育打下了基础。西方高等教育中一直沿袭至今的一些传统,如指定学生必须学习的课程,以及使用的教科书、学生毕业授予学位等,都始于中世纪大学所确立的一些制度。

五、基督教在西方人们日常生活中的影响

西方最隆重的节日,圣诞节(Christmas)和复活节(Easter),分别是跟基督教中耶稣的诞生和复活有关。一定程度上,这两个节日的庆祝活动,已经成为全社会每年的盛事。

无论证人在法庭上作证还是美国总统的就职仪式，都要手抚《圣经》进行宣誓。在美国，很多城镇，教堂是各种社会活动的中心。

总之，基督教思想是欧洲文化的重要渊源之一，对西方历史文化的进程起着举足轻重的作用。作为欧洲文化发展史的一部分，基督教是构筑西方文化的重要组成部分，西方文化中处处渗透着基督教的影响。领悟宗教，尤其是基督教和西方文化的密切关系，对于我们正确、全面认识西方文化大有裨益。

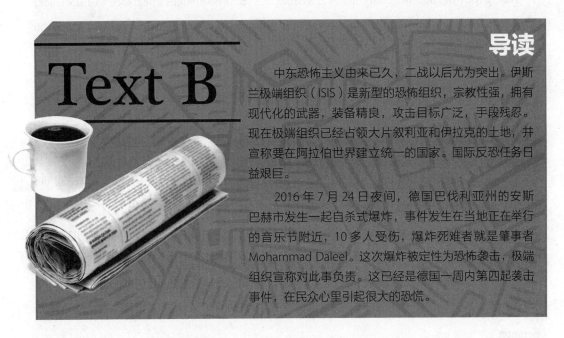

Text B

导读

中东恐怖主义由来已久，二战以后尤为突出。伊斯兰极端组织（ISIS）是新型的恐怖组织，宗教性强，拥有现代化的武器，装备精良，攻击目标广泛，手段残忍。现在极端组织已经占领大片叙利亚和伊拉克的土地，并宣称要在阿拉伯世界建立统一的国家。国际反恐任务日益艰巨。

2016 年 7 月 24 日夜间，德国巴伐利亚州的安斯巴赫市发生一起自杀式爆炸，事件发生在当地正在举行的音乐节附近，10 多人受伤，爆炸死难者就是肇事者 Mohammad Daleel。这次爆炸被定性为恐怖袭击，极端组织宣称对此事负责。这已经是德国一周内第四起袭击事件，在民众心里引起很大的恐慌。

ISIS[1] release chilling video of Ansbach suicide bomber[2] warning "you will not live peacefully" before attack

By Anthony Bond, Gareth Browne

The 27-year-old man, named as Mohammad Daleel, also threatens ISIS will use car bombs to strike in the heart of Europe.

Twisted terror group ISIS has released a video allegedly showing Ansbach suicide bomber warning the West that "you will not live peacefully" before claiming the Islamists would soon use car bombs to wreak havoc across Europe.

This video is alleged to be the final words of Mohammad Daleel before he launched his attack—which injured 15 people but mercifully only claimed his own life.

In the video, which ISIS claims shows the 27-year-old failed asylum seeker, Daleel issues a

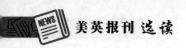

chilling threat where he says "This operation is carried out with an explosive device, but next time it will be with (car) bombs."

He adds: "To the German people, your country is killing you by its actions.

Islamic State did not start this war with you."

Daleel is seen with his face entirely covered with a black scarf as he sits in front of a white sheet.

Barely moving, and with only his eyes visible, the terrorist pledges allegiance to ISIS leader Abu Bakra Al-Baghdadi[3] and his fellow savage and senior member of the murder cult Abu Mohammed Al-Adnani.

Entitled "Germany—VIdeo of Mohammad Daleel the Islamic State Soldier Who Carried out the Attack in Ansbach", the video has the suicide bomber attempting to justify his acts.

He says at one point: "And to the German youth: your planes that are shelling us don't distinguish between men, women and even children".

The video comes at the same time as ISIS released a picture allegedly showing the face of the man who detonated explosives strapped to himself.

Daleel killed himself and injured 12 others, three of them seriously, when he detonated an explosive device near a bar in central Ansbach on Sunday evening.

News sites linked to ISIS have tonight published the picture, claiming it is Daleel.

ISIS have said he was a "soldier of Islamic State'"and describe the attack as a "martyrdom operation".

Police have also discovered a chilling video of the attacker pledging his allegiance to ISIS.

He threatened to attack Germany on mobile phone footage discovered by police, in which he declares his membership to ISIS.

The 27-year-old failed asylum seeker, who was about to be deported to Bulgaria, had gasoline, acid, alcohol cleaner, soldering iron, wires and pebbles in his flat.

In the video found on his phone today, Daleel pledges his allegiance to ISIS leader Abu Bakr al-Baghdadi.

The phone and his laptop were seized by police and are being examined by experts with Arabic skills.

Bavaria's[4] top security official Joachim Herrmann said this morning that the attack was motivated by religious extremism.

"My personal view is that I unfortunately think it's very likely this really was an Islamist suicide attack," he said.

Justice Minister Winfried Bausback added: "Islamist terrorism has reached Germany."

The ISIS-linked Amaq Agency[5] has claims the suicide bombing was carried out by "soldier of Islamic State".

Police raided Daleel's home in Ansbach as German authorities revealed he was due to be deported to Bulgaria.

German police said today that Daleel has a roll of 50 euro notes on him at the time of the attack and had filed a compliant about someone he "claimed was a member of Hezbollah".

Hermann added that police found violent videos and bomb-making material at the home of the attacks.

Around 2,500 people were evacuated from a nearby open-air music event where Daleel, who had been in Germany for more than a year, tried to gain entry.

Witnesses of the incident described seeing a rucksack explode, killing the man.

He was already known to police for drugs possession of drugs and had also spent time in a psychiatric unit after attempting suicide twice.

Local reports claim Daleel was angry at being denied asylum and the prospect of being deported to Bulgaria.

Bavarian police said the bomber had six Facebook accounts, including one under a false identity.

The attack comes as Germany reels from Friday's massacre in Munich that left nine dead and dozens injured.

It is the third attack to hit Bavaria in a week, following an IS-inspired axe rampage by a teenager on Monday.

Previously German authorities refused to speculate on any Islamic link to the attack with Michael Schrotberger, a spokesman for the prosecutor's office in Ansbach, saying Daleel's motive was unclear.

"If there is an Islamist link or not is purely speculation at this point," he said last night.

Police were alerted to a blast near the festival shortly after 10pm, with initial reports suggesting the incident was a gas explosion.

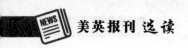
Witness Thomas Debinski described the "disturbing" scene as people in the small city came to realise a violent act had taken place.

"People were definitely panicking, the rumour we were hearing immediately was that there had been a gas explosion," he told Sky News[6].

"But then people came past and said it was a rucksack that had exploded. Someone blew themselves up. After what just happened in Munich it's very disturbing to think what can happen so close to you in such a small town."

Around 200 police officers and 350 rescue personnel flooded the scene and investigators later confirmed the blast had been caused by a bomb.

Police said there is no direct connection between the bomber and terrorist groups and they are now investigating if other people were involved in the attack.

The latest incident will add to a feeling of grief and insecurity in a country rocked by a spate of violent extreme acts.

On Monday a 17-year-old Afghan asylum seeker launched an axe and knife attack on passengers on a train in Wuerzburg.

Islamic State claimed responsibility for the attack in which five people were injured. The teenage axeman, Riaz Khan Ahmadzai, was shot dead by police.

On July 14 more than 80 lives were lost when a lorry ploughed into crowds watching a Bastille Day[7] firework display in Nice, France. IS said it was also responsible for the attack by 31-year-old Mohamed Lahouaiej Bouhlel .

Earlier on Sunday a Syrian asylum seeker killed a woman with a machete and wounded two others outside a bus station in the south-western German city of Reutlingen before being arrested.

Witnesses said the 21-year-old man, who was known to police, was having an argument with the woman before attacking her. Police said the motive behind the attack is still not clear.

(From *The Mirror*, July 25, 2016)

NOTES

1. ISIS 伊斯兰极端组织，全称为"伊拉克及叙利亚的伊斯兰国"，由中东地区伊斯兰教极端分子组成，是伊斯兰武装中的一支，宣称为伊斯兰信仰而战。是一种新型的恐怖主义组织，极端、狂热、残忍是其特点，拥有大量的现代化杀伤武器，经常发生自杀式袭击，对中东地区，乃至整个世界的和平有极大的威胁。近年来，随着叙利亚内战的爆发，力量发展很快，影响力越来越大。其目标是在阿拉伯世界建立一个逊尼派（Sunnite）神权国家。

2. Ansbach suicide bomber 安斯巴赫市自杀爆炸者，指的是 2016 年 7 月 24 日，27 岁的叙利亚难民 Mohammad Daleel 在德国南部安斯巴赫（Ansbach）引爆炸弹，Daleel 当场身亡。爆炸造成 10 多人受伤。

3. Abu Bakra Al-Baghdadi 阿布·伯克尔·阿尔·巴达迪，1971 年出生，伊拉克人，在伊斯兰大学获得法学博士学位。2003 年，加入基地组织。2005 年，被美军俘虏，在伊拉克南部的博卡营监狱关押四年。自称是先知默罕默德的直系后裔。2014 年，他自称为"哈里发"，将政权更名为"伊斯兰国"（ISIS）。

4. Bavaria 巴伐利亚州，德国南部的一个州，同时是德国面积最大的州。7 月 24 日发生自杀爆炸的安斯巴赫市就位于巴伐利亚州。

5. Amaq Agency ISIS 的通讯社，一个支持 ISIS 的伊斯兰国家恐怖组织机构，专门负责传播激进组织活动的消息。

6. Sky News 英国的天空新闻台，1989 年 2 月 5 日开始正式运营。进行 24 小时不间断的新闻报道，口号是"first for breaking news"。

7. Bastille Day 巴士底日，1789 年 7 月 14 日，法国市民攻陷象征封建主义的巴士底狱，推翻专制，揭开了法国大革命的序幕。7 月 14 日被定为法国的国庆日，是法国最隆重的节日。

USEFUL WORDS

alleged	[ə'ledʒd] *adj.*	declared but not proved 声称的
asylum	[ə'saɪləm] *n.*	refuge; safety; protection from persecution, etc 庇护；安全；避难
blast	[blæst] *n.*	an explosion 爆炸
chilling	['tʃɪlɪŋ] *adj.*	provoking fear terror, frightening 令人恐惧、害怕的
cult	[kʌlt] *n.*	devotion to a person (esp a single deity) or practice 对某人（尤其指对某神）或风尚的崇拜
deport	[dɪ'pɔːrt] *v.*	to legally force (a foreigner, criminal, etc.) to leave a country 将……驱逐出境
detonate	['detəneɪt] *v.*	to burst and release energy as through a violent chemical or physical reaction 使爆炸；使爆裂
evacuate	[ɪ'vækjueɪt] *v.*	to withdraw or leave from a place 撤离，疏散
footage	['fʊtɪdʒ] *n.*	film that has been shot 连续镜头
havoc	['hævək] *n.*	widespread damage; destruction 大破坏；混乱
machete	[mə'ʃeti] *n.*	a large heavy knife used as a weapon or for cutting vegetation 大砍刀
martyrdom	['mɑːrtərdəm] *n.*	death that is imposed because of the person's adherence of a religious faith or cause 殉难，牺牲
psychiatry	[saɪ'kaɪətri] *n.*	the study and treatment of mental illness 精神病学，精神病治疗学
psychiatric	*adj.*	of psychiatry 精神病学的，精神病治疗的
rampage	['ræmpeɪdʒ] *n.*	violently angry and destructive behavior 暴怒，狂暴行为

reel	[riːl] *v.*	(here) to be shaken (physically or mentally) by a blow, a shock, rough treatment, etc.（身体或心理方面）因被打击或惊讶或粗暴对待等而震颤
rucksack	['rʌksæk] *n.*	canvas bag strapped on the back from the shoulders, used by people on a walking holiday, etc 一种帆布背包（步行、度假者等用之）
spate	[speɪt] *n.*	a large number or amount or extent 泛滥
speculation	[ˌspekju'leɪʃn] *n.*	a message expressing an opinion based on incomplete evidence 猜测，推测，臆断
strap	[stræp] *v.*	to fasten or tie in place with a strap 用带子绑住
wreak	[riːk] *v.*	to cause to happen or to occur as a consequence 造成（破坏等），带来（灾难性的后果）

EXERCISES

I. Vocabulary

Choose among the four alternatives one word or phrase that is closest in meaning to the underlined part in each statement.

1. ISIS release <u>chilling</u> video of Ansbach suicide bomber warning "you will not live peacefully" before attack.

   A. imposing   B. compellent

   C. frightening   D. delightful

2. Twisted terror group ISIS has released a video allegedly showing Ansbach suicide bomber warning the West that "you will not live peacefully" before claiming the Islamists would soon use car bombs to wreak <u>havoc</u> across Europe.

   A. keen interest   B. widespread damage

   C. ardent love   D. joyless atmosphere

3. He says at one point: "And to the German youth: your planes that are <u>shelling</u> us don't distinguish between men, women and even children".

   A. bombarding   B. saluting   C. shocking   D. coalizing

4. The video comes at the same time as ISIS released a picture allegedly showing the face of the man who detonated explosives <u>strapped</u> to himself.

   A. stripped   B. tied   C. sketched   D. grabbed

5. Police have also discovered a chilling video of the attacker <u>pledging</u> his allegiance to ISIS.

   A. asserting   B. cursing   C. vowing   D. displaying

6. The 27-year-old failed asylum seeker, who was about to be <u>deported</u> to Bulgaria, had gasoline, acid, alcohol cleaner, soldering iron, wires and pebbles in his flat.

   A. imported   B. exported   C. banished   D. embarked

7. Around 2,500 people were <u>evacuated</u> from a nearby open-air music event where Daleel, who had been in Germany for more than a year, tried to gain entry.

A. transferred　　　B. transplanted　　C. routed　　　　D. withdrawn

8. Police were alerted to a <u>blast</u> near the festival shortly after 10pm, with initial reports suggesting the incident was a gas explosion.

A. massacre　　　　B. assassination　　C. explosion　　D. kidnapping

9. "People were definitely <u>panicking</u>, the rumour we were hearing immediately was that there had been a gas explosion," he told Sky News.

A. scared　　　　　B. vexed　　　　　C. impatient　　D. rattled

10. Earlier on Sunday a Syrian asylum seeker killed a woman with a <u>machete</u> and wounded two others outside a bus station in the south-western German city of Reutlingen before being arrested.

A. a short pointed knife　　　　　　　B. a cavalry lancer

C. a large heavy knife　　　　　　　　D. a big gun

II. Comprehension

Decide whether the following statements are true or false according to the information given in the press clipping. Mark T or F to each statement.

1. Before the Ansbach suicide bombing, Mohammad Daleel had alleged he would launch the attack in this place.

2. He adds: "To the German people, your country is killing you by its actions. Islamic State did not start this war with you." From these remarks, we can tell it is German that started the war with Islamic State.

3. The 27-year-old Mohammad Daleel, was denied asylum, and was due to be deported to Bulgaria.

4. The Syrian asylum seeker—named as Mohammad Daleel—had enough material to build another bomb and a wad of €50 notes in his hands.

5. Asked whether the bomber might have links to ISIS, Bavaria's top security official Joachim Herrmann said that couldn't be ruled out, because there was concrete evidence for this.

6. The bomber tried to get into the open-air festival but was turned away, and he was raged for that, which was the direct reason he conducted the suicide bombing.

7. When the suicide bombing first happened, the initial reports suggested the incident was a gas explosion, but later when people in the city realized this violent act, they were definitely panicking.

8. Germany has suffered several violent extreme acts, and the Ansbach suicide bombing just added a feeling of grief and insecurity.

9. Before the suicide attack, Mohammad Daleel had suffered some mental illness, and attempted to commit suicide several times.

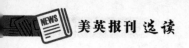
10. On Sunday a Syrian asylum seeker killed a woman with a machete and wounded the two other outside a bus station in the south-western German of Reutlingen, which is just a prelude to Ansbach suicide bombing.

III. Questions for discussion

1. How much do you know about ISIS? Please distinguish the terms among IS, ISIS and ISIL.

2. Terrorism has haunted hideously around the world. For people in some area, life is just like a nightmare, for they frequently suffer the violent acts from terrorists. What are the effective and efficient means to fight against terrorism?

3. Mohammad Daleel, a 27-year-old young man, killed himself in the suicide attack. Please illustrate your ideas about this.

4. After the outbreak of Syrian civil war, some Syrian refugees fled to Europe, seeking for asylum, but not everyone could make it. Is it the responsibility of European countries, such as Germany, to offer unconditional help for them? Please refer to the Internet and find more evidence to support your idea.

《镜报》简介

英国报纸按照版面内容可分为严肃性报纸和通俗性报纸。严肃性报纸通常篇幅较长，刊登的新闻内容深刻、严肃，偏重于社会政治生活的主题，也刊登关于高雅文化的评论文章和特别报道，读者多是受过良好教育的中产阶级。通俗性报纸通常版面尺寸较小，有更多的图片和醒目的标题，文章篇幅短，通俗易懂，内容娱乐性强。《镜报》是全国通俗性日报。

《镜报》（The Mirror）原名为《每日镜报》（Daily Mirror），是英国销量最大的日报之一，由 Alfred Harmsworth 于 1903 年创刊，初期是为女性而创办的小型报纸，这同时也是《镜报》名字的来源，"让这份报纸成为女性的一面镜子，既照出女性暗淡的一面，也照出光彩的一面……娱乐但不轻佻，严肃却不呆板"是一直被秉承的办报目标。此报成立后不久，改为画报。后来版面越来越丰富，目标读者群也不再局限于女性，图片篇幅越来越大，内容包括新闻、娱乐和体育等。

　　1951年，塞西尔·金（C.King）任《每日镜报》董事长，建立了镜报集团。1984年，罗伯特·马克斯韦尔（Robert Maxwell）买下镜报集团报业公司。1999年镜报集团和三一集团合并成为英国最大的报纸出版商——三一镜报集团（Trinity Mirror），镜报是该集团的旗舰级报纸。几经易手和合并，《镜报》已逐渐变成英国有影响的大报，其姐妹报纸为《星期日镜报》。《镜报》上发布的消息被公认为具有较高的可靠性和权威性。

　　登录《镜报》的官方网站，可以阅读该报刊的电子版。

Keys to Exercises

Unit 1

Text A

I. Vocabulary

1–5 DABAB   6–10 DBABC

II. Comprehension

1–5 FTTFF   6–10 FFFFT

Text B

I. Vocabulary

1–5 CBABB   6–10 DCCDC

II. Comprehension

1–5 FFTTT   6–10 FTFFF

Unit 2

Text A

I. Vocabulary

1–5 ACADD   6–10 AAADB

II. Comprehension

1–5 FFTFT   6–10 FFFTT

Text B

I. Vocabulary

1–5 ACCDA   6–10 BCABD   11–12 CA

II. Comprehension

1–5 FTTFT   6–10 FFTTT   11–12 TF

Unit 3

Text A

I. Vocabulary

1–5 CADBA   6–10 CDBCD

II. Comprehension

1–5 FTFTT   6–10 TFFFT

Text B

I. Vocabulary

1–5 CDABA   6–10 DCABD

II. Comprehension

1–5 TFTFT   6–10 TFTFT

Unit 4

Text A

I. Vocabulary

1–5 ACBAC   6–10 DBDCA

II. Comprehension

1–5 TFFTT   6–10 FTFFT

Text B

I. Vocabulary

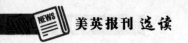

1–5 BADBC   6–10 DACBD

II. Comprehension

1–5 FTTFT   6–10 FTTFT

Unit 5

Text A

I. Vocabulary

1–5 CABCA   6–10 BABDD

II. Comprehension

1–5 TFFTF   6–10 TFFTF

Text B

I. Vocabulary

1–5 CABCA   6–10 DABBD

II. Comprehension

1–5 FTTFF   6–10 TTTFF

Unit 6

Text A

I. Vocabulary

1–5 CBBDC   6–10 ABDAA

II. Comprehension

1–5 TFTTF   6–10 TFTFF

Text B

I. Vocabulary

1–5 ACCAD   6–10 BBDAB

II. Comprehension

1–5 TFTTT   6–10 FTTFT

Unit 7

Text A

I. Vocabulary

1–5. CDBDB   6–10. BDAAC

II. Comprehension

1–5. FFTTF   6–10. FTFTF

Text B

I. Vocabulary

1–5. DCDAA   6–10. BBCBA

II. Comprehension

1–5. TFFTF   6–10. TFFTF

Unit 8

Text A

I. Vocabulary

1–5. BADCA   6–10. BCDCA

II. Comprehension

1–5. TFFTF   6–10. TFFTT

Text B

I. Vocabulary

1–5. DACAB   6–10. DCABC

II. Comprehension

1–5. TFFTT   6–10. FFFFT

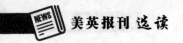

Unit 9

Text A

I. Vocabulary

1–5 BCCBD   6–10 ACDAB

II. Comprehension

1–5 TTFFF   6–10 TFFFF

Text B

I. Vocabulary

1–5 BCDAD   6–10 ABBCD

II. Comprehension

1–5 FTTFF   6–10 FTFTT

Unit 10

Text A

I. Vocabulary

1–5 DCABB   6–10 ABDDD

II. Comprehension

1–5 FTTTT   6–10 FTTTF

Text B

I. Vocabulary

1–5 CBABC   6–10 CDCAC

II. Comprehension

1–5 FFTTF   6–10 FTTFF

Bibliography

[1] 陈明瑶，卢彩虹. 2006. 新闻英语语体与翻译研究. 北京：国防工业出版社.

[2] 安义宽. 2003. 公司债券及其相关品种发展. 经济管理（11）：6-14.

[3] 陈仲利. 2013. 最新英美报刊选读. 北京：中国人民大学出版社.

[4] 储昭根. 2015. 冷战后美国的经济安全与外交. 国际观察（4）：142-157.

[5] 从莱庭. 1999. 比喻——当代报刊英语文体修辞的灵魂. 山东师大外国语学院学报
（1）：32-36.

[6] 戴炜华，陈宇昀. 2004. 批评语篇分析的理论和方法. 外语研究（4）：12-16.

[7] 端木义万. 2005. 美英报刊阅读教程（中级本）（精选版）. 北京：北京大学出版社.

[8] 端木义万，赵虹. 2013. 美英报刊阅读教程（普及本）（修订本）. 南京：南京大学出版
社.

[9] 邓友平. 2014. 美国"课程现代化"的科学主义内核研究. 东北师范大学博士论文.

[10] 高攀，郑启航. 2016. 美国参议院通过波多黎各债务重组法案. 经济参考报（7月1日）.

[11] 黄萍. 2006. 新闻英语中新词汇的造词分析. 黑龙江社会科学（2）：132-133.

[12] 侯维瑞. 1988，英语语体. 上海：上海外语教育出版社.

[13] 金灿荣. 1995. 美国政党制度简介. 国际社会与经济（1）：25-26.

[14] 理查德·卡特，张民强. 2004. 现行美国教育体制. 河北师范大学学报（教育科学版）
（6）：100-102.

[15] 李孔岳. 2006. 科技成果转化的模式比较及其启示. 科技管理研究（1）：88-91.

[16] 廖维娜，杨静. 2008. 高效阅读英美报刊文章. 西南民族大学学报（人文社科版）
（12）：142-145.

[17] 林克勤. 2005. 当代报纸专栏的类别及其特点. 新闻界（3）：125-126.

[18] 刘大保. 2000. 社论写作. 北京：中国广播电视出版社.

[19] 刘凤鸣. 2005. 英语报纸词、句特征. 西南民族大学学报（人文社科版）（3）：305-308.

[20] 刘燕华，王文涛. 2013. 第三次工业革命与可持续发展. 中国人口·资源与环境（4）：3-7.

[21] 那明. 2014. 金融危机背景下国家主权信用评级影响因素分析——基于27个OECD国家面板数据的研究. 世界经济研究（10）：28-33.

[22] 人民教育出版社历史室. 2006. 世界近代现代史（第2版）. 洛阳：人民教育出版社.

[23] 唐军，李政. 2011. 我国发展对冲基金的必要性分析及前景预测. 商品与质量（1）：43-44.

[24] 王长勤，纪海涛. 2015. 科技创新与国际竞争格局演变. 紫光阁（11）：29-31.

[25] 王劲松. 2009. 对我国发行市政债券若干问题的思考. 财政研究（5）：31-34.

[26] 王克俊. 2007. 报刊英语语言特色研究. 四川理工学院学报（社会科学版）（1）：109-112.

[27] 王明明. 2009. 跨境贸易人民币结算试点——突破和改变. 中国金融家（6）：45-47.

[28] 王振华，马玉蕾. 2009. 英语报刊选读. 北京：高等教育出版社.

[29] 王志捷. 2009. 概论宗教与民族文化的关系. 宗教与民族（6）：103.

[30] 隗静秋. 2010. 中外饮食文化. 北京：经济管理出版社.

[31] 晓晓. 2012. 英国教育体制：现状、学制、体制、特点. 内蒙古教育（3）：38-40.

[32] 熊易. 2016. 国际开放科学数据实证资源及利用研究. 图书馆理论与实践（1）：12-14.

[33] 肖小月. 2013. 英美新闻标题语言特色分析. 重庆交通大学学报（社科版）第13卷（2）：133-136.

[34] 徐明初. 2002. 论英语成语比喻的文化特色及其翻译. 宜宾学院学报（2）：59-61.

[35] 余翔. 2015. 美国经济增长新特征与前景. 国际问题研究（4）：82-95.

[36] 张宏菊. 2010. 美国联邦行政学院领导人才培训的历史与现状. 华东师范大学硕士论文.

[37] 张卫平. 2006. 英语报刊选读. 北京：外语教学与研究出版社.

[38] 赵敬. 2010. 中美饮食文化差异. 学术论坛（13）：227.

[39] 周学艺. 2010. 美英报刊导读（第2版）. 北京：北京大学出版社.

[40] 周学艺，赵林. 2013. 美英报刊文章阅读（第五版）. 北京：北京大学出版社.

[41] https://en.wikipedia.org/wiki/Reader%27s_Digest

[42] http://baike.baidu.com/link?url=DYMac9J2gifweY888pQLrkchILUpuq_e6sMD_6Q3aapADVRnRSaiwUZvYYt7qUp

[43] http://baike.baidu.com/link?url=FNDmKpru2ugLUHp-WBC5402mJNIlhk4hqO0kOGBdGn56YM
     FDO3Uay5vDi7-tz

[44] http://baike.so.com/doc/5387772-5624315.html

[45] http://news.sohu.com/61/52/news147095261.shtml

[46] http://student.zjzk.cn/course_ware/bjjy/images/052.htm

[47] https://en.wikipedia.org/wiki/Sam_Allardyce

[48] https://en.wikipedia.org/wiki/The_Times

[49] http://student.zjzk.cn/course_ware/bjjy/images/052.htm

[50] Rifkin J. 2011. *The third industrial revolution: how lateral power is transforming energy, the economy, and the world.* London: Macmillan.